Social Change in India

SOCIAL CHANGE IN INDIA

Geetanjali

CENTRUM PRESS
NEW DELHI-110002 (INDIA)

CENTRUM PRESS
H.O.: 4360/4, Ansari Road, Daryaganj,
New Delhi-110002 (India)
Tel: 23278000, 23261597, 23255577, 23286875
B.O.: No. 1015, Ist Main Road, BSK IIIrd Stage,
IIIrd Phase, IIIrd Block, Bangalore-560085 (INDIA)
Tel: 080-41723429
Email: centrumpress@gmail.com
Visit us at: www.centrumpress.com

Social Change in India

First Edition, 2011
ISBN 978-93-80921-70-9

PRINTED IN INDIA

Printed at Tarun Offset Printers, Delhi-110053

Contents

Contents

Preface

Indian society is multifaceted to an extent perhaps unknown in any other of the world's great civilizations. Virtually no generalization made about Indian society is valid for all of the nation's multifarious groups. Comprehending the complexities of Indian social structure has challenged scholars and other observers over many decades.

Social change is common to all societies. Its nature, pattern, and causation are linked with certain historical and societal condition located in time and space which form its framework. The material and subjective factors are shaped by the socio-historical circumstances of a particular society. Each of the material and subjective factors develops relatives autonomy in influencing the pattern of change. That, however, comes into play at a particular historical juncture. A society may also have wide regional variations in terms of the nature of social formation as well as patterns of change. This book is devoted to the understanding of change in Indian society which is both large and complex.

The book, on the basis of empirical and historical investigations, convincingly demonstrates that the process of change in India involved a great degree of ambivalence, but there is no clear-cut indication except that various strategies have tended to strengthen the position of the society.

Author

1

Vision of Social Change in India

INDIA: AN OVERVIEW

India, officially the Republic of India is a country in South Asia. It is the seventh-largest country by geographical area, the second-most populous country with over 1.2 billion people, and the most populous democracy in the world. Mainland India is bounded by the Indian Ocean on the south, the Arabian Sea on the west, and the Bay of Bengal on the east; and it is bordered by Pakistan to the west; Bhutan, the People's Republic of China and Nepal to the north; and Bangladesh and Burma to the east. In the Indian Ocean, mainland India and the Lakshadweep Islands are in the vicinity of Sri Lanka and the Maldives, while India's Andaman and Nicobar Islands share maritime border with Thailand and the Indonesian island of Sumatra in the Andaman Sea. India has a coastline of 7,517 kilometres (4,700 mi).

Home to the ancient Indus Valley Civilisation and a region of historic trade routes and vast empires, the Indian subcontinent was identified with its commercial and cultural wealth for much of its long history. Four of the world's major religions-Hinduism, Buddhism, Jainism and Sikhism-originated here, while Zoroastrianism, Judaism, Christianity and Islam arrived in the first millennium CE and shaped the region's diverse culture. Gradually annexed by the British East India Company from the early 18th century and colonised by the United Kingdom from the mid-19th century, India became an independent nation in 1947 after a struggle for independence which was marked by a non-violent resistance led by Mahatma Gandhi. India is a federal constitutional republic with a parliamentary democracy consisting of 28 states and seven union territories. A pluralistic, multilingual and multiethnic society where more than 300 languages are spoken, India is also home to a diversity of wildlife in a variety of protected habitats. The Indian economy is the world's eleventh largest economy by nominal GDP and the fourth largest by purchasing power parity. Since the introduction of market-based economic reforms in 1991, India has become one of the fastest growing major economies in the world; however, the country continues to face several poverty, illiteracy, corruption and public health related challenges. India is classified as a newly industrialised country and is one of the four BRIC nations. It is the world's sixth de facto recognized nuclear weapons state and has the third-largest standing armed force in the world, while its military expenditure ranks tenth in the world. India is a regional power in South Asia.

It is a founding member of the United Nations, the Non-Aligned Movement, the World Trade Organization, the South Asian Association for Regional Cooperation, the East Asia Summit, the G20 and the G8+5; a member of the Commonwealth of Nations; and an observer state in the Shanghai Cooperation Organisation.

FUTURE OF INDIA

India has a promising future, given the unprecedented growth in economy and its clout in the global issues. India is now riding on the wave of a gigantic boom in computer driven new economy. Many developed countries of the world are seeking the huge pool of English speaking talented software professionals in India. Premier professional institutes like IIT and IIM have become the source of big international corporates' human resource need, both overseas and within India. India is also a nuclear power. Its security concerns have been to some extent allayed by the possession of nuclear weapons, though fears remain of an expensive military expenditure to sustain the nuclear programs. India is also poised to become the entertainment superpower. Already the

Bollywood is churning out hundreds of films annually. With improvements in the technical and artistic aspects India can well give a stiff competition to western productions. Indian culture is influencing the western world in dress, food and festivals. The Indian Diaspora is increasing in economic prosperity and status. The Indian community is a force to reckon with in every country because of its contribution to the country concerned. Indian lobby groups are funding partly some of the elections in vital countries of the world. The 21st century could well belong to India if it fully utilize its resources and expertise. India's population is an asset and not a pull down factor. Finally India is going to prove just that.

A VISION FOR INDIA

In formulating our vision of the future India, it is important to see beyond the limits of the immediate past to rediscover the greatness that is India. Although the present Republic of India is a young developing nation, our people have a rich and illustrious history as one of the longest living civilizations in the world. In 1835, even the British historian and politician, Lord Macaulay, admitted before the British Parliament: "I have traveled across the length and breadth of India and I have not seen one person who is a beggar, who is a thief. Such wealth I have seen in this country, such high moral values, people of such caliber... the very backbone of this nation, which is her spiritual and cultural heritage....." Thus, it would be wrong to state that in 1947 India started to construct a modern nation from scratch. Rather, it began the process of rediscovering its rich cultural and spiritual values that had formed the foundation of India in the past. It is on this foundation that we seek to formulate our vision of India 2020. It is indeed a challenge to formulate a cohesive vision for India in 2020. Therefore, we thought it appropriate to seek inspiration from one who had a clear vision and possessed the gift to articulate it in a manner that has inspired the hearts and minds of countless Indians. The vision articulated by Rabindranath Tagore is all encompassing in every sense.

THE CHALLENGES AHEAD

India's per capita income has doubled over the past 20 years. With population growth slowing now to about 1.6 per cent per annum, a growth rate of the gross domestic product of around 9 per cent per annum would be sufficient to quadruple the per capita income by 2020. Opinions on achievable rates of economic growth have a tendency to swing along with the short-term economic performances. Two years ago, the global boom, the IT revolution and the all-around optimism led many to believe that in the coming decade India could mimic the 9-10 per cent growth rates that China achieved over a twenty year period. Such optimism is out of fashion today. But there is ample evidence showing that if we can adopt a longer term perspective that is not blinded by immediate circumstances and fluctuating moods, higher rates of growth should be achievable for India in the coming years. This is not a prediction—it is a potential. The reality will depend on how effectively we seize the opportunity to do so.

From a historical perspective, global rates of development have been increasing for more than a century. The dramatic rise of Japan and the East Asian tigers, and most recently China, are illustrative of this point. An objective assessment reveals that all the major engines of economic growth that have accelerated growth up till now, will be present in greater abundance in the coming years than they had been in the past.

Engines of Economic Growth:

- Educational levels are rising rapidly.
- Rates of technological innovation and application are accelerating.
- Cheaper and faster communication is dissolving physical and social barriers, both within the country and internationally.
- Information is being made available in greater quantity and quality than ever before.
- Globalisation is opening up new markets.

A vision is a statement of aspirations and intentions, and therefore, it is essential that we fully recognise the need for determined effort to transform all these potentials into realities. Ultimately, it is not our capacity for prediction but our action that will determine the outcome. That action needs to be based on proper appreciation of the forces available for accelerating our progress.

Assuming that India achieves this quadrupling of per capita income by 2020, it would attain a level of development far higher than where China is today, and on par with upper-middle income countries such as Argentina, Chile, Hungary, Malaysia, Mexico and South Africa. One day India will rise higher still, and having achieved such a target, will know HOW she achieved it. But such knowledge could be acquired even now from the experiences of the many nations that have already passed through these stages of development. From their experiences India should endeavour to acquire the underlying principles and theoretical knowledge that can then be applied appropriately to our own specific case.

Therefore, we refer to the average performance of this group of UMI countries as a benchmark for our development challenges and achievable goals by 2020. Table compares India's current status on some key parametres of development with the average level achieved by a group of UMI countries. It may be noted that we are not holding up the UMI countries as the goal for India in 2020, but merely using them as a reference point to indicate the magnitude of progress India needs to make in different fields. Our vision is not only to reach these reference levels but to surpass them in many cases.

Table. Developmental Parametres at a Glance India Present vs. UMI Reference for India 2020

Developmental Parametres	India Present	UMI Reference for India 2020
Poverty as% of population below poverty line	26.0	13.0
Income distribution (gini index 100 = equality)	37.8	48.5
Unemployment rate (% of labour force)	7.3	6.8
Male adult literacy rate ((%)	68.0	96.0
Female adult literacy rate ((%)	44.0	94.0
Net primary school enrolment ratio	77.2	99.9

Public expenditure on education as% GNP	3.2	4.9
Life expectancy at birth in years	64.0	69.0
Infant mortality rate per 1000 live births	71.0	22.5
Child malnutrition as% of children under 5 years based on weight for age	45.0	8.0
Public expenditure on health as% GNP	0.8	3.4
Commercial energy consumption per capita (kg of oil equiv.)	486.0	2002.0
Electric power consumption per capita (kwh)	384.0	2460.0
Telephones per 1000 population	34.0	203.0
Personal computers per 1000 population	3.3	52.3
Scientists and engineers in R&D per million population	149.0	590.0
Sectoral Composition of GDP in%		
Agriculture	28.0	6.0
Industry	26.0	34.0
Services	46.0	60.0
International trade in goods as% of ppp GDP	3.6	35.0
Foreign direct investment as% of gross capital formation	2.1	24.5
Gross FDI as% of ppp GDP	0.1	3.5

Striving to achieve these reference levels and surpass them in some cases will present very significant challenges insofar as the determination and resourcefulness of the country is concerned

Major Challenges for India:

- A targeted approach to bring millions of families above the poverty line.
- Generation of nearly ten millions of new employment opportunities per annum, especially for those in the lower income groups.
- Eradication of illiteracy.
- A concerted effort to raise primary and secondary enrolment rates and minimise dropouts.
- Improved public health to reduce infant mortality and child malnutrition.
- Massive investment in power generation, telecommunications and other physical and social

infrastructure.

- Accelerated acquisition of technology capabilities to raise productivity in agriculture, industry and services.
- Becoming a more important player in the world economy in terms of both trade and investments.

We are confident that we can and will meet these challenges. We also feel that we have the knowledge and the capacity as a nation to achieve food for all, health for all, and jobs for all. What we do not know for sure however is, how long it will take us to accomplish them. We need, therefore, to affirm the will and the determination to do it rapidly and achieve it now rather than sometime later.

UNCOMMON OPPORTUNITIES

KNOWLEDGE AND INFORMATION TECHNOLOGY

An essential requirement for envisioning India's future is to recognise that the equations which determine national development have changed in recent years, opening up greater possibilities than before. The same factors continue to be at work, but their relative contribution and importance is rapidly shifting along several dimensions.

The sectoral composition of the GDP changes with economic development. The predominance of agriculture in the least developed economies is reduced by the increasing importance of manufacturing, and subsequently, services, as they move up the ladder of development. As this occurs, the rates of economic growth tend to increase. This transition is now occurring globally and is reflected in the explosive growth of the services sector, especially in the fields of financial services, information and communication technology (ICT), insurance, education and health. India's services sector has already become the dominant contributor to GDP, accounting for 46 per cent of the total, but its share is still far below the UMI reference level of 60 per cent. The country very soon will get the opportunity to skip the long slow phase of industrialisation that the most developed nations have passed through, and transit rapidly into a predominantly service economy by 2020, creating services that meet human needs, generate employment covering the large unorganised segment of the economy, raise incomes and increase purchasing power.

Even our notion of services may need to evolve further to recognise the importance of the emerging knowledge-intensive services. Knowledge has replaced capital as the most important determinant of development. In a path breaking study in mid-1950s, Nobel laureate economist Robert Solow showed that seveneighth of the growth of US from 1900 to 1950 was accounted for by technical progress, while only one-eighth was driven by capital.

A study by Denison, of factors contributing to the growth of the US economy from 1929 to 1982, attributes 94 per cent of that growth to factors relating to knowledge generation and dissemination: 64 per cent of this is linked to advances in knowledge generation (*i.e.*R&D) and another 30 per cent to advances in education.

Better resource management, which is an application of knowledge, is also identified as a more important factor than capital. This fact bodes well for countries whose economic planners are able to escape from their earlier faith in capital and fully tap the enormous productive potential of non-material, knowledge resources.

India's Green Revolution is a dramatic example of how the input of greater knowledge in the form of improved production technologies can rapidly increase the productivity of scarce land resources. India's IT Revolution is a striking instance of how the importance of human capital has come to acquire a higher position than that of material plant and machinery.

All efforts to project India's future progress get at times blinded by the question of resources, more specifically, the financial resources needed for all plan activities. We start with the conviction that financial (capital) resources will not be the key factor that decides the course of our future progress. If we fail, it will be mainly for want of a vision of what is possible, knowledge of how to realise it, belief in ourselves, commitment to achieve, will for the effort or skill in implementation —and not for lack of finance.

The knowledge revolution is not just a short-term blip on the radar screen which peaked in 2000 with the boom in dot com companies. It is a real and profound opportunity for countries around the world to increase the pace and scope of the benefits of development. It marks a significant shift in the relative importance of different resources or factors of production in the development process.

This shift from material to knowledge-based resources opens up vast opportunities for the developing countries to accelerate the pace of development. India's rate of economic growth can be substantially increased if the country becomes a superpower in knowledge and if the potentials of information and information technology are fully understood and exploited. Thus far, the potentials have been narrowly focused on the export potentials of the IT sector. But far greater potential lies in the extension and application of IT to stimulate the development of other sectors of the domestic economy. Information is a revolutionary force in bridging the digital divide that currently separates the advantage and the disadvantaged of our nation. Apart from generating new employment opportunities, the application of IT can vastly extend access to education, health care, markets, financial services, vocational skills, administrative services and other aspects of modern society, to many more people at far lower cost. It can dramatically reduce the cost of communications, improve access to technology and marketing capabilities for the rural poor, eliminate intermediary exploitation in the production and distribution chains, increase government accountability and stimulate democratic participation. Therefore, rather than addressing IT as a specific sector, in this report, we have chosen to highlight its significant contributions under different headings, like employment, education, infrastructure and governance.

KNOWLEDGE RESOURCES

There are a host of non-material, knowledge-based human resources that we possess in abundance and can apply to achieve far greater results.

Knowledge Resources:

- Technology
- Organisation
- Information
- Education
- Skills

Technology

Knowledge in the form of information technology (IT) has opened up the opportunity for India to become the premier, low-cost provider of computer software and IT-enabled services to the industrialised world. It can not only provide high paying jobs and rising exports, but also transform the way we educate our youth—increasing the speed, quality and efficiency of learning manifold. In addition, it can and is already transforming the way we communicate among ourselves and with the rest of the world, shrinking the distances between hemispheres, providing instantaneous access to the whole world's knowledge base and customer base.

Knowledge in the form of biotechnology offers not only a lucrative field for employment and economic growth, but a means for improving the health of our people and the productivity of our fields. In the form of agricultural technology, knowledge can increase crop yields from the present level, which is far below world averages, to levels two, three or four times higher. Pioneering Indian farmers have already achieved it for a variety of crops. What they have done individually, we can do as a nation. Finally, knowledge in the form of manufacturing technology will raise the competitiveness of the Indian manufactures to international standards of costs and quality.

Organisation

Technology is not the only knowledge resource now abundantly at our disposal. Today we have access to the whole world's experience in organisation. Organisation is nothing but the know-how for carrying out work most efficiently and expeditiously. India's highly successful Green Revolution and White Revolution were the results of organisational innovations as much as technology. We have the opportunity to fashion new and better forms of organisation to carry out the tasks of education, health-delivery, governance, commerce, industry and social welfare.

Information

Physical and biological reactions require the presence of catalytic agents to set them in motion and speed completion. Human social processes depend on a catalytic agent too and that catalyst is information. Free movement of information releases society from fear of uncertainties. Information about prices and market potentials spurs an entrepreneur into commercial activity. Information about scientific and technological discovery prompts a scientist or an engineer to adopt new innovations and practical applications.

Widely disseminated public information about proper health care and nutrition contributes more powerfully to the general health of the community than does a hospital or medical innovation. Information about government policies enables individuals and communities to fully exercise their rights and take advantage of public programmes. Information about distant places spurs tourism and trade. Information in all forms and all fields—administration, commerce, education, finance, health, science and technology—is the very source from which we shape our dreams, plans, decisions and actions. The more and better the quality of that information, the more enlightened, expansive, productive and effective will be our efforts at individual and social advancement. Today, the average Indian citizen has access to a wider range of timely and reliable information than had the government leaders in the world's most advanced nations a few decades ago. The fairly easy access to computers and the Internet has placed the world at our fingertips. Spread of information is further facilitated by the advancement of telecommunications technology, rapid expansion of cellular telephone networks, as well as the recent legalisation of Internet telephony, that makes live voice communication possible at a fraction of the cost, both within the country and internationally.

Education

What is true of information is true of education as well. Dissemination of useful information can be said to constitute the so-called unorganised sector of public education. The formal educational system is its organised counterpart. Education is the process whereby society passes on the accumulated knowledge and experience of past generations to its youth in a systematic and abridged form, so that the next generation can start off where past generations have ended and move on from there.

Today, through education we have access not only to the knowledge of our own direct ancestors but to the accumulated experience and wisdom of people the world over. With the development of modern media that brings sound and video images into every household, and with the advent of the Internet that enables us to reach out to sources of knowledge around the world, education offers both unprecedented richness of content and the capacity to deliver it. If only we could break free from the limitations of out-dated curriculum and out-moded delivery systems, we could utilise the opportunity to close the education gap that separates the world's most prosperous communities from their poorer cousins.

Skills

Productive skills form another component of the precious human resource that we can and must fully utilise as leverage for national development. Skill is the ability to direct human energy efficiently to achieve desirable goals. A large reserve of unskilled people may be perceived as a problem, but a large population of skilled workers is a huge asset. It takes both knowledge and skill to train people and we have these in abundance. Imparting employable skills to our entire workforce is not only highly desirable but highly achievable as well.

All the resources that we have enumerated—technology, organisation, information, education and skill—are knowledge-based resources. Knowledge-based resources differ significantly in character from material resources. While material resources are consumed when they are utilised, knowledge resources increase when shared. Material resources are costly to transport and store, whereas knowledge resources are easily transportable at rapid speed and can be stored at negligible cost.

Historically, development has occurred under conditions in which access to critical resources was restricted to a relatively small portion of the population. The distinct characteristic of knowledge as a resource makes it possible, for the first time, to spread and share a resource among the entire population. The pace of India's future progress will depend to a large extent on its ability to make available the latest and most useful knowledge to vast parts of the population.

HUMAN DEVELOPMENT

THE PEOPLE

Human beings are distinguished among all living species by their capacity to develop and think. Though development is often measured in terms of so many miles of roads, number of tall buildings, airports, cars, TVs, computers etc., it is not things and places alone that define development. Development must be people centric. Twenty years hence, the people of India will be more numerous, better educated, healthier and more prosperous than at any other time in our long history. Having eradicated the scourge of famine that plagued the country for centuries, we still confront the challenging tasks of providing a nutritious diet to all our children, educating our teeming masses, abolishing epidemic diseases and creating employment opportunities for all our citizens. Today India is the second most populous country in the world, with about 1.04 billion people, home to a-sixth of humanity. Although it is difficult to accurately predict population growth rates 20 years to the future, we expect this number to rise by another 300-350 million, in spite of continuous efforts to reduce fertility rates. This would raise the total population to about 1330 million by 2020.

India is in the process of a demographic transition from high fertility, high mortality and stable population to low fertility, low mortality and stable population. This transition is a global phenomenon generated by the improved availability and access to modern health care that sharply reduced mortality rates and increased life expectancy. The Crude death rate has declined to one-third of its level in 1941 and the expectation of life at birth has nearly doubled during this period.

Falling mortality rates have been followed by a steady decline in birth rates, but this decline has not been as steep as the fall in death rate; even after reaching the replacement fertility rates, the population will continue to grow because of large numbers of young persons entering reproductive age. While assessing future prospects, it is necessary to take into account the vast regional differences in demographic parametres. Population growth has recently decelerated below 2 per cent for the first time in four decades, but not uniformly across the length and breadth of the country.

Several states in south India have already reached, or are about to attain, the replacement level of fertility that would ensure a zero growth rate of population in the long run. On the other hand, in many states in north India, characterised by high fertility rates, it may take several decades to reach the replacement level of fertility. There are also similar differentials in levels of mortality, especially in infant and child mortality. At the national level, two alternate scenarios for achieving population stabilisation have been considered. In the optimistic scenario, which is based on achieving the demographic goals of the National Population Policy 2000, life expectancy is assumed to rise to 71 for males and 74 for females by 2020. Under the realistic scenario, life expectancy is assumed to reach 65 for males and 69 for females by 2020.

Under either scenario India's population would exceed

1.3 billion in the year 2020. In both cases the sex ratio of population (females per 1000 males) would marginally increase from 932 in 2000 to 950 in 2020; reversing the historical trend of falling sex ratio is expected in the 21st Century. We can be more certain of the changes in the age structure of the population as given in Table.

Table. Population Projections (millions)

Year	2000	2005	2010	2015	2020
Total	1010	1093	1175	1256	1331
Under 15	361	368	370	372	373
15-64	604	673	747	819	882
65+	45	51	58	65	76

Actually, the population under-15 years is expected to increase only marginally over the next 20 years. This means that pressure for expansion of the educational system will come only from increasing enrolment and efforts to reduce drop-out rates. The largest growth of population will be in the 15-64 year age group, which will expand by about 46 per cent by 2020 (*i.e,* annually by 1.9 per cent as against the population growth of much lower, at 1.4 per cent). It is expected to rise from 604 million in 2000 to 883 million in 2020, *i.e.,* from 60 to 66 per cent of the total population.

This rise will accentuate the need for challenge of reducing fertility and increasing employment opportunities, so that the family size comes down and incomes rise. The elderly population is also expected to rise sharply from 45 to 76 million, (*i.e.,* by 2.6 per cent per annum) and their share in the total population would rise from 4.5 to 5.7 per cent. As a consequence of these age structural changes, the age-dependency ratio of non-working age population to working age population) is expected to fall from 67 per cent in 2000 to 46 per cent in 2020, although the percentage of elderly people to population will increase.

FOOD SECURITY

The single most important implication of India's rapid population growth during the second half of the twentieth century was the threat it posed to national food security. That threat reached dangerous proportions in the mid-1960s, leading to the launching of the Green Revolution, achievement of food self-sufficiency, and subsequently, a growing stock of surplus food grains by the mid-1970s.

Happily, such a threat no longer exists for the country. Growth of food production has exceeded population growth for each of the past three decades. Statistics present a confusing picture of India's progress on food security. Both per capita food grain consumption and total calorific intake have declined slightly in recent years among all levels of the population. At the same time, grain surpluses have reached peak levels and real per capita expenditure on food is rising among all income groups.

The factors influencing this trend are numerous and complex, however, it can be primarily attributed to:

- Reduction in calorie requirement due to a more sedentary life style among both the rural and urban population. Bicycle and bus travel, mechanised pumps and equipments, access to telephones and newspapers have reduced the physical work to a greater or lesser extent for most Indians.
- Diversification of the Indian diet to include a larger intake of fruits, vegetables, dairy products, sugar, oil and pulses, eggs, fish and meat products, thereby reducing the required intake of calories from cereals.

However, the challenge of achieving food security for all our people remains a real one even today, and will continue to demand our attention in the coming decades. Food security depends on both availability of food and access to it. Long-term food security requires not only producing sufficient food to meet the market demand, but also ensuring that all citizens have the required purchasing power to obtain the food they need for a nutritious and healthy life. India has won the first battle, but the second still looms large. By best estimates, nearly half of the population still suffers from chronic under-nutrition. The most vulnerable are children, women and the elderly, specially among the lower income groups. While the number of children suffering from severe malnutrition declined significantly in the 1990s, the prevalence of mild and moderate under-nutrition, especially among those in the lower 30 per cent income group, is still high. Prevalence of micro nutrient deficiencies such as anaemia is also very high.

The problem of chronic macro and micro nutrient under-nutrition cannot be addressed simply by increases in food production or the accumulation of larger food buffer stocks. Nor has the public distribution system been able to effectively target the most needy in an effective manner. Targeted food for work programmes and targeted nutrition programmes can alleviate the problem temporarily. But in the long run, the solution is to ensure employment opportunities for all citizens so that they acquire the purchasing power to meet their nutritional requirements.

Thus, employment or livelihood security becomes an essential and inseparable component of a comprehensive strategy for national food security and must be considered as one of the nation's highest priorities. Increasing food consumption alone is not a sufficient condition for overcoming malnutrition in India. It is also necessary to address the factors responsible for the high incidence of gastrointestinal and respiratory infections as well as cultural factors responsible for faulty child feeding and weaning practices. Assured provision of safe drinking water, improved health care and education for all women are necessary elements of a comprehensive strategy to eliminate malnutrition and achieve the goal of Food for All before 2020.

India's population is still rapidly expanding. Living standards are rising and slated to rise faster than in the past. As they rise, both calorific intake and diversification of diet will increase significantly. Although a portion of this increase can and will be obtained from abroad, a fulfilling vision of India 2020 depicts this nation—with its conducive and varied climate, the largest irrigated area in the world and a vast farming population—as a major food exporter. Both as a challenge and as an opportunity, India can and must do much more to modernise and diversify its agriculture to meet the increased domestic and international demand for a wide variety of food products. Continued growth of the agriculture sector is particularly important because it plays such a vital role in generating purchasing power among the rural population. Therefore, it is essential that agricultural development strategies for the 21st Century focus on generating both higher incomes and greater on-farm and off-farm employment opportunities. India is now entering the fourth stage of agricultural transformation. The Green Revolution phase spread in the north-western and southern states from the mid-1960s to the mid-1980s.

From the early 1980s, it spread rapidly in the central, and to a lesser extent the eastern states. This, coupled with a further growth of productivity in the north-western and southern states, enabled India to achieve a 3.77 per cent annual growth rate in agricultural production during the 1980s. The overall growth slowed to 2.72 per cent in the 1990s, which was associated with a reduction in public investment in both agriculture and agricultural research, slower growth of fertilizer consumption and the area under high yielding varieties, and degradation of soils.

Stages of Agricultural Development:

- *Pre-Green Revolution*: Boost in productivity growth of coarse grains and pulses per unit of land.
- *Green Revolution*: Expansion of area and rapid growth in productivity of wheat and rice, made possible by widespread adoption of improved varieties, expansion of agricultural research, demonstration and education, and investment in irrigation, supported by establishment of a national infrastructure to produce and supply inputs and to warehouse, distribute and market outputs.
- Post-Green Revolution Continued growth in productivity through intensification of chemical and labour inputs, followed by a gradual deceleration in productivity growth. Expansion of area under maize, cotton, sugarcane, and oilseeds.
- Commercialisation Further diversification of

cropping patterns from low value to high value crops such as fruits, vegetables, flowers and other horticulture crops for domestic consumption, processing and export.

There is enormous scope for accelerating growth in agriculture, through improved soil nutrition and pest management, diversification into higher value-added crops, expansion and more efficient use of irrigation potential, rainwater harvesting, and infrastructure development for agroprocessing industries. India's productivity on major crops ranks far below the world average. This low productivity contributes to low farm incomes and wages, lower on-farm employment generation, and relatively high food prices for all Indians.

Average yields from tomato cultivation, for example, are 76 per cent higher in Mexico and more than four times higher in the USA, while average yields on seed cotton are more than four times higher in Mexico and three times higher in USA. Even within India, some progressive farmers have achieved yields comparable to their foreign counterparts till recently; but these high achievers are a rare exception. Progressive farming must become the rule and the standard.

Raising the productivity of our soil and water resources is an effective way to increase the profit margins of farmers, while at the same time reducing the cost of farm produce, so that it is more affordable to the masses. A minimum target should be to double or triple the average yields of major commercial crops. This will reduce pressure on scarce land and water resources as well as enable the country to utilise less fertile areas for other purposes. Tapping the full potential of Indian agriculture to meet the rising domestic demand and to take advantage of the liberalisation of international trade will require, first and foremost, the recognition of the vital role that agriculture can continue to play in national development.

The other necessary conditions are: greater public investment in research; expansion and development of rural infrastructure including roads, storage capacity and organised markets; improved farmer education; effective involvement of the private sector to provide technology, investment and organisational expertise for commercialisation; and modification of land regulations to achieve greater production efficiency. A suitable land use pattern will also need to be implemented, based on the principle that each region would focus on crops best suited to their agro-climatic characteristics, soil types and water resources.

Strong measures will also be needed to address the problem of land degradation that affects an estimated 45 per cent of total land area. India's objective for 2020 must not only be to produce the food its population requires but also to fully exploit the comparative advantages it possesses—agro-climatic variety, irrigation, scientific capabilities and low labour cost—to become a low cost, high profit producer for the world market.

Figure depicts the projected food production under two scenarios, together with estimates of food demand in 2020. Business-as-usual (BAU) assumes that growth of production continues at the same rates as during the 1990s.

The Best-case scenario (BCS) assumes that production grows at the higher rates achieved during the 1980s. Even under the BAU, India will be able to meet the projected demand in all five food categories. This indicates that more emphasis can be placed on diversifying production to other value added agricultural products.

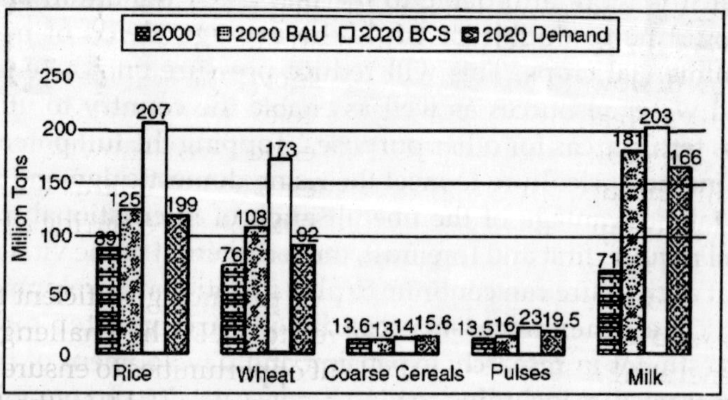

Fig. Current and Projected Food Production vs. Demand in 2020

India needs to sustain an agricultural growth rate of 4.0

to 4.5 per cent in order to reduce food insecurity and poverty, while increasing rural purchasing power. At this growth rate, agricultural development could more rapidly diversify into horticulture, fishery, dairying, animal husbandry and other areas. It would also spur the growth of agro-processing industries in rural areas. Such an achievement is well within reach, provided there is the requisite commitment to raising crop productivity through dissemination of advanced technologies; increasing investment in irrigation, research and training; water harvesting and improved access to credit. While food production should be able to comfortably meet the total domestic demand, there will still be parts of the population that require assistance in order to meet their nutritional requirements.

In view of the high cost and inefficiency of the public food distribution system, reform should directly target the most vulnerable parts, which can be more effectively accomplished through programmes such as food vouchers or food stamps. For the vast majority of the population, food security can best be achieved by ensuring creation of gainful employment opportunities for all job seekers.

EMPLOYMENT

Population, food security, education and remunerative employment opportunities are closely interconnected. Rising levels of education and rising living standards are powerful levers for reducing birth and mortality rates. As population growth slows to replacement levels over the next two decades, India's greatest challenge will be to expand the opportunities for the growing labour force, to enrich their knowledge and skills through education, raise their living standards through gainful employment and make provisions for ensuring a good life for the aged.

India has met the challenge of producing sufficient food to feed everyone, but it has yet to meet the challenge of generating sufficient employment opportunities to ensure that all its people have the purchasing power to obtain the food they require. Gainful employment is one of the most essential conditions for food security and economic security. Conversely, food security is an essential requirement for raising the productivity of India's workforce to international levels. India's labour force has reached 375 million approximately in 2002, and it will continue to expand over the next two decades. The actual rate of that expansion will depend on several factors including population growth, growth of the working age population, labour force participation rates, educational enrolment at higher levels and school drop-out rates. Projections based on these parametres indicate that India's labour force will expand by 7 to 8.5 million per year during the first decade of this century, and will increase by a total of about 160-170 million by 2020, *i.e.*, 2.0 per cent per annum.

Total unemployment in India has been estimated to be about 35 million persons in 2002. This figure takes into account the significant level of underemployment and seasonal variations in the availability of work. It also reflects wide variations in the rate of unemployment among different age groups and regions of the country. Approximately three-fourth of the unemployed are in rural areas and three-fifth among them are educated. The recent trends towards shedding excess labour to improve competitiveness and increasing capital intensity have further aggravated the situation. A clear consensus is now emerging that major changes in economic policy and strategy will be needed to meet the country's employment needs.

Future rates of unemployment will depend on a range of factors, including the growth rate of the labour force and changes in the structure of employment between different sectors, as well as the growth rate of the economy. Adopting the higher number takes us closer to understanding the full magnitude of the challenge the country faces for providing employment opportunities for all its people. India needs to generate on the order of 200 million additional employment opportunities over the next 20 years.

The first question that inevitably arises is whether generating nine or ten million jobs a year is feasible, and that naturally budgets the question of what rates of economic growth would be required for achieving this. However logical and inevitable it may sound, we believe this is the wrong way to approach the problem. The right question to ask is: How important is it to us as a nation to create employment opportunities for all? The answer here is simple. It is extremely important. It is as important to create job opportunities for all citizens in a market economy as it is to provide universal suffrage to all adults in a democracy. Access to employment is an essential component of freedom of economic choice. Absence of such opportunity means depriving our young not only of economic freedom but of hope as well. India's vision for 2020 must be founded on the premise of gainful Jobs for All. Access to employment should not only be a top priority of the government but a constitutionally guaranteed fundamental human right.

But can we possibly achieve such an ambitious goal and that too within the framework of a non-subsidised market economy? In order to answer this question, first of all we need to recognise that the economy we build over the next two decades and the jobs we create will be products of the decisions we make, not some irreversible logic of economic science. It is we, the nation, that have to decide what we want to accomplish and how serious we are about doing it, how willing we are to change our attitudes and to alter our policies to achieve this desirable goal.

We conclude that if the will and determination are present, the goal is achievable. Achieving full employment will require a reorientation of national priorities, technology policy and government action. Until now, planning to achieve national goals has been largely done on a sector-wise basis by respective ministries assigned with the responsibility. These parallel lines of planning need to be integrated around a central vision and set of goals, of which full employment must be one. As we have incorporated an environmental analysis into all our planning, every plan initiative needs also to be re-evaluated to consider its impact on employment.

Despite a persistent tendency to associate employment

with large industry in the organised sector, an in-depth examination of employment potentials makes it evident that the largest share of new jobs will come from the unorganised sector. In evaluating the importance of developing each sector, we must include an assessment of its potential contribution to employment. Such an assessment will have to be made for the unorganised sector, which currently contributes 92 per cent of the country's employment and generates seven times greater labour intensity per unit of production, as compared to the organised sector.

The public organised sector has been and will continue to shed jobs. Although the private organised sector will contribute significantly to the growth of the economy, its contribution to the overall employment generation will be quite modest, since total employment in this sector currently represents only 2.5 per cent of all jobs. Even if this sector grows by 30 per cent per annum, over five years it will contribute less than one per cent to the growth of the workforce.

International comparisons reveal that small and medium enterprises (SMEs) create the majority of jobs. In the USA, nearly half of the private workforce is employed in small firms, of which three-fifth have less than five employees. In Japan, 78 per cent of jobs are generated by small and medium enterprises. The small and medium manufacturing enterprises in Korea account for 99 per cent of all manufacturing enterprises and 69 per cent of employment in this sector. Therefore, the unorganised sector, including small and medium enterprises, must play a central role in the country's employment strategy.

This will require modification of policies and programmes to level the playing field, improve availability of credit, increase productivity, raise quality consciousness and competitiveness, and enhance job quality. Recent experiences of different countries in the context of globalisation also demonstrate that SMEs are better insulated from the pressures generated by the volatility of world trade and capital markets. They are more resistant to the stresses, and more responsive to the demands of the fast-changing technologies and entrepreneurial responses.

Indeed, they are observed to be a very important vehicle for new technology adoption and entrepreneurial development. What is true of the most developed countries today will be true for India in 2020.

SMEs will play a crucial role in ensuring India's international competitiveness and its rapid assimilation of new technologies. An assessment of the different sectors reveals a vast untapped employment potential in a wide range of fields for unskilled, semi-skilled, skilled and professionally educated workers. A list of specific sectors with the largest gross employment potential per unit of output.

High Employment Potential Sectors:

- Commercial agriculture
- Agro-industry and agri-business
- Afforestation for pulp, fuel and power
- Retail and wholesale trade
- Tourism
- Housing
- Construction
- Garment industry
- Other small scale and medium industries
- IT and IT enabled services
- Education
- Health
- Financial services
- Transport
- Communications
- Community services

The growth of food grain production may not lead to a significant growth in on-farm employment opportunities. However, there is substantial scope for creating new jobs through watershed development programmes, expansion of the area under irrigated cultivation, raising crop yields which increases labour intensity, and diversification of cropping patterns into cash crops—especially vegetables and horticultural crops. Together, these could generate upwards of 20 to 30 million new on-farm employment opportunities during the next decade.

India processes less than 2 per cent of its fruit and vegetable products, as compared with 70 to 80 per cent in countries such as Brazil, Malaysia and Philippines. The development of downstream processing, packaging and distribution activities can generate millions of additional off-farm jobs. Policies are needed to attract greater private sector participation in terms of land development, production and processing technologies, investment, management and marketing.

A concerted effort to fully develop the potentials of agri-business could generate millions of additional jobs. The recorded forest area constitutes about 23 per cent of the geographical area (about 71 million hectares) of the country, but half of this area is degraded. Hence, it is unable to play an important role in environmental sustainability and in meeting the forest produce needs of the people, the industry and other sectors. India has more than 50 million hectares of degraded wasteland that lie outside the national forests, in addition to 30 million hectares within protected areas.

In spite of this huge expanse, the country is a net importer of forest products to the extent of ₹2.5 billion annually. Afforestation of India's vast expanse of wastelands and depleted forest areas for production of wood pulp, timber, fuel, fodder, biomass power, edible and fuel soil, fuel, herbs and medicinal plants for exports can create millions of jobs, while reversing environmental degradation and supporting industrial development.

Every two hectares of additional area placed under plantation of forest crop such as bamboo, casuarina, eucalyptus or oil-bearing plants can generate year-round employment for one person. Development of forests can generate 10 to 15 million additional employment opportunities over the next five year plan period and increase the livelihood opportunities of low income families during the transition period, while educational levels are rising and other sectors of the economy are developing.

The contribution of primary sector employment to the total workforce has been coming down very slowly, to 56-57 per cent in 1999-2000, and should decrease to about 51 per cent by 2006-2007. This slow rate of decline is likely to continue for at least a decade, because of the hidden under-employment in the agriculture sector, partly compensated for by the vast potential for additional job creation by crop diversification and afforestation. Increasing prosperity in agriculture will naturally lead to the growth of non-farm jobs in agri-industries, agro-business and other occupations required to meet the needs of an increasingly prosperous farming community.

During the second decade of the 21st Century, increasing domestic demand for manufactured products and services, coupled with more rapid mechanisation of agriculture will draw in more and more people to non-farm occupations. By 2020, total employment in agriculture may fall to less than 45 per cent, while the share of the services sector increases proportionately. The small scale industries (SSI) sector accounts for 95 per cent of industrial units, 40 per cent of value addition, 35 per cent of exports, and 80 per cent of manufacturing employment.

Registered SSI units provide nearly 18 million jobs in the country at this time. Among manufacturing sectors, the single largest employment potential is in textiles, which is slated to generate 7 million jobs over the next five years alone. More than 40 per cent of these jobs are in garment production units in the SSI sector. A healthy and rapidly expanding small sector is essential for a vibrant growth of the Indian economy as a whole. This sector serves as the field for entrepreneurship to flourish, as an entry point for new entrepreneurs who can start small and then grow, as a vehicle for extending the regional spread of industry, as a labouratory for development of innovative products and services, and as an essential support to attract large manufacturing assembling industries from overseas.

Since SSIs are generally more employment intensive per unit of capital than large scale industry, they are also a source of much needed employment. Employment in the registered SSI sector has nearly tripled over the past 20 years. A repetition of this performance would generate an additional 36 million jobs over the next 20 years. A comprehensive package of venture capital, credit, liberalisation of controls, technical training, marketing and management measures is needed to ensure the continuous expansion of this sector.

By far, the largest number of new jobs will be in the services sector. Over the past 100 years, the US economy has more than quadrupled the total number of those employed, yet the percentage of the US workforce engaged in manufacturing is now back to the same level as it was in 1850, while agricultural employment has shrunk to less than 3 per cent of the US workforce. Today, the fastest growing job categories in the USA are in services industries such as financial services, insurance, education, health, construction and real estate.

Rapid growth is slated for a wide range of services in India, including professional, computer-related research and development, real estate, leasing, advertising, printing and packaging, marketing, telecommunications, postal and courier, audiovisual, engineering and construction, wholesale and retail distribution, all levels and types of education, environment, banking, insurance, health, travel, sports and recreation, and all categories of transport services. By the year 2020 more than 120 million jobs will come from the services sector alone.

Tourism-related occupations, including hotels and restaurants, employ 10.8 per cent of workers globally, compared to only 5.6 per cent in India. Domestic tourism will rise rapidly as living standards increase. India's domestic tourist sector is the fastest growing in the world, but with the lowest level of investment. The potential for international tourism too has not yet been exploited properly. China currently attracts more than five times as many foreign tourists, excluding visitors from Hong Kong.

Thailand, Malaysia, and Turkey attract three to four times as many. By one estimate, development of India's tourism infrastructure such as roads, airports and medium priced hotels, combined with modifications in air and hotel pricing and tax policies, could generate more than 20 million additional employment opportunities in tourist related businesses within a decade. Numerous studies have been undertaken to assess the potentials of the IT industry and to identify specific strategies needed to accelerate development of this sector. The NASSCOMMcKinsey study in 1999 projected creation of a ₹70 billion IT industry, employing more than two million persons within 10 years.

The worldwide market for IT services is expected to exceed ₹900 billion by 2010. The recent growth of IT-enabled service businesses in India—call centres, medical transcription, technical support and back office processing, engineering and design, geographic information services, payroll and other human resource services, insurance claim processing, legal databases—is powerful evidence that the potential of IT technology and knowledge based industries extends far beyond the development of software and hardware. The US experience shows that, as the application of information technology spreads and encompasses traditional industries, it can generate new employment opportunities ten times greater in number than those directly involved in core IT industries. IT is also a stimulant to the growth of home-based employment opportunities, especially suitable for women. The trend towards tele-working, which is growing rapidly in USA and some other countries, is just beginning in India. The lower cost and greater convenience of home-based employment is bound to open up greater job opportunities for educated women with children. IT services will be a powerful engine of job growth, but the term 'Knowledge-based industries' includes a much wider range of commercial opportunities.

It encompasses all fields in which the application of mind, judgment and skill, rather than the application of mechanised production technology is the core resource. Education, health services, biotechnology, pharmaceuticals, insurance and financial services are among the leading industries in this category. They are also among the fastest growing industries in the world. Added to these, there is enormous scope for other knowledge intensive activities such as clinical drug trials and many other types of scientific research.

The management of all types of information is emerging as a major growth industry worldwide and India is well poised to become a global leader in this field. Increasing demand for education within the country and worldwide will create tremendous demand for qualified teachers with adequate language skills. An estimated two million additional teachers will be needed in India to support 100 per cent primary school enrolment and to reduce the teacher-student ratio for improved quality of teaching.

Another two million or more will be required to support higher rates of upper primary and secondary school education and to reduce teacher-student ratios at those levels. Teaching staff for vocational training and higher education need to be expanded as well. Demand for health services is increasing worldwide. Already nurses and medical technicians are in short supply. The USA has a doctor-nurse ratio of about twice that of India. Yet the US currently faces a shortfall of nurses, that is more than three times India's total annual production of new nurses. Physicians, nurses, medical technicians and other scientific occupations will become growth industries to rival the IT sector within the next decade. Creation of new jobs in existing industries can and should be supplemented by creation of new services industries that will in turn stimulate increased employment opportunities.

It is extremely difficult to project unemployment rates 20 years into the future, when so much doubt exists even about current levels of unemployment and underemployment. However, it is clear that rising levels of education and growth of the 60 plus age group will mitigate to some extent the growth of the labour force. Combined with the enormous opportunities for creation of new employment opportunities, the incidence of unemployment should be almost eliminated during the second decade of the century.

EDUCATION

Successful population policy is directly linked to successful education policy. Success in raising literacy rates and school enrolment rates while reducing drop-out rates, especially for women, are closely correlated with the delayed onset of marriage and child birth, improved mortality for both mothers and children, and reduction in family size. In fact, a successful education policy forms the bedrock of all fields of national development—political, economic, technical, scientific, social, and environmental.

Education is the foundation for a vibrant democracy in which informed citizens exercise their franchise to support the internal growth of the nation and its constructive role in the world community. It is the foundation for growth in productivity, incomes and employment opportunities and for the development, application and adaptation of science and technology to enhance the quality of life. Education is the foundation for access to the benefits of the information revolution that is opening up vistas on the whole world. Education is also the foundation for improved health care and nutrition.

Literacy, the basis of all education, is as essential to survival and development in modern society as food is to survival and development of the human body. Literacy rates in India have arisen dramatically from 18 per cent in 1951 to 65 per cent in 2001, but these rates are still far from the UMI reference level of 95 per cent. Literacy must be considered the minimum right and requirement of every Indian citizen. Vast differences also remain among different parts of the population. Literacy among males is nearly 50 per cent higher than females, and it is about 50 per cent higher in urban areas as compared to the rural areas. Literacy rates range from as high as 96 per cent in some districts of Kerala to below 30 per cent in some parts of Madhya Pradesh. Rates are also significantly lower among scheduled castes and tribes than among other communities.

These differential rates of progress leave approximately 300 million illiterate adults in the country, the largest number of illiterates in the world. For these people, the traditional avenues of knowledge dissemination through education and printed information are ruled out. These are the people who are most vulnerable to the challenges of development, because they are least equipped to rapidly expand their knowledge base. Since many of them are relatively young adults who will still be active in 2020, the country cannot afford to ignore them or leave them behind. The Government has already set a goal to achieve 75 per cent literacy by the end of the Tenth Five Year Plan. A 100 per cent literate India is of paramount importance for realising the vision for the country in 2020 as presented in this document. Even when this goal is achieved, innovative approaches will be needed to increase knowledge dissemination through TV and other means, to literate adults with little or no formal education. Literacy is an indispensable minimum condition for development, but it is not sufficient. In this increasingly complex and technologically sophisticated world, ten years of school education must also be considered as an essential prerequisite for citizens to adapt and succeed economically, avail of the social opportunities and develop their individual potentials.

Education is the primary and most effective means so far evolved for transmitting practically useful knowledge from one generation to another. India's education system has expanded exponentially over the past five decades, but its current achievements are grossly inadequate for the nation to realise its potential greatness. The net enrolment rate in primary schools is around 77 per cent and in secondary schools it is around 60 per cent. These compare with the 99.9 per cent primary and 69 per cent secondary enrolment for the UMI reference level. The drop out rate was 40 per cent at the primary level and 55 per cent at the upper primary level in 1999-2000. These high drop out rates from both primary and secondary school, combined with low enrolment rates at the higher levels deprive tens of millions of children of their full rights as citizens.

Out of approximately 200 million children in the age group 6-14 years, only 120 million are in schools and net attendance in the primary level is only 66 per cent of the enrolment. Further, less than 7 per cent of the children ever pass the 10th standard public examination. Apart from addressing the needs of a large illiterate population, India's knowledge strategy must also develop innovative approaches to enhance knowledge acquisition among the large community of school drop-outs. Unless something is done to drastically reduce drop-out rates, by the year 2016 there will be approximately 500 million people in the country with less than five years of schooling, and another 300 million that will not have completed high school.

In other words, about two-thirds of the population will lack the minimum level of education needed to keep pace with and take advantage of the social changes occurring within the country and worldwide. Extending the primary school system to over 500,000 villages in India has brought education to the masses. Unfortunately, this huge quantitative expansion has been accompanied by a tremendous dilution in the quality of schooling. High drop out rates in rural areas is one result of single room schools, with few teaching aids and inadequate instruction both in terms of quantity and quality.

Qualitative improvement in the system can be accomplished by promoting centralised schools serving clusters of 10 or more villages, wherever distances and transportation links make that feasible. This will permit greater investment in educational infrastructure, including introduction of computers. Achieving 100 per cent enrolment of all children in the 6 to 14 year age group is an ambitious but achievable goal for 2020. This must be coupled with efforts to increase the quality and relevance of school curriculum to equip students not only with academic knowledge but also with the values and practical knowledge needed for success in life. A business-as usual scenario for primary and secondary education in 2020, based on recent trends as well as an alternative scenario designed to radically enhance the quantity and quality of school education in the country.

A tremendous expansion of schools and classrooms will be required to support a quantitative and qualitative improvement in the country's school system. In order to achieve the best-case scenario total school enrolment would have to increase by 75 million or 44 per cent. That will require a proportionate expansion in the number of classrooms. In addition, efforts to improve the quality of education by reducing the class size would require a further 20 per cent increase in the number of classrooms. Together, this will necessitate increasing the total number of classrooms by 65 per cent within 20 years.

Table. Education Scenarios in 2020

	1980 Actual	2000 Estimated	2020 Business-as-usual	2020 Best-case Scenario
Primary enrolment (1-5)	80%	89%	100%	100%
Elementary enrolment (1-8)	77%	79%	85%	100%
Secondary enrolment (9-12)	30%	58%	75%	100%
Drop-out rate (1-5)	54%	40%	20%	0%
Drop-out rate (1-8)	73%	54%	35%	0%

An enormous increase in the number of teachers will also be required to achieve the alternative scenario, *i.e.*, eliminating primary school drop outs and reducing the teacher-pupil ratio from the present high level of 1:42 down to around 1:20, which is the UMI reference level. Together, this will require an additional three million primary school teachers, more than twice the number currently employed.

Similar increases will be required at middle and secondary school levels. The training of such large number of teachers will require the establishment of additional teacher training colleges and much larger budget allocations for teachers' salaries. Qualitative improvements in education should reflect a change in pedagogical methods and lay emphasis on several dimensions, including:

- A shift from methods that emphasize passive learning to those that foster the active interest and ability of children to learn on their own.
- A shift from rote memorisation to development of children's capacity for critical thinking.
- A shift from traditional academic to practically relevant curriculum.
- A shift from imparting information to imparting life values such as independent thinking, self-reliance

and individual initiative that are essential for success in any field of endeavour.

An important role of education is to foster in each child the attributes and values of a responsible, capable, active and healthy member of the family and society. The rigidity of curriculum, testing and teaching methods need to be relaxed so that innovative methods and new models of education can be evolved, tested and perfected. Vocational streams have to be developed and expanded to equip iarger numbers of high school students with occupation-related knowledge and skills. Experimentation is needed with new methods for knowledge delivery. Television can be a very effective means for educating both school going and non-school going children and adults. It can deliver teaching materials in a more dynamic, entertaining, and interesting manner, utilising the nation's best teachers and multimedia teaching materials on each subject. A TV based curriculum can help slow learners to supplement classroom teaching, fast learners to learn at much faster rates than the rest of the class, drop outs to acquire knowledge they missed out in school, and adults to expand their level of education without returning to school.

New methods of delivery will be particularly necessary to augment access and improve delivery at higher levels of education. Although India's college and university network has expanded dramatically, it is able to accommodate only a tiny fraction of the college-age population. In addition, the quality of facilities, teaching and course materials leaves much to be desired. Recruitment and promotion are highly politicised; seniority rule precludes merit advancement; and the cost of delivery is beyond the means of the vast majority of young Indians.

Table. Growth of Higher Educational Institutions

Years	Colleges for General Education	Colleges for Professional Education	Universities
1951	370	208	27
1998	7199	2075	229

India in 2020 must be a nation in which all those who aspire for higher education have access to college and university level courses. A national network of community colleges, similar to the highly successful American system, is needed to provide knowledge and job-oriented skills to millions of young people who lack interest in or capacity for more stringent academic studies. The advent of computer and the Internet-based educational methods offer an exciting new learning medium that can literally transform our concept of school and classroom from physical into virtual realities.

Studies in the USA project a radical reshaping of higher education over the next two decades as a result of the digital revolution. Many traditional colleges will close as more course works are delivered at a distance through alternative channels. The traditional boundaries between education and other sectors will fade, as publishers, for-profit and non-profit organisations, offer accredited, multimedia-enhanced courses directly to students, by-passing the university.

The traditional classroom type of education, which is most useful for students that require personal attention and assistance and for subjects that involve hands-on experimentation, will no longer be the predominant model of education. For all other purposes, it is very costly and not very efficient in the way it uses the time of both teachers and students. Experience shows that computer-based educational methods can lead to much faster rates and higher quality of learning, which is more interactive and motivating for students at all levels of education from pre-school to post-graduation. It is extremely effective for enhancing reading and language skills and general knowledge among the very young and even for some sophisticated professional courses such as medicine and engineering.

Given the huge number of young students that will quest for all levels of higher education in the coming decades and the severe shortage of qualified instructors, and in the light of India's outstanding expertise in the IT industry, the country needs to embark on a massive programme to convert the entire higher educational curriculum into a multi-media, web-based format and to establish accreditation standards for recognition of the distance education so imparted. Our vision of India in 2020 is predicated on the belief that human resources are the most important determinants of overall development.

As India's IT revolution has been fuelled by the availability of a very large reservoir of well-trained engineers, its future development in many different spheres will depend on commensurate development of sufficient and surplus capabilities. Full development of India's enormous human potential will require a shift in national priorities, to commit a greater portion of the country's financial resources to the education sector. India currently invests 3.2-4.4 per cent of GNP on education. This compares unfavourably with the UMI reference level of 4.9 per cent, especially with countries such as South Africa, which invests 7.9 per cent of GNP on education. A near doubling of investments in education is the soundest policy for quadrupling the country's GDP per capita.

S&T CAPABILITIES

Literacy and general education form the base of the knowledge pyramid that is essential for rapid and sustained development in the 21st century. The continuous advancement of science and application of improved technology form the middle rung; and social ideals and spiritual values form the apex. Technical education, both vocational and professional, constitutes the foundation for development of science and technology. India is rightly proud of the international standing of its IITs, but a handful of world class technical institutions is not sufficient. A large number of the country's approximately 500 engineering colleges need to be upgraded to quality standards nearer to those of the IITs, and given similar autonomy.

Private sector initiative and investment, whether from Indian corporates or NRIs or reputed foreign universities, need to be fully encouraged. Close links need to be fostered between technical institutions and industry. India's enormous manpower base of scientists and engineers is often coveted. President Kalam observed that India's human resource base is one of its greatest core competencies. This is true in absolute terms, but as a percentage of the total population, we are at 1/100th of the US levels and 1/50th of the Korean level. Even China's manpower base of scientists and engineers as a percentage of its population exceeds ours by more than three times. Absolute numbers do count, but manpower alone is not sufficient to excel in the development and application of science and technology.

In terms of total investment in R&D, India's expenditure is 1/60th of that of Korea, 1/250th of that of the USA, and 1/340th of that of Japan. More significantly, atomic energy, space and defence research account for 71 per cent of all central spending on science and technology, which means that relatively little is left for investment in agriculture, energy, telecommunications and other crucial sectors within the sphere of science and technology. R&D expenditure even in India's fast-growing IT sector has been averaging around 3 per cent of sales turnover (STO), which is much lower as compared to the 14-19 per cent expended by internationally reputed software firms.

These low figures reflect on our R&D performance. India's share of global scientific output in 1998 was only 1.58 per cent of the world's total. Out of 500,000 new patent applications filed globally each year, China accounts for 96,000 and Korea accounts for 72,000, while India accounts for only 8,000. Of greater concern has been the country's inability to capitalise on our huge pool of manpower and extensive network of scientific research organisations for transferring proven technologies from the lab to the land and to the factory.

Despite possessing the world's largest cadre of agricultural scientists, we have not been able to extend the momentum of Green Revolution to other regions and crops and to update the scientific practices of our farmers to levels comparable with most other nations. Crop productivity remains far below and production costs far above world averages. A similar gap exists in the application of science and technology for food processing and many other industries. High technology exports account for only 6 per cent of total manufacturing exports for India, compared to over 20 per cent for the UMI reference level. India has a number of premier universities for scientific and technical education which produce world class scientists and engineers, but the national research system rarely produces world class results. One reason is the missing link between scientists in universities and research institutes and practitioners in agriculture and industry.

Another is that non-teaching research institutes lack the continuous inflow of young talented researchers required to challenge assumptions and infiltrate new ideas and approaches. Bureaucracy, tenure and lack of accountability minimise the pressure for practical application of scientific knowledge. Other countries have done a much better job of providing optimum incentives to their scientific community and creating close linkages between science and industry. The management of technology and the administration of government require different sets of skills and a different culture.

Management of technology demands innovation, global competitiveness, and wide latitude for individual freedom, characteristics that are difficult to foster under an administrative regime. The objectives of many institutes and the mechanisms for achieving them need a radical reorientation to bring them in tune with the changing environment brought about by liberalisation of imports, technology tie-ups with foreign agencies and foreign direct investment in key sectors. If the national R&D bodies do not reorganise themselves to face globalisation and global competition, nor take into consideration the nature of the factor endowment of the country along with many existing indigenous technologies so far neglected, then they risk becoming irrelevant to the mainstream activities of industrial development.

The nature of service offered by these institutions has to undergo a sea change. Grass-root consultancy and turnkey project consultancy, including project implementation and monitoring are increasingly in demand. Another essential step is to improve the linkages between technology development and technology application by fostering close ties between basic research and business. In the USA, a large proportion of scientific research at the university level is financed by business, and most leading universities operate technology incubators designed to promote commercialisation of new products and processes. India's recent experiment with the Science and Technology Entrepreneur Parks (STEPs) has been successful in promoting application of technologies, new business start-ups, and employment. The STEPs in combination with technology incubators need to be rapidly multiplied around the country. Effective R&D management backed by suitable incentives for commercialisation are essential for bridging the gap between the lab and the land or factory. R&D is not only essential for propelling growth in industrial fields. It can also become a growth industry on its own. Much of the work done by Indian software companies for overseas clients and parent companies rightly fall under the category of new product development. Vast potential exists for complementing India's strengths in IT with corresponding strengthening of fields such as biotechnology, pharmaceuticals, designer-made materials, and others.

India's investment in the biotechnology sector is expected to increase five-fold by the end of the current decade largely as a result of growing collaboration between multinational corporations and indigenous research efforts. Huge opportunities also exist for R&D in the field of genomics, bioinformatics, DNA technologies, clinical studies and genetically modified crops. Rationalisation of procedure, backed by effective bio-safety regulations are needed to govern testing and approval of biotech products. India has the potential of converting its strong R&D infrastructure into a global research, design and development platform.

VOCATIONAL TRAINING

The knowledge and skill of our workforce will be a major determinant of India's future rate of economic growth as well as the type and number of jobs we create. The greater that knowledge and skill, the higher will be the productivity, the better the quality, and the lower the cost of the products and services we generate. Similarly, the better the quality and lower the cost, greater will be the comparative advantage and market potential. Currently only 5 per cent of the country's labour force in the 20-24 age category have undergone formal vocational training, compared with 28 per cent in Mexico, 60 to 80 per cent in most industrialised nations, and as much as 96 per cent in Korea.

A strategy to achieve full employment must include as an important component, a strategy to ensure that all new entrants to the workforce are equipped with the knowledge and skill needed for high productivity and high quality. India has over 4,200 industrial training institutes (ITI) imparting education and training in 43 engineering and 24 non-engineering trades. Of these, 1,654 are government run ITIs, while 2,620 are private.

The total seating capacity in these ITIs is 6.28 lakh. Most of this training is conducted in classroom style in the form of one to two year diploma courses. In addition, about 1.65 lakh persons undergo apprenticeship vocational training every year in state-run enterprises. If a wider definition of applied courses is taken that includes agriculture, engineering and other professional subjects, the total number receiving job related training is about 17 lakh per annum, which still represents only 14 per cent of new entrants to the workforce. The nature of vocational skills makes it impossible for vocational schools to fully address the nation's needs.

The variety of skills needed by the workforce is far too great. The changes in technology and work processes are too rapid for training courses and their instructors to stay up-todate. The cost of training is also relatively high as it often demands full time enrolment for a prolonged period. Some vocational fields do not lend themselves to classroom or laboratory study at all. A comprehensive strategy is thus needed to enhance the nation's employable skills. It must begin by preparing a catalogue of the entire range of vocational skills needed to support the development of the country. The network of vocational training institutes and the range of vocational skills taught needs to be expanded substantially to impart those skills for which institutional training is most suitable.

The private sector, which promoted the rapid proliferation of computer training institutes throughout the country, should be encouraged to recognise the commercial potential of vocational training in many other fields. In addition, it is essential to fashion more effective and efficient mechanisms for disseminating useful knowledge and skills, especially through the TV media and through computerised vocational training. The importance of computer has been widely recognised as a means to improve efficiency in business, government and formal education, but its application in vocational training is not fully appreciated.

Use of Computers in Vocational Training:

- Rates of learning on computer for both academic as well as vocational or skill-based subjects are four to ten times faster than they are in a classroom setting, and learning retention is likely to be much higher.
- Computers can provide multimedia, interactive, customised and individually paced learning with instantaneous feedback and testing.
- It eliminates the need for producing and deputing a large number of highly skilled instructors. Course contents can be rapidly modified to reflect changing needs.
- For many types of vocational skills, computerised training also offers specific advantages over the live delivery of skills in a classroom.
- Training can be delivered wherever computers are available. A nationwide network of 50,000 computerised vocational centres, run as private self-employed businesses similar to the STD booths and Internet cafes, can deliver low-cost, high-quality training to 10 million workers every year—more than five times the total number covered by existing programmes.

Although 58 per cent of Indians are engaged in agriculture, vocational training for farmers is one of the weakest links in the Indian educational system. Agricultural universities cater to the nation's need for agricultural scientists and extension officers. An extensive network of more than 300 Krishi Vignan Kendras (KVK) offers short and medium term courses for farmers on specialised subjects. The KVK network provides training to several hundred thousand farmers each year, but it can cater to the needs of only a miniscule percentage of all farmers.

Agricultural education can be moved from the campus into the village by establishing a national network of farm schools, offering practical demonstration and training on lands leased from farmers in the local community. The prime objective of the schools would be to impart knowledge and skills designed to double yields on important commercial crops. Educated farmers can be trained as self-employed instructors to operate the farm schools as private enterprises on a commercial basis.

HEALTH FOR ALL

The health of a nation is difficult to define in terms of a single set of measures. At best, we can assess the health of the population by taking into account indicators like infant mortality and maternal mortality rates, life expectancy and nutrition, along with the incidence of communicable and non-communicable diseases. The health of the Indian population has improved dramatically over the past fifty years. Life expectancy has risen from 33 years to 64 years.

The infant mortality rate (IMR) has fallen from 148 to 71 per 1000. The crude birth rate (CBR) has declined from 41 to 25 and the crude death rate (CDR) has fallen from 25 to under 9. The couple protection rate (CPR) and total fertility rate (TFR) have also improved substantially. Despite these achievements, wide disparities persist between different income groups, between rural and urban communities, and between different states and even districts within states. The infant mortality rate among the poorest quintet of the population is 2.5 times higher than that among the richest. Maternal mortality remains very high. More than one lakh women die each year due to pregnancy-related complications.

Like population growth and economic growth, the health of a nation is a product of many factors and forces that combine and interact with each other. Economic growth, per capita income, employment, levels of literacy and education—especially among females—age of marriage, birth rates, availability of information regarding health care and nutrition, access to safe drinking water, public and private health care infrastructure, access to preventive health care and medical care, health insurance, public hygiene, road safety, and environmental pollution are among the factors that contribute directly to the health of the nation.

Communicable diseases such as malaria, kalaazar, tuberculosis and HIV infection remain the major causes of illness in India. During the next five to ten years, existing programmes are likely to eliminate polio and leprosy and substantially reduce the prevalence of kalaazar and filariasis. However, TB, malaria and AIDS will continue to remain major public health problems. India has about 1.5 million identified cases of TB that are responsible for more than 3,00,000 deaths annually. Improved diagnostic services and treatment can reduce the prevalence and incidence of TB by 2020. About 2 million cases of malaria are reported in India each year. Restructuring the "malaria workforce" and strengthening health infrastructure can reduce the incidence of this disease by up to 50 per cent within a decade.

Assessing the impact of HIV epidemic is more difficult; there are about 4 million persons infected with HIV. The National Health Policy aims at achieving a plateau in the prevalence of HIV infection by 2007. Childhood diarrhoea, another major cause of illness, is largely preventable through simple community action and public education, and deaths due to diarrhoea can be eliminated by 2010. Childhood under-nutrition, the other major area of concern, can be addressed by targeting children of low birth weights and employing low-cost screening procedures to detect under-nutrition at an early age. Given the projected improvement in living standards, food security, educational levels and access to health care among all levels of the general population, substantial progress can be made in reducing the prevalence of severe under-nutrition in children by 2020.

China's remarkable success in combating disease over the past two decades is proof that a determined commitment to improving public health can dramatically reduce the incidence of infectious diseases within one or two decades. With the demographic and epidemiological transition taking place in the coming years, non-communicable diseases are also likely to emerge as major public health problems. Modernisation of life styles will further aggravate health problems. The rapid proliferation of two and four wheel motor vehicles, increasing congestion on city roads and intercity highways have all contributed to an increasing number of deaths and serious injuries from traffic related accidents.

Greater emphasis on education and enforcement of road safety rules by both drivers and pedestrians is an urgent need of the hour. As already noted, there will be a massive increase in population in the 15-64 age group. Reproductive and Child Health care programmes must meet the needs of this rapidly growing clientele.

The population in this age group will be more literate and have greater access to information. They will have greater awareness and expectations about access to quality services for maternal and child health, contraceptive care, management of gynaecological problems, etc.

A major focus of vision 2020 must be on improving access to health services to meet the health care needs of women and children. India's significant achievements in the field of health have been made possible by the establishment of a huge rural health infrastructure, along with the formation of a massive health care manpower consisting of over five lakh trained doctors working under plural systems of medicine, and a vast frontline of over seven lakh nurses and other health care workers; 25,000 primary and community health care centres; and 1.6 lakh sub-centres, complemented by 22,000 dispensaries and 2,800 hospitals practicing Indian systems of medicine and homeopathy.

This infrastructure remains under-equipped, under-manned and under-financed to cope with the challenge of eradicating major threats to human life. The inadequacy of the current health care system is starkly showed by the fact that only 35 per cent of the population have access to essential drugs, while the UMI reference level is above 82 per cent. Infant immunisation against measles and DPT for children under 12 years is only 60 per cent and 78 per cent compared to the UMI level of over 90 per cent for both diseases. As a larger proportion of the population reaches middle class standards of living, an increasing number of people will turn to private health care providers.

This development is welcome, because it will permit the public health care system to concentrate more resources on meeting the needs of the poorer parts. But at the same time, the level of public expenditure on health care needs to rise about four-fold from the current level of 0.8 per cent of GDP to reach the UMI reference level of 3.4 per cent. Rapid growth of the private health care system, however, requires the formulation of competence and quality standards to check and balance the increasing emphasis on health care as a business.

Criteria for a More Equitable and Effective Health Care System:

- Universal access and access to an adequate level of health care without financial burden.
- Fair distribution of financial costs for access and fair distribution of burden in rational care and capacity.
- Ensuring that providers have the competence, empathy and accountability for delivering quality care and for effective use of relevant research.
- Special attention to vulnerable groups such as women, children, the disabled and the aged.

Development plans for India's health care systems need to place greater emphasis on public health education and prevention. The wide dissemination of health and nutrition related information through traditional channels should be supplemented by an ambitious and persistent programme of public health education through the print, television, radio and electronic media. Health insurance can play an invaluable role in improving the overall health care system. The insurable population in India has been assessed at 250 million and this number will increase rapidly in the coming two decades.

This should be supplemented by innovative insurance products and programmes by panchayats with reinsurance backup by companies and government to extend coverage to much larger parts of the population. The life expectancy of the Indian population is expected to reach above 65 years in 2020, which compares favourably with the UMI reference level of 69 years. Mortality rates for infants is expected to decline to about 20 per 1000 in 2020, which compares favourably with the UMI reference level of 22.5.

VULNERABILITY

Economic growth, rising levels of education among the young, expansion of employment opportunities for the working age population, slower population growth, and declining infant mortality, however, will not eliminate and may even aggravate, inequalities between different age groups, the sexes, income groups, communities and regions, unless specific corrective steps are taken for levelling the different degrees of capacity and opportunity. The Vision 2020 must have special focus on bridging the existing gaps in the various levels of development and endeavour its best to fulfil the Constitutional commitment of raising the status of the vulnerable groups vis-a-vis the rest of the society.

During the next 20 years, the aged population in India will nearly double, placing much greater demand on the infrastructure of hospitals and nursing homes, while at the same time shifting the profile of health disorders from problems of the young to those of the aged. The population above 65 years of age will increase from 45 to 76 million persons by 2020. Reference has already been made to the very high incidence of malnutrition among this group and the growing incidence of diseases associated with aging, such as cancer and cardiovascular diseases.

A disproportionate number of the aged population are illiterate and living below the poverty line. While majority of these people live in rural areas where the extended family system remains prevalent, increasing urbanisation and mobility will destabilise their situation in future. The problem of coping with a larger aged population will be partially solved by a big surge in the size of the working age labour force and a reduction in the dependency ratio, meaning that there will be a larger proportion of workers to support the aged. Specific strategies will be needed to provide targeted assistance for the most vulnerable members of this group, including research on the disabilities of the aged, greater development of geriatric medicine, training of minders for the aged, and establishment of innovative support systems such as the highly successful Japanese model.

Like the aged, the disabled persons also form another subgroup that is particularly vulnerable and unlikely to benefit directly from the general advance of society, unless specific provisions are made to address their particular needs, including a special system of schools, clinics and homebased learning programmes, combined with therapeutic and institutional care. Increasing gender equity is an important challenge of the coming years. Literacy rates for females are 40 per cent lower than for males. Females represent only 43 per cent of all students at primary level, 37 per cent at higher secondary level, and 35 per cent of those in higher education. Drop out rates are also higher for girls. The UNDP's gender development index ranks India 108th among 174 countries in terms of gender equity.

It is no coincidence therefore that countries ranking highest on this index are among the most prosperous in the world. Gender equity and social development are inseparably interlinked. Reducing the disparity in nutritional, literacy and educational levels between the sexes is essential for realisation of the country's full potentials. Children being the supreme assets of the country, the 'Rights' based approach will continue to play an important role in ensuring their 'survival', 'protection' and 'development', with special attention to the girl child. Our vision for 2020 in this regard is to see a nation free from all forms of child labour.

However, complete elimination of child labour through legal means is not only difficult to implement but may also prove to be counter productive in protecting the interest of these very children. While legal enforcement can contain the demand for child labour, it may leave the poor households supplying child labour more vulnerable rather than addressing the underlying socio-economic compulsions generating the supply of such labour. Indeed, poverty eradication combined with educational reforms to provide free (or affordable) access to quality education with an interesting, innovative and job-oriented curriculum for all can effectively eliminate child labour once and for all.

The other categories of the vulnerable groups include the scheduled castes (SC), scheduled tribes (ST), other backward classes (OBC) and minorities, constituting nearly three-fourths of the country's total population. They require special attention in order to narrow down the disparities between them and the more privileged part of the population. Literacy rates for SCs and STs are 25 per cent lower than for other communities. Education enrolment rates among this group, especially for females, lag significantly behind that of other communities. Low levels of education lead to lower paying employment opportunities and lower incomes.

Thus, it becomes exceedingly difficult for these communities to come out of the vicious circle. Large number of people in other communities also suffer from similar disparities. Regional disparities in rates of development are of similar concern. Regardless of the community or the region, the overall progress of the nation will depend to a large extent on its ability to provide increasing opportunities for the disadvantaged to take initiative for their self development. Otherwise, these disadvantaged will exact an increasing toll on the stability, well-being and development of the country as a whole.

It is notable that rising levels of violence and crime in society are not so much associated with overall low levels of development, as they are with wide disparities between levels of development, which create frustration and resentment. The progress of the whole will ultimately depend on the progress of its weakest links. India's vision of 2020 must be one in which all levels and parts of the population and all parts of the country march forward together into a more secure and prosperous future.

INFRASTRUCTURE

URBAN DEVELOPMENT

Disparities between the social and physical infrastructure of the urban and rural areas are common to all countries. In India they are a continuing source of concern and will become further aggravated unless innovative strategies are evolved to accelerate the development of rural infrastructure. A Vision of India 2020 must assess and try to anticipate the complexion of the future urban-rural divide. Recent evidence confirms that the rate of growth of urban centres in the country is declining more rapidly than was previously anticipated, though the proportion of people living in urban areas continues to rise. The 2001 Census, 27.8 per cent of the Indian population reside in cities, compared with 25.5 per cent in 1990.

The urban population is expected to rise to around 40 per cent by 2020. As India's cities continue to swell, the challenge of improving the urban infrastructure will be magnified. For instance, only 73 per cent of India's urban population has access to improved sanitation facilities, compared to the UMI reference level of 95 per cent. The trend towards concentration of urban population in a small number of large urban centres has been taking shape over a century. While the number of urban centres doubled between 1901 and 1991, the urban population increased eight-fold, resulting in a top heavy urban hierarchy.

Future demographic and economic growth is likely to concentrate in and around 60 to 70 large cities in the country having a population of a million people or more. The demographic trends towards urbanisation are accompanied by a change in the management and financing of urban development as a result of liberalisation. Decentralisation of municipal governance has led to a substantial reduction in budgetary allocations for infrastructural development. Greater reliance is now placed on institutional financing and capital markets for resource mobilisation and on private companies for service delivery.

Disparities in infrastructure between large and small urban areas have always been prevalent, but these disparities can be expected to increase significantly in future years. The stricter fiscal disciplines imposed by government and credit rating agencies will make it increasingly difficult for all but the largest urban centres to attract finance for infrastructural development. The large cities may be expected to experience modest to high rates of growth and to absorb a large part of the incremental migration in their peripheries and neighbouring towns.

Being linked to the national and global economy, these large areas are likely to attract investment from the corporate sector and experience a stable demographic growth, while small and medium towns, particularly in backward regions, attract little industrial and infrastructural investment and report low and unstable demographic growth. This almost exclusive focus on improving infrastructure and basic amenities in the large cities is misplaced.

Still greater inequality may be expected in the level of basic services across urban centres of different sizes by the year 2020, unless concerted initiative is taken to reverse the trend. The gross inadequacies of infrastructure, especially those of public transport, water supply and sanitation, demand corrective action. A strategy for developing capabilities within the urban local bodies to cope with the infrastructural deficiencies must be adopted, with genuine decentralisation of financial and administrative powers and restructuring of the entities on the basis of sound management practices.

The face of urban poverty in 2020 is unlikely to be very different from what it is today, given that the largest indicator of poverty in cities is not so much lack of income, as lack of decent housing and civic amenities. These call for a change in a number of policies, especially those relating to land regulation, zoning, and development. The activities relating to provision of health care, water supply and sanitation, education and vocational training need to be carried out with higher levels of efficiency, to help the urban poor upgrade themselves. While improving infrastructure in existing cities/ towns is not to be ignored, in the next two decades there will be need to encourage growth of new townships and take up regional urban development plans where growth corridors can be identified and public-private partnerships promoted for investment in alternative nodes of development. Such centres will have considerable impact in improving the urban profile of the country. They will, however, need to make provision for adequate supply of water and sanitation as well as other civic amenities. They will also need to chalk out more liberal policies towards education and health care in order to attract a cosmopolitan group of investors, professionals and providers of other services.

While a large part of it will cater to the affluent, through imaginative planning the new centres can serve the needs of the hinterland also by offering avenues for employment, housing and other needs of a large workforce. Urban development represents one of the great challenges for India over the next two decades. Given the socio-political reality in India, it will be difficult for the private sector to bring about changes in the pattern of investment in infrastructure without the state becoming an active partner, bringing about the required legislative and administrative changes.

A satisfying outcome will depend on the formulation of effective public policy to accelerate all-round development of smaller urban centres and to refashion the role of the state as an effective facilitator to compensate for the deficiencies of market mechanisms in the delivery of public goods. Anti-poverty programmes should primarily be directed towards creation of a community-based infrastructure.

RURAL INFRASTRUCTURE

Along with the development of urban infrastructure,

simultaneous efforts are also needed for strengthening rural infrastructure. Specific aspects of the rural infrastructure are discussed elsewhere in this report under the headings of education, health care, transport, telecom, power and water. Our vision is to create a rural infrastructure which connects every village with paved roads and telecommunication facilities, provides electricity and an assured supply of safe drinking water to all rural households, offers access to quality primary and secondary education to all children and medical services to all citizens. The rural electrification programme, launched in 1951, has succeeded in bringing electricity to more than 5 lakh villages.

However, 80,000 villages are yet to get electricity connections. Out of these, 18,000 are in remote areas where electrification through the conventional electricity grid may not be feasible. To achieve 100 per cent rural electrification, we must rely on non-conventional sources of energy, especially for the remote villages. A detailed discussion regarding the potential for such energy sources is given elsewhere in this report. But the problem of rural infrastructure cannot be viewed or tackled in terms of a composite of separate services or in isolation from changes affecting the urban landscape.

A comprehensive and integrated strategy is required. The future development of urban centres will widen the disparities in civic infrastructure that exist between urban and rural communities, thereby stimulating greater migration to the cities and rapid expansion of urban slum areas. The natural growth of urban areas will make this trend inevitable unless bold steps are taken to promote an alternative, more geographically dispersed and equitable development paradigm.

Past efforts to develop satellite townships and growth centres in the vicinity of large cities have mitigated the concentration of population in central urban business districts to some extent, but in the process it has furthered the concentration of population in mega cities. Rural livings offer several considerable advantages over their urban counterparts: However, any successful alternative approach must address the crucial issues of infrastructure and civic amenities that make urban areas so attractive.

Comparative Advantages:

- Urban
  - *Domestic services*: Piped water, electricity, telecommunications and sanitation.
  - *Primary or localised services*: Shops, dispensaries, and playgrounds.
  - *Secondary services*: Schools, police stations, railway, fire-fighting services, and hospitals, which need not be local but must be readily accessible when required.
  - *Tertiary services*: airports, wholesale markets, referral hospitals, etc. which are less frequently demanded.
- Rural
  - Living space is much cheaper and more abundant.
  - The environment is much healthier.
  - Commuting times between work and home are much shorter.

One promising alternative is to link clusters of ten villages together by a high speed circular highway, thereby bringing 100,000 or more people into a circular community that can be crossed within 30 minutes travel time, and promoting a balanced and well spread out development of urban services along the periphery of the ring road. This arrangement would vastly reduce the length and cost of constructing good roads between all the villages, and enable establishment of quality services at any point around the ring to be accessible to all members of the linked community.

Telecom links and sanitation systems would naturally develop around the ring at far lower cost, and better quality schools and hospitals could develop to support the larger community. Industrial parks could be established to utilise the large workforce available within the ring. These and similar models need to be tried and modified, on a priority basis, otherwise it requires little stretch of imagination to anticipate the increasing congestion and immobility of large urban areas that is bound to occur in the near future.

TELECOM

Telecom acts as a stimulus for the development process. Over the past decade, India's achievement in this sector has been quite impressive. In terms of the overall size of main telephone lines in operation, the country rose from its 14th rank in the world in 1995 to 7th in 2001. India has adopted a gradual approach towards telecom sector reforms, through selective privatisation and managed competition in different market segments.

Since the early 1990s, it has introduced private competition in value-added services, and national and international long distance telephony. Two state-owned public sector incumbents with a large existing subscriber base still dominate the fixed line service, in which they own about 35 million direct exchange lines (DEL).

While the number of DELs has multiplied six-fold since 1991, demand for new lines has grown nearly as fast, resulting in persistent shortfall of supply and a current waiting list of nearly 3 million lines. India has also achieved significant quality upgradation of its network in the 1990s, achieving almost 100 per cent conversion to digital lines. At the same time there has been a significant reduction in telecom rates paid by consumers. The opening up of the cellular market has unleashed real dynamism in the marketplace. Cellular mobile telephone subscribers in India increased from 77 thousand in 1995 to 7.3 million by June 2002, rising from a 0.6 per cent of the total subscribers to 17 per cent.

This level is still relatively low compared with the average level of about 25 per cent achieved by low-income countries, 42 per cent by middle-income countries, and upwards of 50 per cent by upper middle income and high-income countries. The mobile explosion is helping in improving telecom penetration, bringing along the concomitant economic benefits of enhanced telecom accessibility, while at the same time promoting a better entrepreneurial culture, generating additional employment, and fostering a shift in the investment burden from the state to the private sector and the consumers.

Table. Number of Main Telephone Lines per 100 Inhabitants

Country	2001
USA	66.45
Germany	63.48
Japan	59.69
UK	57.78
France	57.35
Korea, Rep.	47.60
Russia	24.33
Turkey	28.52
Brazil	21.69
China	13.81
India	3.38

In spite of a significant expansion of capacity, however, India's tele-density remains appealingly low and closing the digital divide in terms of tele-density remains a daunting task. In order to attain the current network size of UMI countries by 2020, India will have to increase the number of telephone lines seven-fold in 18 years. Targeted intervention through access promotion can be an important strategy for achieving growth with greater equity. The launching of private franchises for public call offices (PCOs) handling both domestic and long distance services has resulted in an increase in the number of PCOs from 0.2 million in 1993 to 0.9 million in 2001, including 0.4 million in villages. The presence of the private sector is widespread in PCOs and Internet Kiosks in the cities and towns, but remains insignificant in rural areas which account for only about 23 per cent of the country's fixed phone lines.

The aggressive expansion of public sector telecommunications infrastructure in geographically remote parts of the country, where private industry cannot venture profitably, is essential for unleashing the latent economic energies and market forces in these regions. Looking forward from now to 2020, the rapid expansion of India's fixed line network is likely to continue. As the fixed line market matures, more and more users will cross over to mobile communications as well, spurring a mobile revolution in India. Mobile telecommunications and the Internet are going to set the contours of further technological progress over the next two decades.

The recent convergence of voice and data transmission, global satellite systems, mobile handsets and calling cards have overcome the technological barriers of distance, topography and remoteness. By 2020, third generation (3G) mobile devices with access to mobile data and voice should be within the reach of wider parts of the Indian population. The last decade also witnessed a phenomenal growth in the use of Internet. Private Internet service providers have been allowed to set up international Internet gateways, as well as both satellite and landing stations for submarine optical fibre cables. Internet telephony is also opening up.

India must strive to complete the transition into digital switching and transmission, voice over Internet protocol (VoIP), broadband and 3G by 2020. Despite differences across countries, the global trend is towards growing privatisation and competition in telecommunications. Global experience suggests that this process is likely to undergo alternating cycles of differentiation and convergence. The convergent nature of technology may dictate mergers and acquisitions between companies in certain cases. Network operators and service providers may have to merge with content developers to add value to their services.

This may create temporary conditions of oligopoly until the emergence of new firms, offering multiple services, intensifies competition. India in 2020 is likely to see competition among big firms offering innovative value-added services to capture market share. The regulatory environment should therefore foster maximum flexibility and freedom to encourage innovation and expansion, consistent with this process of evolution. Rapid flow of information is a catalyst for social development. Vision 2020 conceives of India evolving into an information society and knowledge economy built on the edifice of information and communication technology

(ICT), of which telecommunications is the springboard. Telecom is improving opportunities for people across different social strata.

A whole range of information based industries and applications have come up, creating new sources of employment and earnings with welfare enhancing consequences for both the poor and the wealthy. As a meta technology, ICT has caused rapid innovations to occur in other areas of material sciences. It has improved access in the fields of education, healthcare, governance and business services. It has also enhanced the ability of the poor to manage risks and mitigate vulnerabilities through provision of timely information. Rapid expansion and extension of the country's fixed and mobile telecom infrastructure is essential for stimulating growth of both the ICT sector and the economy as a whole.

TRANSPORT

Development involves a continuous increase in the number of physical transactions and the speed with which they occur, both of which are highly dependent on the size and quality of the nation's transport system. India's network of roads, railways, air services and ports is one of the largest in the world, serving a land mass of 3.3 million square km and a population of over one billion. Over the last 50 years, the growth of this network and of the demand for transport services has been enormous. The volume of railway freight has increased five-fold and passenger kilometres nearly seven-fold. The length of surfaced roads has multiplied nine-fold. The number of goods vehicles has increased 40-fold, buses 20-fold and four-wheel passenger vehicles 30-fold.

The tonnage of freight handled by the nation's expanding system of major and minor ports has grown more than 16-fold. Air-freight tonnage has increased about 30-fold. Currently, about 800 billion tonne km of freight and 2,300 billion passenger km are handled by the transport system, with the total transport demand growing at around 10 per cent a year for the past decade. The modal growth rates have varied, with road transport and air services growing at a much faster rate than the railways. The relative share of railways in total freight and passenger traffic has declined dramatically over the past five decades, from 90 to 25 per cent of inland freight and from 75 to 18 per cent of inland passenger.

Meanwhile, the share of road transport has increased from 12 to 60 per cent of freight and from 32 to 80 per cent of passenger business. Growing urbanisation is a natural phenomenon and despite all its implications has beneficial effects on economic growth. Increasing population combined with continued urbanisation are likely to raise India's urban population to around 540 million over the next two decades, resulting in the emergence of about 60 to 70 cities with population of more than a million. Lack of adequate public transport has resulted in a rapid increase in private ownership of vehicles, particularly two wheelers, with consequent adverse effects of air and noise pollution.

In most cities, two wheelers comprise more than 70 per cent of total motor vehicles. Based on current growth rates, two-wheeler ownership in cities with more than 100,000 inhabitants is likely to rise from 102 to 393 per thousand population in the next 20 years, while the number of cars increases from 14 to 48 per thousand. To contain this explosion of personal vehicle movement in cities, massive investment in mass transport services will become necessary. Public investment in transport has declined steadily over the past four decades from 23 per cent of the total plan funds in 1960 to around 12 per cent in the 1980s and 1990s. Considering the developing nature of the country and the deficiencies in its transport system, a larger proportion of resources will need to be invested in improvements to the transport infrastructure.

Among the most daunting problems faced by India's cities are the inadequate public transport infrastructure, long travel times and high transport cost for both passenger and goods traffic. The growth of cities has been haphazard, expanding around a compact central core with industrialisation and migration bringing about rapid change in peripheral land use, resulting in urban sprawl. No organised, viable and significant public transport system is available in major cities, except the four metro areas of Mumbai, Kolkata, Chennai and Delhi. Bus and rail systems are the mainstay of public transport in these cities. Transport planning must go hand-in-hand with land use planning. Specific plans will need to be formulated by each urban authority, starting with the provision of bus services, developing intermediate public transport and identifying corridors for future growth, including reserving land for such activity. In the long run, rail-based mass transport systems appear to be the only viable solution to the problems of urban transport in India's major metropolitan areas. Where flexibility of land use is possible, electrified surface rail transport can be adopted. In the case of highly developed and congested areas, underground or fly over systems will have to be considered. On medium density corridors, electric trolley buses or CNG operated buses may be best suited.

A key component of rural development is the provision of roads for connectivity, access being essential for social and economic well-being. Families residing along side roads benefit from better health, greater educational opportunities, smaller sized families and higher ownership of assets, compared to those families living in remote villages. While almost all villages with population above 1,500 are now connected by road, more than 45 per cent of villages with less than 1,000 people still need to be connected.

There are also significant regional imbalances in the connectivity of villages. Poor road maintenance is a related problem. The Government has allocated resources to achieve all-weather road access to all villages with population above 1,000 by 2003, and for villages with population between 500 and 1,000 by 2007. While the progress made in the transport sector has been significant, it has not been able to meet the growing demand, particularly in the last decade when economic reforms triggered an unprecedented growth of GDP. Efforts to achieve even higher GDP growth rates in future years cannot be sustained without correspondingly greater efforts to strengthen the nation's transport system. The existing issues and concerns, the congestion and constraints in movement leading to higher transport costs, and other unfinished tasks will be some of the challenges that need to be met during the next two decades. A huge increase in demand for both railways and road transport will require not only massive investments but also modification in pricing policies, increasing customer focus, improved terminal management, enhanced safety, reduced transit times, and other changes required to provide adequate and efficient services for meeting the growth in demand and public expectations.

Based on projected GDP growth of 8 per cent per annum, the total freight traffic is likely to reach about 5,500 billion tonne km by the year 2020, five times the level in year 2000. If a 10 per cent growth is achieved, the traffic demand would exceed 10,000 billion tonne km. Assuming that railways retain a 20 per cent market share, rail freight traffic, measured in ton km, will increase three to six-fold. The proportion of manufactured products to bulk cargo will also rise, with a larger proportion of liquids being carried through the pipelines. General merchandise will travel longer distances and in much smaller consignments, favouring smaller carrying units.

The rising value of consignments will place a higher premium on the speed of transit in order to minimise inventories. The total logistical management of transportation, marketing and distribution will become commonplace for most general merchandise. These changes, together with the impact of other factors such as energy efficiency, environmental pollution, and technological changes in each mode, will result in changing preferences for alternative modes of transport.

For medium distances up to 500 kms—with four-lane highways connecting the country, expressways coming up close to the main metro cities, and car ownership increasing rapidly—the bulk of the passenger travel may start moving towards 'own vehicle travel', a phenomenon already observed in most countries. Fast inter-city rail services will have an edge over air travel for this segment of traffic. Road transport is best suited for short distance traffic, except where volumes increase to very high levels and rail-based mass rapid transport offers a cost-effective alternative.

Future Trends in Transport:

- Improvement in the length, quality and speed of transport networks.
- Increase in productivity and economic efficiency of transport.
- Higher frequency and quality of services.
- Better control of air and noise pollution.
- Increased mobility for commuters, business and recreational travel.
- Improved urban transport systems.
- Corresponding improvements in rural transport.
- Fewer transport constraints to trade.
- Reduced transport transit times in general and at initial loading and terminal points.
- Better energy efficiency.
- Improved safety with fewer accidents.

Our vision of India 2020 is of a country with a well-developed network of roads and railways and adequate capacity to handle the growth in demand for transport. The volume of road traffic will multiply about five-fold, carried over a 70,000 km network of National Highways, including 5,000 to 10,000 km of expressways, linking the golden quadrangle of Delhi-Mumbai-Chennai-Kolkata-Delhi as well as northern, southern, eastern and western portions of the country, mostly with four or more lanes. State Highways with at least two way lanes will link most districts. Rural roads will provide access to the furthest outlying villages. Technological progress will generate vehicles that are pollution free and fuel-efficient.

An efficient public transport system will lead to a reduction in the population of two-wheelers in major urban areas. The railways will have to be expanded to handle a three-fold increase in traffic. Improved customer service, comfort and safety, a reduction in freight costs and tariffs, elimination (or at least reduction) of the uneconomic services, non-paying projects and subsidies will be necessary for this. India will need airports of international standards for passenger and cargo handling and modern handling systems at major ports to reduce delays in berthing. Institutional arrangements will need to be in place with adequate funds for proper maintenance, especially of roads. Urban transport systems will be needed in all cities with a population of a million plus. We envisage that connection of several distributaries of the rivers through a network of canals will give impetus to the development of inland water transport. Investment requirements to meet these needs will increase to levels three to four times higher than the present in real terms. While the government will continue to be a major source of funds for infrastructure, internal generation of resources by the transport services will have to increase, supported by more realistic pricing of transport services and reduction in operating costs. The private sector will need to play a more central role in the development and operation of transport systems.

ENERGY AND THE ENVIRONMENT

Economic growth the world over is driven by energy, whether in the form of finite resources such as coal, oil and gas or in renewable forms such as hydroelectric, wind, solar and biomass, or its converted form, electricity. This energy generation and consumption powers the nation's industries, vehicles, homes and offices. It also has significant impact on the quality of the country's air, water, land and forest resources. For future growth to be both rapid and sustainable, it needs to be as resource-efficient and environmentally benign as possible.

POWER

India's installed capacity for power generation has tripled over the last 20 years and now exceeds 101,000 MW. However, the total demand is expected to increase by another 3.5 times in the next two decades, even under a best-case scenario that envisions intensified efforts to modernise power plants, improve transmission and distribution efficiency, and adopt more efficient generation technologies. Figure depicts power consumption by various sectors in 1997 compared to a business as-usual (BAU) and an alternative scenario which as suggested, consider as the best-case scenario (BCS) for 2020.

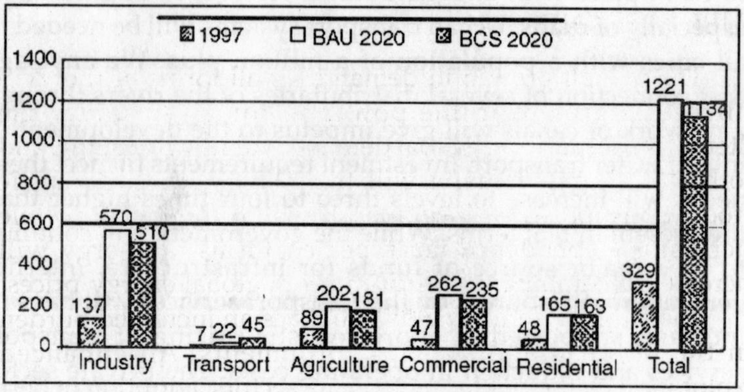

Fig. Projected Power Demand (TWh)

The soaring demand for power will necessitate a tripling of the installed generation capacity from 101,000 to 292,000 MW over the next two decades. The projected fuel mix for power generation from various sources is shown in Figure. At least two-thirds of this power will have to come from thermal sources—coal, oil and gas—even under the BCS. This will mean a spiralling cost for imported fuels, including coal, since even a doubling of domestic coal production would not be sufficient to meet the demand. It will also mean a surge in emission of environmental pollutants. Even under this alternative scenario, the contribution of renewable energy does not exceed 5 per cent of the total production.

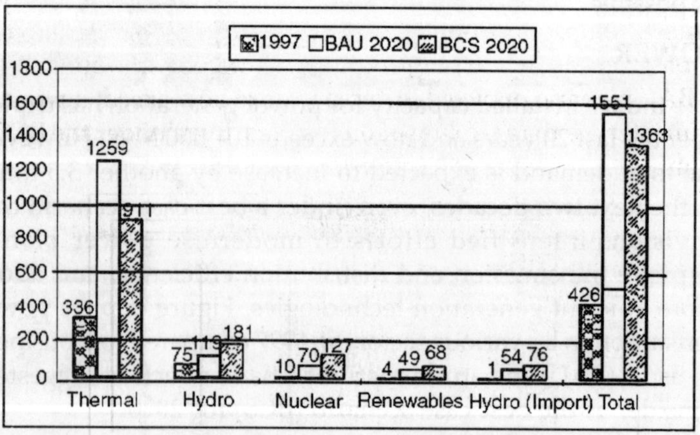

Fig. Fuel Mix for Power Generation (TWh)

FUEL DEMAND

The overall growth in demand for all forms of fuel will mirror the growth in the power sector. Even under the alternative scenario, total coal demand will nearly double, and both oil and gas demand will triple. Expanding domestic production capacity will require substantial investments, while increasing dependence on imported forms of energy will increase vulnerability to fluctuations in global energy prices.

The surging demand will also place an increased burden on the physical and social environments. An enhanced exploration by the public and private sectors, adoption of best practices and environment-friendly technologies, more efficient use of energy, promotion of private sector investment, and greater efforts to protect the environment will be required to cope effectively with the nation's growing energy needs.

Table. Projected Fuel Demand

	Coal (million tons)	Oil (million tons)	Gas (billion cubic mtrs)
1997	311	83	21.5
2020 BAU	688	245	70.8
2020 BCS	538	195	64.7

The growth in demand for oil depicted in Figure shows that the largest increases will be for transportation and industry. Domestic oil production has remained relatively constant over the past decade, while oil imports have more than doubled. If the BAU scenario depicted in Table were to be realised, it would require a more than tripling of oil imports. Even under the BCS, oil imports would have to increase two-fold.

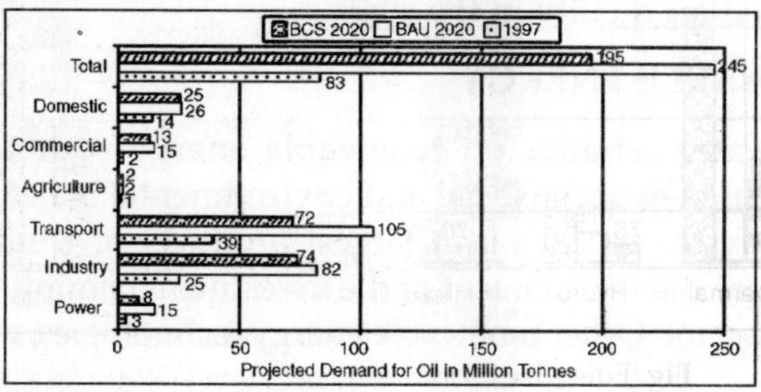

Long-term forecasts for the price of oil are at best precarious. A recent forecast by the Institute of Energy Economics of Japan shows the price fluctuating within a band from ₹765 to ₹1035 per barrel over the next 20 years. The growth in demand for natural gas depicted in Figure shows that the largest increases will be for power and industry, especially fertilizers. Domestic gas production is expected to meet around 20 per cent of the total demand, thereby requiring massive import of gas. Plans for gas pipeline projects from Bangladesh and Iran as well as LNG terminals along India's coastlines are already being contemplated.

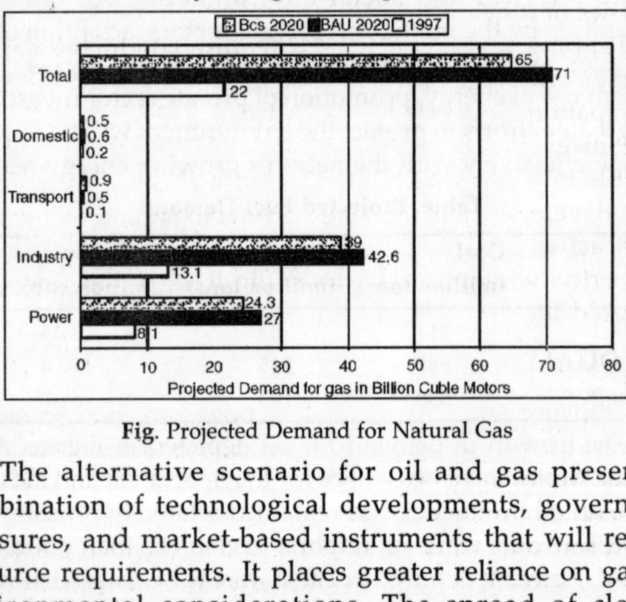

Fig. Projected Demand for Natural Gas

The alternative scenario for oil and gas presents a combination of technological developments, governance measures, and market-based instruments that will reduce resource requirements. It places greater reliance on gas for environmental considerations. The spread of cleaner technologies among transport vehicles should lead to improved air quality in the cities.

RENEWABLE ENERGY

Greater reliance on renewable energy sources offers enormous economic, social and environmental benefits. India is already the world's fifth largest producer of wind power, with more than 95 per cent of the investment coming from the private sector. Other renewable energy technologies, including solar photovoltaic, solar thermal, small hydro and biomass power are also spreading. Under the BAU scenario the contribution of renewable forms of energy is expected to be quite modest, but a concerted effort to implement a more visionary plan could significantly alter this outcome.

Apart from reducing India's dependence on imported fuels and the strain on the environment, some forms of renewable energy such as biomass power production and ethanol motor fuel offer the added advantage of potentially creating millions of rural employment opportunities and contributing to higher rural incomes, rather than higher outflows of foreign exchange.

Tapping this potential will require conducive national policies and programmes designed to attract active participation from the private sector.

However, a far more aggressive alternative scenario is also possible in which the country makes a massive commitment to the development of biomass power, biogas and biofuels that could act as a powerful stimulus to rural job-creation and prosperity, while radically reducing India's dependence on imported fuels.

AIR QUALITY

Transport, manufacturing, the power sector, commercial and residential energy use, all contribute to problems of air quality. Motor vehicles contribute to all forms of air pollution. Residential burning of unprocessed biomass fuel is the single largest source of carbon monoxide and suspended particulate matter. Power generation contributes most of the nitrogen oxides and sulphur dioxide.

The escalating demand for power, rapid proliferation of motor vehicles, expansion of industries and rising living standards will all combine to have significant impact on the quality of air, especially in urban areas, as depicted in Figure. Appropriate strategies and actions are required to address the various forms of pollution in each of these sectors. Stricter enforcement of environmental regulations, rapid adoption of pollution-free and more efficient technologies, and higher standards for fuel quality are needed to reduce the environmental costs of growth.

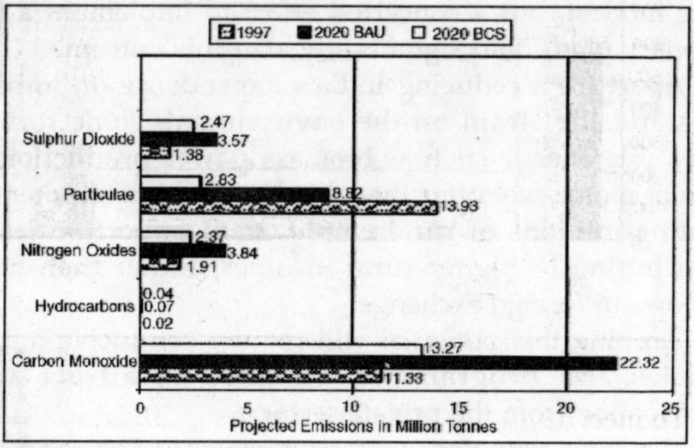

Fig. Projected Air Emissions

WATER MANAGEMENT

India possesses 16 per cent of the world's population but just 4 per cent of its water resources. Overall, at the national level, current water resources are more than sufficient to meet the demand, but future studies project that the supply situation could become difficult over the next half century.

However, water shortage has already become a serious and recurring source of concern for a large number of people in different parts of the country and for a number of the major metropolitan areas.

Only 70 per cent of the people in urban areas have access to basic sanitation services. A large number of rural habitations remain without any identified source of safe drinking water. Groundwater tables are receding, rivers are silting up, and leaching of chemical fertilizers is polluting drinking water supplies.

The rising consumption will further aggravate water scarcity as population, food production, industrialisation and living standards continue to rise over the next two decades. The total water consumption in India is expected to rise by 20-40 per cent over the next 20 years. Figure shows the current and projected consumption of water for different categories of use.

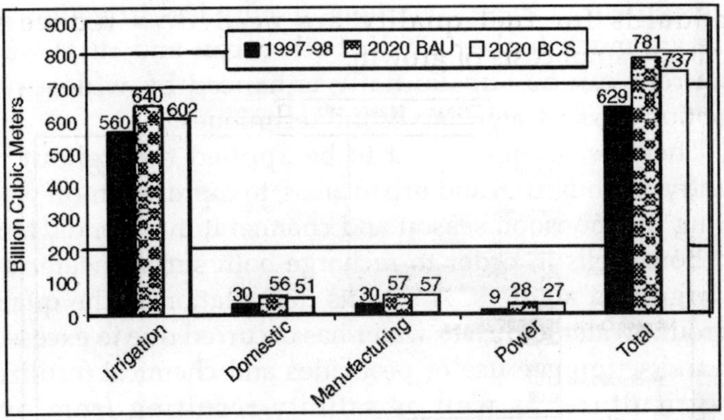

Fig. Projected Water Consumption

To meet the rising demand for water in 2020, it is essential to develop potential storage capacities and strengthen existing storage facilities. Agriculture accounts for 89 per cent of the total water consumption and domestic consumption accounts for 4.8 per cent. Subsidised or free supply of power and water has resulted in over exploitation and inefficient use of water in agriculture, leading to water-logging and salinity on 5.76 million hectares.

Tremendous wastage occurs as a result of evapostranspiration, distribution losses, seepage through unlined channels and excess application. Canal-irrigation efficiency in India is estimated at around 35 to 40 per cent, which is below international standards. Government policies need to be revised to provide incentives for efficient use of water, including appropriate water pricing and more effective institutional mechanisms for water management. India is not poor in water resources.

What it lacks is the ability to efficiently capture and effectively utilise the available resources for the maximum benefit. Enormous potential exists for increasing the productivity of water in agriculture by raising crop productivity, combined with better water management. Deep soil chiseling prior to planting can dramatically improve water retention by the soil, while reducing run-off and flooding. Crops grown in these conditions require less irrigation and generate much higher yields. Both urban and rural water resources can be substantially enhanced by widespread adoption of rainwater harvesting techniques.

These techniques need to be applied throughout the country, in both rural and urban areas, to capture run-off water during the monsoon season and channel it into ponds, tanks and bore wells in order to recharge both surface water and underground aquifers. A serious degradation in the quality of groundwater and river water has occurred due to excessive and indiscriminate use of pesticides and chemical fertilizers in agriculture, as well as salinity resulting from over exploitation of groundwater.

The deterioration of water quality is compounded by lack of proper effluent treatment for domestic waste water and industrial wastes. Stricter enforcement of environmental regulations is essential for stemming further degradation, and enactment of groundwater legislation is necessary to check over exploitation. Given the enormous cost of major water projects, emphasis needs to shift from large scale projects for augmenting water supply to decentralised projects designed to manage water demand and conserve water resources.

The National Water Policy 2002 advocates an integrated approach to water resources development with a river basin as a planning unit. The Policy emphasises community participation in management of water resources, appropriate pricing for water, tackling of pollution of surface and ground water bodies, and encouragement to the private sector to invest in water resources development. What is now required is to operationalise the policy by preparing state level policies and drawing up action plans to implement the various recommendations.

For the past fifty years, public imagination has been stirred by proposals to link major rivers together in a manner that would channel surpluses from flood-prone areas into drought prone regions, create millions of hectares of additional irrigated land, provide an inexpensive system of inland water transport, and generate millions of additional employment opportunities in construction, agriculture, trade and industrial development.

The high cost estimates of such a system–recent estimates place the cost at more than ₹500,000 crores–as well as some technical and political issues involved have been perceived as serious obstacles to implementation. However, the potential benefits to the nation of linking even some of the major rivers, subject to technical feasibility, are so vast that pragmatic proposals demand serious consideration. Given the vision and political will, India can convert the present water problem into a huge opportunity.

LAND, FOREST AND BIODIVERSITY

India's wide range of agro-climatic regions, vast extent of land and forest, and rich variety of biodiversity, rank it among the most naturally endowed nations of the world. But its huge and still expanding human and animal populations and its urge for industrialisation tax these resources to the limit.

Competing uses of land for agriculture, forestry, pastures, human settlements and industries exert increasing pressure on the country's finite land resources, influencing land-use patterns and sometimes causing degradation of forests and soils.

Changes in land use and land cover, together with land degradation have adverse impacts on forest resources and biodiversity. Increasing demand for forest resources is of particular concern. Yet the potential exists for dramatically reversing this pattern of degradation during the next two decades. It can be done by a concerted and systematic effort to halt soil erosion, restore precious nutrients and organic material to crop lands, recharge groundwater tables, and re-establish depleted forest lands, together with a holistic approach to land management that combines technologies and policies to integrate ecological, socio-economic, and political principles. Figure shows current and projected land use pattern under the business-as-usual and alternative scenario.

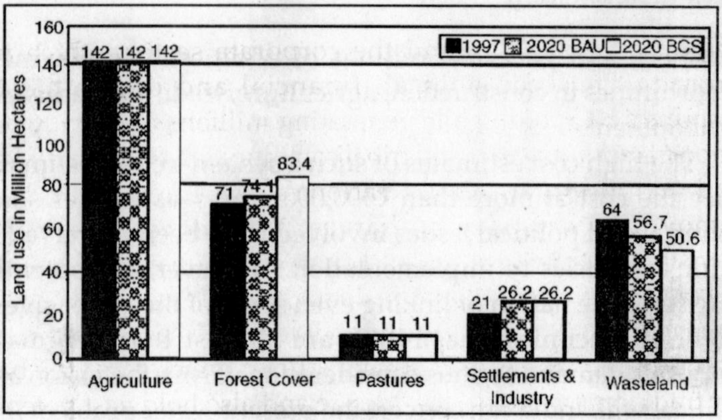

Fig. Projected Land Use

The most significant improvement under the alternative scenario is the increase in land under forest and tree cover from the current level of 71 million hectares to 83 million hectares.

Table. Projected Land Use -Percentage Distribution

	1997	2020 BAU	2020 BCS
Agriculture	45.9	45.8	45.3
Forest Cover	23.0	23.9	26.6
Pastures	3.5	3.5	3.5
Settlements and Industry	6.8	8.5	8.4
Wasteland	20.7	18.3	16.2

At present, 40 per cent of the commercial demand for timber and less than 20 per cent of the demand for fuel wood are being met by sustainable supply from the forests. Population growth will result in rising demand for both. Overgrazing and over-extraction of green fodder lead to forest degradation through decreased vegetative regeneration, soil compaction and erosion. Combating the pressure on forests requires a combination of measures.

A superior genetic stock is required to correct the poor productivity of Indian forests, which is a third below world averages. Extensive areas should be brought under joint forest management and plantation forestry. Plantation forestry can be expanded through the combined efforts of local communities, NGOs, and the corporate sector, which will provide the technological, financial and organisational resources required, while generating millions of employment opportunities for rural and tribal communities. Removal of legal and technical barriers by rationalising land-ceiling laws, removing restrictions on harvest and sale of timber, and devising incentives to attract private investment are essential for achieving these goals. The degradation of land and forest is also endangering India's rich biodiversity. Maintaining viable populations of plant and animal species which form the basis for traditional systems of medicine and also hold vast potential for modern science, requires the conservation of important ecosystems, habitats and the ecological processes of which they are a part. While the country has nearly achieved the international goal of reserving 5 per cent of its area as protected, some important biomes and species are not yet covered. This can be accomplished by an expansion of the system of national parks and sanctuaries combined with enhancing control and enforcement of wildlife trade, creation of new conservation reserves, conservation forestry, integration of rural development and biodiversity strategies, and a range of other legal, administrative and technical measures.

GLOBALISATION

India's progress over the next 20 years will be intimately linked to events within the region as well as around the world. Both opportunities and challenges will arise as the result of transformations in the regional and global political and security environments. World trade under WTO will determine access to markets and international competitiveness, particularly after the ascension of China.

The economic growth rates of other regions will influence demand for exports and foreign capital flows. Some other developments that will influence India's progress in the coming two decades are: pressure on energy prices as a result of global economic growth; continued spread of the information revolution; and technological innovations, such as those with regard to disease prevention and treatment.

GLOBAL TRENDS AND INSTITUTIONAL FRAMEWORK

Although these external factors are too many and too complex for us to reliably predict their impact, what we can do is recall some of the most significant and broad global trends that are likely to exert a powerful influence on India's progress over the coming two decades.

Population Growth

Global population will continue to grow from 6 billion to around 7.5 billion people, fuelling a large increase in global demand for food, goods and services. Life expectancy will rise significantly, leading to a larger proportion of the aged in all regions. At the same time a swelling of the working age population will lead to a significant increase in the global labour force.

Economic Expansion

The phenomenal achievements of the last half century have been the results of a fortuitous blend of forces—the absence of a world war, the spread of democracy to countries around the globe, rising levels of education everywhere, rising social aspirations and expectations, rapid technological development and diffusion, advances in the science and the practice of management, and development of a more efficient and sophisticated economic and financial organisation for global commerce.

All of these driving forces should continue to exert strong positive pressure for global economic expansion in the next century. If world real GDP continues to expand at an average rate of 3.14 per cent per annum as it did over the past 12 years, real world GDP will increase by 85 per cent over the next 20 years. A substantial rise in incomes and living standards will act as an additional stimulus to global demand for food, manufactured goods, services and energy.

Growth of World Trade

World trade grew by an average of about 7 per cent per annum in the decade of 1990s. By reducing and eventually eliminating all forms of trade barriers, the emerging institutional framework under WTO is likely to accelerate the expansion of world trade in the coming years. This will open greater opportunities for domestic producers while making them more vulnerable to international competition. At the same time, with the spread of new technologies and production capabilities, economies of scale are becoming increasingly important in reducing costs and prices.

Increasingly, single countries or even single producers are becoming globally dominant in specific product categories. This trend has already resulted in global surpluses in categories such as steel, basic chemicals and computer memory chips. Growing surpluses will bring even greater competition between companies and countries producing the same products, as well as cheaper products for consumers, and higher standards of living. Opportunities in business will gradually shift from volume production to special value-added categories of products and services.

Growth of Services Sector

The driving force for economic growth and employment will increasingly come from the services sector. Rising living standards will fuel the demand for commercial, social and community services. Construction, retailing, education, health, entertainment and tourism will expand more rapidly than ever before. The incorporation of services under the WTO framework has opened up enormous opportunities for hitherto non-tradable sectors to expand their horizons across borders. This will enhance the quality, range and affordability of services to the domestic economy and add a further stimulus to a service-led economic growth around the world. At the same time, the efforts will be needed to secure a level playing field and fairness in the trading system.

OECD Labour Shortages

Demographic trends in the OECD countries will create acute labour shortages, opening up unprecedented opportunities for countries that can provide skilled manpower and outsourcing services. A UN study released in March 2000 estimates that the 15-nation European Community would have to accept 150 million new immigrants over the next 25 years in order to maintain the present levels of working population. By 2013, labour force growth in the USA will be zero. The UN estimates that Japan would need to admit 600,000 immigrants annually for the next 50 years in order to maintain the size of its working population at the 1995 level.

Significant labour shortages will develop in the OECD countries unless immigration policies are dramatically liberalised or large numbers of manufacturing and service jobs are shifted overseas. This trend will further accelerate the outsourcing of production of goods and services to locations where infrastructure, ease of doing business, quality, costs and availability of labour are most attractive, which will be beneficial for many labour surplus countries like India.

Capital Flows

The new institutional framework will promote freer flow of capital and foreign investment, both direct as well as portfolio. Capital rich nations will seek out investment destinations generating higher returns. This trend will be reinforced by rising income levels and the aging of the OECD population, which will swell the size of pension, insurance and mutual funds, resulting in a continued increase in international capital flows in search of secure and attractive returns. At the same time, large manufacturing companies will increasingly move from national to global production strategies, resulting in further shifting of production and direct investment in countries or regions in which markets exist or in which production costs are lowest.

Technology and Infrastructure

The TRIPS will promote even faster technological innovation. Application and diffusion of technologies in a wide range of fields across international borders will also accelerate. Agricultural technology, biotechnology, information and communications technology, computerised manufacturing technologies will transform the way human beings learn, communicate, produce, and care for their health. The most important technological breakthroughs of the coming decade are expected in areas such as precision farming, fuel cells, alternative energy, genetic engineering, portable information devices, robotics, mass customisation, and computerised health care.

Application of computers will continue to spread rapidly, influencing all aspects of the global society, especially communication, manufacturing, finance and trade, scientific research, education, and medicine. The cost of global communications will continue to decline rapidly, reducing barriers of distance and making global production, distribution and marketing strategies more viable.

IMPLICATIONS AND OPTIONS FOR INDIA

Trade in Goods

Liberalisation of trade will open up new opportunities for export of goods, while increasing pressures on India's domestic industry to cope with competition from imports, especially from China. The global market for textiles and clothing will expand dramatically and the phasing out of quantitative restrictions will increase trade in these categories. But India's ability to export will depend on its capacity to keep pace with the rising international standards of price, quality, productivity, and service. Global trade in agricultural products will also grow rapidly, though it is not yet clear to what extent the OECD countries will remove the barriers and subsidies that hinder exports to these markets.

However, India's ability to become a major exporter of agricultural products will depend most on its ability to improve crop quality and productivity, while lowering costs to international levels. India missed out on the boom in manufactured exports that occurred from the 1970s to 1990s. Increasing overcapacity in basic manufacturing industries, coupled with mechanisation of processes, which eliminates the advantage of low cost labour, will limit future opportunities and benefits for export of manufactured commodity goods such as cars, TVs, and computers. Future opportunities for manufactured exports will be focused on the high end of the technology chain, computerised, customised manufacturing processes and sophisticated engineering and capital goods, areas in which India has not yet strongly positioned itself internationally.

Trade in Services

The World Bank estimates that India will possess the fourth largest economy in the world by 2020. The emerging global scenario will open up greater opportunities for countries with a surplus of well-educated, highly skilled labour that can provide an attractive commercial environment for the outsourcing of manufacturing and service businesses from high and even middle income countries. India's recent boom in outsourcing of IT services, further facilitated by declining costs of international communication and transportation, only points to the wide range of economic opportunities existing in the manufacturing and service businesses. At the same time, the pressure for export of highly educated and highly skilled individuals will also increase, so that a significant migration of scientific, engineering and medical talent is likely to continue.

Steps however need to be taken to ensure that such migration is not detrimental to the country's development. Export of services is a field in which India can excel. Computerisation, coupled with low cost global telecommunications are generating rapid growth of trade in service businesses, such as software and IT enabled services. This trend will further accelerate, opening up vast opportunities for countries with the capacity to deliver low-cost, high-quality services. India already commands an impressive 18.5 per cent share in the global market for customised software and the Indian software industry is the fastest growing in the world.

A NASSCOM-McKinsey report estimated that by 2008, the global market for IT enabled services alone will exceed ₹1,000 billion, and that India's export of IT services will exceed ₹50 billion, which is double the country's total export of goods and services in 2000. In addition, India's established credentials in IT and IT enabled services can be leveraged to develop a competitive advantage in other fields, including other branches of engineering, branches of scientific research, especially biotechnology, medicine, pharmaceuticals, and agriculture, as well as education. Performance in these sectors will depend on the country's capacity to generate larger numbers of well-educated and competent scientists, engineers and professionals.

Capital Flows and FDI

The enlargement of the international capital market will open up increasing opportunities for India to attract foreign direct and institutional investment. Foreign direct investment (FDI) expanded globally from ₹159 billion in 1991 to ₹1,270 billion in 2000, but with an increasing proportion of these flows moving between developed nations. During this period, FDI flows to India increased six-fold to ₹2.3 billion, which represents less than 0.2 per cent of global FDI.

The amount of capital globally available will continue to grow, but improvements in infrastructure and elimination of bureaucratic barriers will be major determinants of India's success in attracting a greater share of FDI flows. The size and prosperity of China's non-resident population has been a vital link for the channelling of technology, investment and business back to the mainland. A similar mobilisation of India's expatriate population could have momentous impact on the inflow of FDI in 2020. Likewise, multinational investments in India should be encouraged, especially in technology-intensive sectors where they can supplement and strengthen India's technological capabilities.

Technology

India's technology policy needs to be reformulated in the light of the emerging international economic environment, to capitalise on the accelerated global development and diffusion of technologies, and keep pace with more demanding international standards for cost, quality and productivity. India will need to be far more aggressive in acquiring and applying advanced technologies in a wide range of fields, including agriculture, information technology, energy, health and education. At the same time, India can also aspire to become an important contributor to the expansion of global frontiers of technology by building upon and leveraging its already significant achievements in fields such as pharmaceuticals, biotechnology, software, space and energy. It can also revive, simultaneously, it's traditional knowledge and technologies through formal R&D efforts.

PEACE AND SECURITY

India is in the midst of a great experiment. It is in the process of transforming a weak agrarian economy into a modern multi-dimensional economic enterprise and a traditional stratified society into an egalitarian society, while simultaneously fashioning and transforming itself into a modern democracy through consultative politics. It is inevitable that the rapid social, economic, technological and political development of one billion people should cause turbulence.

Yet it is essential that this turbulence be managed and confined within limits that preserve the social fabric and cultural values and permit the nation's transformation to continue. Underlying all our plans and hopes for a better future, underpinning all our efforts to evolve into a harmonious and prosperous democratic nation, is the shared aspiration of all Indian people for peace. Peace is not merely the absence or avoidance of conflict. It is the essential foundation for all human and social development, the fertile ground on which we can strive to elevate our minds in knowledge, hone our productive skills, strengthen our physical infrastructure, and fashion our multitudinous communities into a strong, united and harmonious nation.

The challenges to peace are numerous and they come from all directions—from outside our border and within, as well as from within our minds. Our capacity to preserve and build lasting peace for all Indians will depend on the strength of our military to defend our borders and the potential of our economy to generate increasing employment and income opportunities for all citizens. Our education system will need to inculcate knowledge and skills in our youth. Our legal and judicial system will be required to safeguard the rights of individuals and communities. Our scientists and engineers will have to develop and harness technologies for the benefit of the people. Most of all, the wisdom and determination of our political leaders to remove injustices and to direct the collective energies of the nation for greater achievement in every field of endeavour will go a long way towards maintaining peace and harmony in the country.

REVOLUTION OF RISING EXPECTATIONS

It is widely believed that poverty violence, but if that were true then violence both within the country and around the world would be rapidly diminishing, for both India and the world have attained unprecedented levels of development. But on closer examination it appears that violence is often associated with higher levels of development, because of the widening gap that emerges between peoples' aspirations and their accomplishments. Development leads to an awakening of human aspirations—a raising of expectations that releases people's energy and initiative for improving their lives. Yet, as it proceeds, the gap between those rising aspirations and present conditions widens.

Up to a point, the widening gap acts like a voltage differential, increasing the force available for progress. But beyond that point, the widening gap leads to increasing frustration, resentment, instability and violence. The greatest global challenge facing the international community as well as our own country is this transnational revolution of rising expectations. Recent advances in communications and information, coupled with rising levels of education, have further hastened and intensified this revolution by spreading awareness and raising aspirations. This revolution presents a challenge that must be managed by socio-economic advancement, social justice and political leadership.

The peace of our nation as well as that of the world community will depend on our ability to channel the energies released by this movement into constructive initiatives for national and global prosperity. Conventional wisdom has tended to treat national security and national defence as synonymous, but whereas defence is primarily concerned with military preparedness to combat external threats, national security covers a much broader spectrum of challenges, threats and responses. National security can be conceived of as the preservation of core values and vital interests critical to the nation-state from external and internal challenges and threats. Although we distinguish between the external and internal, in fact the two spheres are closely related. The political, economic, social and military spheres are mutually dependent. Internal security problems in a newly emerging, independent, developing country like India essentially grow out of the laborious processes of nation-state building. At the root of the problem lies the issue of economic disparities and social inequities.

Development tends to reduce the extent of these disparities in some ways while aggravating them in others. It increases the life expectancy, nutritional security, health, education, social and legal protection, and economic opportunities of the masses, while at the same time enabling the more talented, enterprising, fortunate or unscrupulous to derive disproportionately greater benefits and leaving others untouched or even harmed by the general progress. Economic disparities aggravate perceptions of difference between sub-national, linguistic and communal groups, fostering ethnicity and communalism. A positive strategy for national security must reinforce the secular and democratic values of the Indian nation which derive their strength from our culture, civilization and freedom struggle. External security depends on national power. It requires a continuous enhancement of the country's capacity to use its tangible and intangible resources in such a manner as to affect the behaviour of other nations. While power is often conceived in narrow terms as military power, in the world that is emerging it must be much more broadly conceived to include political, economic, technological, social and intellectual dimensions. A vibrant economy and a leading role in international affairs may be as important as a strong military to the preservation and development of national power. International affairs have been altered so radically by the end of the Cold War, and more recently by emergence of an international coalition against terrorism, that it is difficult to anticipate the complexion of the international environment for peace and security two decades hence. However, we can identify several of the factors that have consistently influenced our security environment in the past and which are likely to remain active for years to come.

Factors influencing Security Environment in 2020:

- The twin revolutions of rising expectations and information-communications will continue.
- The fundamental ideological conflict between Pakistan and India is unlikely to be resolved without a major social-political change in Pakistan.
- Territorial disputes with neighbours that have defied resolution for fifty years may not lend themselves for easy solution.
- Religious extremism and radical politics will continue to have adverse impact on our core values.
- Rising dependence on energy imports will make us increasingly vulnerable economically, as well as diplomatically.
- Public opinion, both domestic and international, and the media will be increasingly important forces in international affairs.
- The international order is likely to evolve into a polycentric configuration with its centre of gravity shifting increasingly to Asia, which will include seven out of the ten largest economies and six out of the eight nuclear weapon states.
- The increasing economic and military strength of China may pose a serious challenge to India's security unless adequate measures are taken to fortify our own strengths.

The current global security paradigm is a competitive system founded upon the relative military power of nation states. The competitive security paradigm is a state-centred and egocentric approach in which the security of each nation is perceived in terms of its military superiority over potential adversaries. The push of each nation for unlimited security through military power is inherently de-stabilising, since it inevitably increases the level of insecurity of other sovereign states. In practice, the effort of nations to arm themselves against perceived external threats generates a sense of insecurity among other nations and compels them in turn to increase military preparedness, thus initiating a vicious spiral, as it did during the Cold War. This highly militarised approach contains an in-built mechanism for escalation that was responsible for the growth of global military expenditure to an all time peak of ₹1.2 trillion in 1988. The competitive security paradigm cannot provide a stable basis for global peace and security.

What is needed is a quantum shift from the competitive security paradigm to a cooperative security system in which countries mutually and collectively agree to refrain from acts of aggression and to protect each other from such acts by any nation. We are now at a historic crossroads: one path leads us back to a static, unstable and exclusive competitive security paradigm; the other leads to a far more stable and dynamic cooperative security paradigm, inclusive of all nations and responsive to future needs and challenges.

Human development in all its dimensions is and will remain our highest strategic priority. Peace in search of human development must not only be durable but also seek harmony between peace and security at different levels. Internationally, we must gravitate from a state-centred, egocentric and competitive security paradigm to a cooperative security paradigm that enhances the security of each nation by reducing potential threats to all nations.

GOVERNANCE

India's economic and technological transition is

accompanied by a multifaceted political transformation which may well be slower, less clearly defined and less visible, but will nonetheless have profound impact on the functioning of the government 20 years from now. The main consequences of that transformation are likely to include:

Decentralisation and People's Participation:

- Devolution of power to local bodies will continue at an accelerated rate. Pressure from the grassroots will increasingly supplant governance from the top down.
- Local communities will come to depend less on state and central government action and more on their own initiative and organisational capacity.
- Financial devolution will give local bodies more authority to levy taxes and greater control over the use of local natural resources. It will also make them increasingly responsible for financing local infrastructure.
- Direct democracy through *gram sabhas*, as opposed to representative democracy, will become more prevalent at the local level. People at the local level will be more directly involved in setting priorities for distribution of resources and managing local projects.
- A better educated and better informed electorate will be increasingly demanding of its rights and increasingly critical of non-performing governments and their individual members.

Efficiency, Transparency and Accountability:

- Government agencies of all types at all levels will be more responsive and accountable to the public as customers.
- Mechanisms will be evolved to increase transparency and reduce corruption.
- E-government will improve responsiveness and reduce corruption in some areas. Computerisation of information systems coupled with downsizing, higher recruitment standards and stricter discipline will increase administrative efficiency.

- The educational, technical and professional qualifications of political leaders will rise.

The problems of governance 20 years from now will still include those issues which occupy our attention today–transparency, corruption, non-responsiveness, favouritism, bureaucracy, inefficiency, lack of accountability, ineffectiveness of implementation, etc. But rising expectations, increasing levels of education, greater access to information and greater prosperity will be working to mitigate these factors to a large extent. Worldwide E-governance is such a recent development, that it is difficult to assess its potential impact 20 years hence. However, the plans and projects already being implemented by various state governments within the country suggest that it has the potential, if fully harnessed and rightly utilised, to radically improve the speed, convenience, quality and transparency of public administrative services, while enhancing the ability of individual citizens to express and exercise their democratic rights.

The essence of good governance is the capacity to envision the opportunities that lead to a better future, to build a broad consensus in support of that vision, to take the bold decisions necessary to realise the vision, and to exercise the determination and perseverance required for overcoming obstacles and resistances that arise along the way.

2

Rural Transformation in India

INTRODUCTION

Literally and from the social, economic and political perspectives the statement is valid even today. Around 65% of the State's population is living in rural areas. People in rural areas should have the same quality of life as is enjoyed by people living in sub urban and urban areas.

Further there are cascading effects of poverty, unemployment, poor and inadequate infrastructure in rural areas on urban centres causing slums and consequential social and economic tensions manifesting in economic deprivation and urban poverty.

Hence Rural Development which is concerned with economic growth and social justice, improvement in the living standard of the rural people by providing adequate and quality social services and minimum basic needs becomes essential.

The present strategy of rural development mainly focuses on poverty alleviation, better livelihood opportunities, provision of basic amenities and infrastructure facilities through innovative programmes of wage and self-employment.

The goals will be achieved by various programme support being implemented creating partnership with communities, non-governmental organizations, community based organizations, institutions, PRIs and industrial establishments, while the Department of Rural Development will provide logistic support both on technical and administrative side for programme implementation. Other aspects that will ultimately lead to transformation of rural life are also being emphasized simultaneously.

Though the percentage of persons below poverty level in Tamil Nadu has come down significantly between 1993-94 (35.03%) and 1999-2000 (21.12%) as a result of the implementation of various Central and State sponsored schemes, the level of poverty both in absolute numbers (130.40 lakh persons) and percentage of population below poverty line (21.12%) in Tamil Nadu is highest among the four southern States.

In spite of huge investments on wage and self - employment programmes, the level of unemployment as per the NSSO 55th round (1999-2000) for Tamil Nadu compared to All India is the second highest among major States in 1987-88 and 1993-94 and third highest in 1999-2000.

The Government's policy and programmes have laid emphasis on poverty alleviation, generation of employment and income opportunities and provision of infrastructure and basic facilities to meet the needs of rural poor. For realising these objectives, self-employment and wage employment programmes continued to pervade in one form or other.

As a measure to strengthen the grass root level democracy, the Government is constantly endeavouring to empower Panchayat Raj Institutions in terms of functions, powers and finance.

Grama sabha, NGOs, Self-Help Groups and PRIs have been accorded adequate role to make participatory democracy meaningful and effective.

REVIEW OF NINTH PLAN PERFORMANCE

An outlay of ₹2000 crores was provided for Rural Development sector during Ninth Plan period. The budgetary support and allocation from 1997-98 to 2001-02 for various schemes/programmes was ₹2498.30 crores. The year-wise outlay and expenditure are indicated below:

	Financial Performance	**(₹in crores)**
Year	**Budget Provision**	**Expenditure**
1997-98	330.68	440.76
1998-99	490.51	526.45

1999-2000	498.27	484.27
2000-01	423.31	543.50
2001-02	755.53	725.14
Total	**2498.30**	**2720.12**

Table. Physical Performance

Year	I. R. D. P No. of families benefited	TRYSEM No. of persons trained	DWCRA No. of groups formed	No. of SHGs formed	SGSY economic assistance provided	Families benefited	Individual assisted
1997-98	180696	16479	2041	–	–	–	–
1998-99	142813	12381	2917	–	–	–	–
1999-2000	New scheme-SGSY introduced			18661	3198	47264	18163
2000-01				25324	4712	71503	11890
2001-02				12132	2158	34098	1259
Total	323509	28860	4958	56117	10068	152865	31312

During the Ninth Five Year Plan, under IRDP, income generating assets were provided to 3.235 lakh families through subsidy and credit. Under TRYSEM 28,860 rural youths in the age group of 18 to 35 from the families of below poverty line were provided with training enabling them to take up income generating activities.

Under DWCRA 4,958 women groups covering 12.40 lakh beneficiaries were formed and they were provided with revolving fund, credit and subsidy so as to enable them to participate in social developmental activities towards achieving economic self-reliance. During 1999-2000 the IRDP, TRYSEM, DWCRA were merged to form a new self-employment programme called *Swarna Jayanthi Gram Swarojgar Yojana* (SGSY) with effect from 1-4-99. Under SGSY 56,117 Women Self Help Groups (SHGs) were formed from the families of below poverty line.

Out of this, 10,068 SHGs have been provided with economic assistance under various trades enabling them to take up income generating activities. Under SGSY 31,312 individual beneficiaries have also been provided with economic assistance.

MANDAYS GENERATED AND COMMUNITY ASSETS CREATED UNDER CENTRALLY SPONSORED SCHEMES DURING NINTH FIVE YEAR PLAN

Sl. No.	Name of the scheme	Unit	Mandays generated /Assets created
1	JRY/JGSY	Lakh mandays	1048.95
2	EAS		1344.38
	IAY		
3	New houses	Nos.	2,08,441
4	IAY Kutcha houses	Nos.	41,239
5	PMGY Rural shelter	Nos.	6880
6	Credit cum subsidy	Nos.	5577
7	Million Wells Scheme	Nos.	9588

The total man-days generated under Employment Oriented Schemes like JRY/JGSY and EAS works out to 2393.33 lakhs. These schemes in addition to the creation of infrastructural facilities such as roads, school buildings, improvement of tanks etc. provided employment and income opportunities to the rural poor.

Regarding provision of housing facilities, 2.08 lakh new houses were constructed and 41,239 kutcha houses upgraded under IAY, 6880 new houses were constructed under PMGY-Rural Shelter for benefit of rural poor living below poverty line. Under Credit cum subsidy scheme, 5,577 houses were constructed for the benefit the people above poverty line.

Access to pucca dwelling provides basic housing as well as better environment for the beneficiaries and raises the social status of the members of the household. Under Jeevandhara Irrigation Wells Scheme (Million Wells Scheme), totally 9588 beneficiaries were assisted to dig irrigation wells during 1997-98 and 1998-99.

During the Ninth Five Year Plan, the State Government introduced new schemes such as Member of Legislative Assembly Constituency Development Schemes (MLACDS), Annamarumalrchi Thittam (AMT) and Namakku Naame Thittam.

Under MLACDS, 42,954 works were taken up at a total cost of ₹580.46 crores, 1,05,605 works were taken up a total cost of ₹301.86 under AMT and 28,421 works were taken up at a total cost of ₹157.11 crores under Namakku Naame Thittam.

GOALS, OBJECTIVES AND STRATEGY

The prime goal of rural development is to improve the quality of life of the rural people by alleviating poverty through the instrument of self-employment and wage employment programmes, by providing community infrastructure facilities such as drinking water, electricity, road connectivity, health facilities, rural housing and education and promoting decentralization of powers to strengthen the Panchayat raj institutions.

The Chief Minister's 15 Point Programme is a visionary programme which seeks to make Tamil Nadu the best State in the country by way of creating growth opportunities in rural areas and eradicating rural poverty. To achieve the objectives, the following priorities and thrust areas have been identified during the Tenth Five Year Plan period:

- The goal is reduction of poverty from 21.12% in 1999-2000 to 10% by 2006-07 and near elimination by 2012. Poverty reduction will be attempted
  - By organizing the rural masses into self-help groups and the establishment of micro-enterprises, training, credit linkages, market support, etc.
  - By substantial flow of investment in physical infrastructure like roads, water supply and social infrastructure like health, education and nutrition.
- Special efforts for generation of adequate employment and creation of durable community assets to improve the rural people especially the small farmers, marginal farmers, rural artisans etc., through programmes like Sampoorna Grameen Rozgar Yojana (SGRY).

- Decentralization of the process of planning by entrusting major role to the Panchayat raj bodies in the preparation of local level planning.
- Improving the efficiency and capacity of the officials and elected local body representatives.
- Providing all weather roads to all rural habitations having a population above 500 by 2004.
- Strengthening of Grama Sabha the governing body of village assembly as an agency of social audit and to review the implementation of programmes.
- Special efforts will be made to converge various schemes and programmes for accelerating the development process through special schemes like Village Self-sufficiency scheme etc.
- Emphasis will be given for the maintenance of the assets created under various schemes.

TENTH FIVE YEAR PLAN PROPOSALS

CENTRALLY SPONSORED SCHEMES

Poverty Alleviation Programmes

Swarnajayanthi Gram Swarozgar Yojana (SGSY)

The magnitude of poverty and disparities that existed between the various social groups necessitated planned state intervention to provide succor and relief particularly to the disadvantaged and marginalised groups such as SC/ST, women etc. Keeping this in view and having regard to the positive aspects as well as deficiencies, the earlier self employment programmes like TRYSEM, SITRA, GKY, DWCRA, IRDP and MWS were merged and a new self employment programme *viz.*, SGSY was launched w. e. f.1-4-1999. The SGSY is conceived as a holistic programme of micro enterprises covering all aspects of self-employment and establishing effective linkages between the various components *viz.*, organization of the rural poor into Self Help Groups (SHGs), their capacity building, planning of activity clusters, infrastructure build up, technology, credit and marketing etc. The main objective of the programme is to bring the existing poor families above the poverty line. Among the rural poor, special emphasis will be given for the welfare of SCs/STs, women and disabled. The programme lays emphasis on organization of poor into Self Help Groups (SHGs) and their capacity building.

The SHGs may consist of 10 to 20 persons 4 to 5 key activities will be identified in each block based on the resource endowments, occupational skills of the people and availability of markets and these activities will be implemented in clusters. 10% of the SGSY fund will be set apart for training, wherein emphasis will be given for skill development through well designed courses. SGSY is a Credit cum Subsidy programme with the involvement of banking and financial institutions. The expenditure under SGSY is shared by the Centre and the States in the ratio of 75:25. Subsidy will be provided at 30% of the project cost subject to a maximum of ₹7,500 and 50% for SC/ST subject to a maximum of ₹10,000. For groups, the subsidy is 50% subject to a ceiling of ₹1.25 lakhs.

During the Tenth Five Year Plan under SGSY it has been proposed:

1. To form 1.25 lakhs Self Help Groups benefiting 25 lakh women beneficiaries in rural areas.
2. To impart EDP and Vocational training for about 5 lakh rural women to start micro enterprise for economic independency.
3. To train 3 lakh unemployed youth to take up self-employment.
4. To construct one Self Help Group Centre per Panchayat to conduct meeting, store and display their products and to hold training programmes for the members of SHGs.
5. To establish District Information Service Centre in each district to provide backward and forward linkages in marketing. The State's share of the SGSY scheme during the Tenth Plan will be ₹131.45 crores.

Sampoorna Grameen Rozgar Yojana (SGRY)

Creation of sustained employment opportunities for

securing a minimum level of employment and income for the rural poor necessitated continuous need for special employment programmes.

Keeping the above aim and to strengthen the need based infrastructure at the village level to boost the rural economy the erstwhile wage employment programmes JGSY and EAS were merged and a new scheme namely SGRY was launched from 15th August 2001. The main objective of the new programme is to provide additional wage employment in the rural areas as food security by creation of durable community social and economic assets and infrastructure development in rural areas.

Towards this end the SGRY envisages distribution of food grains @ 5 kg per manday to the workers as part wages. While the cash component will be shared by the Centre and States in the ratio of 75:25, the Central Government will supply the food grains free of cost to the States. The scheme will be implemented in two streams.

The first stream will be implemented at the District and Panchayat Union levels 50% of the funds and food grains available under the programme will be distributed between the District Panchayat and the Panchayat Union in the ratio of 40:60.

The second stream will be implemented at the Village Panchayat level. The entire allocation under this stream will be distributed among the Village Panchayats through the DRDAs/District Panchayats. To augument the storage capacity of the tanks maintained by the local bodies towards increasing the availability of water for drinking, irrigation and other purposes it has been proposed to renovate one tank per panchayat under this scheme. During Tenth Plan, the State's share will be ₹303.80 crores.

Rural Housing

The aim of the State Government is to provide a dwelling for each family giving special emphasis to rural poor and deprived. The on going rural housing programmes will be given a new thrust.

Indira Awaas Yojana

With a view to meeting the housing needs of the rural poor, Indira Awaas Yojana (IAY) was launched in May 1985 as a subscheme of Jawahar Rozgar Yojana. It is being implemented as an independent scheme since 1 January 1996. It aims at helping below poverty line rural households belonging to SCs/STs, free bonded labourers, widows of next of kin of defence personnel, ex-servicemen and retired members of the paramilitary forces and also non SC/ST rural poor by providing them with grant-in-aid for construction of new dwelling units and upgradation of existing unserviceable kutcha houses. 3% of funds are reserved for the benefit of disabled poor below the poverty line in rural areas.

The assistance ceiling for each house in plain area is fixed at ₹20,000/-and for hill/difficult areas ₹22,000. In order to enable fire proof RCC roofed houses to be provided, the State Government provides additionally ₹12,000 per house as additional cost apart from its usual matching share to the Central grant. The expenditure towards provision of RCC roofing is met under Adi-dravida Welfare head.

Therefore, the unit cost including sanitary latrine under this scheme is ₹32,000/-in normal terrain and ₹34,000 in difficult terrain.80% of the IAY funds is earmarked for construction new houses and 20% is towards upgradation of unserviceable kutcha houses at the rate of ₹10,000/-per unit. The funds under IAY are shared between Centre and States in the ratio of 75:25. During the Tenth Plan it has been proposed to construct 1,54,090 new houses and to upgrade 78,970 unserviceable kutcha houses into pucca houses. The proposed outlay during the Tenth plan under IAY under SCP is ₹292.89 crores.

Credit/cum/Subsidy Scheme

The Credit-cum-Subsidy Scheme has been conceived for rural households having an annual income upto ₹32,000/-. Subsidy upto ₹10,000/-and loan up to ₹40,000/-from commercial or co-op banks is provided to eligible households for construction of houses. Out of the total outlay of ₹9.15

crores, 25% share of the State Government will be ₹2.29 crores. The physical target under the scheme will be 914.

Innovative Stream for Rural House and Habitat Development Scheme

This scheme intends to popularize low cost technology and usage of locally available materials in construction of buildings in rural areas.

Innovative technology adopted for the rural house type design in the scheme are:

- Rat-trap bond brick work, hollow blocks and soil stabilized cement mortar for construction of walls.
- Filler slab roofing using Mangalore tiles as filler material for roofing.
- Ferro cement/pre cast RCC doors, window, frame and shelter and
- Brick with plastering for flooring.

Under this scheme free houses are constructed for the rural poor. Infrastructure facilities such as drinking water, drainage, street formation etc., are provided by dovetailing funds under other ongoing schemes in the habitations developed under this scheme. This scheme is fully funded by the Government of India. The scheme will be taken up in the districts of Tiruvannamalai, Salem, Dharmapuri, Nilgiris, Nagapattinam, Tiruvarur, Theni, Ramanathapuram, Sivagangai and Villupuram during the Tenth Plan at a total cost of ₹5 crores.

Pradhan Mantri Gramodaya Yojana (PMGY) (Rural Shelter Component)

This scheme has been introduced by the Government of India under additional Central assistance for providing shelter in the rural areas to supplement the efforts in the sphere of rural housing considering the magnitude of the task.

The guidelines of Indira Awaas Yojana are applied for this scheme also. 60% of the total allocation is earmarked for SC/ST beneficiaries. During Tenth Plan it has been proposed to construct 34,475 rural shelters with an allocation of ₹111.14 crores.

Member of Parliament Local Area Development Programme

The Government of India introduced this scheme in 1993. Each MP (Lok Sabha and Rajya Sabha) was allotted ₹2 crore per annum to take up developmental works in his constituency.

The District Collectors and in respect of Chennai, the Commissioner of Chennai Corporation implement the scheme. In Tamil Nadu, there are 39 Lok Sabha MPs and 18 Rajya Sabha MPs and hence ₹114 crores is received annually from Government of India under this scheme.

A Member of Rajya Sabha may select any district of the State for exercising the choice of works under the scheme. The executive authorities concerned after studying the feasibility of the proposals of members will execute the works by following open tender system. The list of works that can be taken up under this scheme includes school buildings, village roads/approach roads, and irrigation canals, bus shelters, desilting of village ponds etc. An outlay of ₹570 crores has been proposed under this scheme during Tenth Plan period, which will be directly released to the District Collectors by GOI for executing the works.

Pradhan Manthri Gram Sadak Yojana (PMGSY)

The Pradhan Mantri Gram Sadak Yojana (PMGSY) is a Government of India Scheme introduced in the year 2000-2001 with the objective of providing road connectivity through good all weather roads to all unconnected rural habitations having population above 1000 by 2003 and all unconnected habitations having population of 500 and above by end of Tenth Plan period (2007). Under this programme the approved works are grouped into packages costing more than ₹1 crore but less than ₹5 crores and executed through tender system. The guidelines stipulate that district master plans would be prepared. A District Rural Road Plan is prepared for each district indicating the habitations in each block with the existing status of road connectivity. The scheme will be fully funded by the Government of India and an allocation of ₹750 crores has been proposed for the Tenth Plan.

National Project on Biogas Development

Biogas Development programme aims to promote an eco-friendly Non-conventional Energy Source with multiple benefits. The role of biogas as a major source of renewable energy has been recognized by the Government of India by including this scheme as an item in the 20 Point Programme. Prevention of deforestation, production of enriched manure and to improve sanitation and hygiene by linking sanitary toilets with biogas plants are the objectives of this rural energy programme.

This is a Centrally sponsored programme with a subsidy component of ₹1800/-for general category and ₹2300/-for scheduled category and ₹3500/-for hilly areas. An amount of ₹500/-is provided in addition for installation and maintenance of the plant to the Turnkey agent. 10,000 bio-gas plants will be constructed during the Tenth Plan. The scheme is fully funded by the Government of India and ₹8.05 crores is provided for the Tenth Plan which will be directly released to the District Collectors.

Eleventh Finance Commission Grant

This grant is provided to Village Panchayats and Panchayat Unions for maintenance of civic services. Under Eleventh Finance Commission grant, a sum of ₹186.45 crores for 2000-01 and 2001-02 was allocated. Out of this, ₹171.92 crores is provided to Village Panchayats and Panchayat Unions for maintenance of civic services and ₹14.53 crores for maintenance of accounts and audit and for development of database. An outlay of ₹659.47 crores has been proposed during the Tenth Plan period under this scheme.

Rashtriya Sam Vikas Yojana (RSVY)

During Tenth Plan a new scheme viz, Rashtriya Sam Vikas Yojana (RSVY) Development and Reform Facility will be launched by Government of India. The prime objective of RSVY is to address the problems of pockets of high poverty, low growth, low agricultural productivity, unemployment and poor governance by putting in place programmes and policies, which would remove barriers to growth and accelerate the development process.

An amount of ₹15 crores per year will be provided for implementation of various developmental programmes such as drought proofing (soil conservation, afforesation, social forestry, wasteland development and minor irrigation), agriculture, horticulture etc. infrastructure (road and power), social sector (health and education) and livelihood support (income generating activities such as handloom, information technology, agricultural processing etc.). Under the scheme 15% of the funds will be earmarked for maintenance of assets in health, education and veterinary sectors.

The main focus and strategy of the scheme will be on infrastructure development and income generation for under-privileged. The scheme will be implemented through people's participation, involvement of PRIs, NGOs and Self Help Groups at every stage including plan formulation, implementation and monitoring. Tiruvannamalai district has been selected on pilot basis for implementation of RSVY scheme. During Tenth Plan period the total amount of ₹225 crores is proposed under the scheme.

STATE SCHEMES

Construction of office Buildings for Village Administrative Officers

Administration at the door steps of the people is the slogan of the Government. In order to achieve this objective the scheme for construction of buildings for the office of the Village Administrative Officers has been proposed during Tenth plan period. There are about 16000 revenue villages in the state, each having a Village Administrative Officer.

The VAO's office buildings would be constructed adjacent to every panchayat office building so that public can have easy access to both. It has been proposed to construct the VAO's office building through state budgetary support and by dovetailing funds under MLA Constituency Development Scheme. The outlay proposed for the scheme during the Tenth Plan is ₹19.80 crores.

Village Fair Development Scheme

The Agro-based industries play a vital role in the development of rural economy. It is essential that the farmers should have remunerative returns and the agricultural labourers should have high wages.

To enhance the livelihood security of the farmers and agricultural labourers, the Village Fair Development Scheme has been launched. Presently the agriculture produces are marketed in shandies maintained by village panchayats and panchayat unions.

These shandies are being maintained without adequate infrastructure facilities. It is proposed to provide facilities such as stalls, drinking water to cattle/people, public convenience, lighting facilities, improvement to inner roads between the stalls etc., These will also facilitate the rural masses to have an access to agriculture produce besides improved income to the local bodies. The scheme will be implemented in 25 districts with (NABARD) assistance costing ₹5.00 crores during the Tenth Plan period.

Village Self-sufficiency Scheme

The main objective of the Scheme is to promote self-reliant and self help attitude among the rural people. This scheme attempts to reverse growing dependency syndrome in the rural areas on Govt. and bring back to the mainstream of development process by inculcating community involvement and participatory approach in development. Community needs are articulated by the public through Grama Sabha and after thorough deliberations, their needs are prioritized and converted as implementable projects where the public themselves actively contribute in cash, kind or through labour to supplement the government funds and execute the works. The Government provides necessary technical support to execute the works.

This scheme maximizes the utility value of the funds allocated by the Government. Apart from expediting the execution and improving the quality of work, it also promotes the concept of community maintenance of public assets. The outlay proposed for this scheme during Tenth Plan period is ₹120 crores.

Member of Legislative Assembly Constituency Development Scheme (MLACD)

The Member of Legislative Assembly Constituency Development Scheme is fully funded by the State Government. The main objective of the scheme is to bridge the critical infrastructural gap in the Assembly Constituencies.

Under this scheme each member of Legislative Assembly shall identify the works that should be executed in his constituency. The allocation for each Assembly Constituency is ₹82 lakhs.

Important works like Integrated Sanitary Complexes for Women, construction of hostels for SC/STs, BC/MBCs students, construction of office buildings for VAOs and provision of drinking water in drought-affected areas are taken up on priority basis. The remaining works will be proposed by MLA should be in accordance with the guidelines issued in this regard. An outlay of ₹1059.85 crores has been proposed under the scheme during Tenth Plan period.

State Finance Commission Grant

A devolution formula has been adopted for devolving resources to urban and rural local bodies based on the recommendations of the Second State Finance Commission for the award period 2002-07 coinciding with the Tenth Plan period. The rural and urban local bodies will receive 8 per cent of the States' Own Tax Revenue after excluding Entertainment Tax receipts.

The vertical sharing of resources between rural and urban local bodies will be in the ratio of 58:42. Of the total devolutions to the urban local bodies, the resources will be shared between the Corporations, Municipalities and Town Panchayats in the ratio 31:34:35. The devolution to rural local bodies will be shared among the Village Panchayats, Panchayat Unions and the District Panchayats in the ratio of 47:45:8. Further the State Finance Commission grants will be released to the local bodies on a monthly basis. An outlay of ₹659.47 crores is provided for this purpose

Integrated Sanitary Complex for Women

Tamil Nadu's coverage in rural sanitation is presently at 11% which is lower than national average of 15%. To protect dignity and privacy of the women the Government have launched a new scheme called the Integrated Sanitary Complex for women to provide toilets and facilities for bathing and washing for women under one roof. Each sanitary complex will be spread over approximately 750 sq. ft. with 10 toilets and 3 cubicles for bathing. Each complex has an independent water connection to ensure that the users have a steady and continued supply of water.

A pump room and water tank will also form part of the sanitary complex. The operation and maintenance of these sanitary complexes will be the responsibility of the village panchayats and self-help groups.

Monitoring committees will also be formed for proper maintenance of these sanitary complexes. An outlay of ₹284 crores has been proposed under this scheme during the Tenth Plan period.

Other Programmes/Schemes

The outlay proposed in respect of other Rural Development programmes during Tenth Plan is as follows:

Sl. No.	Name of scheme/programme	Proposed outlay (₹in crores)
1	Capital programme of Infrastructure Development by rural local bodies	100.00
2	DRDA Administration cost	20.08
3	Other Rural Development Programmes	113.14
	Total	**233.22**

Area Development Programme

Western Ghats Development Programme

Provision of infrastructure facilities like drinking water,

street lights, formation of link roads, construction of school buildings and health subcentres have been proposed to be taken up in the Western Ghats taluks under WGDP. These works will be planned and executed by the concerned local bodies. The outlay proposed under the above head during the Tenth Plan period is ₹1.90 crores.

Drought Prone Area Programme

The Drought Prone Area Programme (DPAP) is an integrated watershed development programme with the prime objective of promoting the over all economic development of watershed community by optimally utilizing natural resources so as to mitigate the adverse effects of drought, prevent further ecological degradation and create employment through non-farm activities.

This programme is being implemented in 16 districts viz:

- Dharmapuri (14),
- Thoothukudi (18)
- Sivagangai (7),
- Ramanathapuram (7),
- Virudhunagar (7),
- Pudukottai (4),
- Tirunelveli (1),
- Salem (5),
- Namakkal (3),
- Coimbatore (5),
- Thiruvannamalai (1),
- Dindigul (3),
- Vellore (6),
- Tiruchirappali (1).
- Perambalur (6), and
- Karur (2).

This programme is sponsored by the Government of India and the expenditure is shared in the ratio of 75:25 between and Central and State Governments.

The DPAP is implemented on watershed approach. Each watershed covers an area of approximately 500 ha. The allocation per hectare is ₹6,000.

This programme consists of 5 major components, namely,

1. Entry point activity
2. Community organization,
3. Training,
4. Developmental activities and
5. Project administration.

The Developmental works carried out under DPAP are as follows:

- Land Development including land levelling, summer ploughing, institutional and moisture conservation measures like contour and graded bunds fortified by vegetation, bench terracing in hilly terrain.
- Drainage line treatment with a combination of vegetative and engineering structures.
- Development of small water harvesting structures such as low cost farm ponds, nulla bunds, check dam and percolation ponds.
- Nursery raising for fodder, timber, fuelwood and horticultural species.
- Afforestation activities including block plantations, avenue plantation, shelter belts, sand dune stabilization etc.,
- Agro-forestry and horticultural development.
- Pasture development either by itself or in conjunction with plantations.
- Repair, restoration and upgradation of existing common property assets and structures in watershed to obtain optimum and substained benefits from previous public investments.
- Crop demonstration for popularizing new crops/ varieties or innovative management practices.

Proposals

Development works in 297 watersheds sanctioned in the first batch during 1995-96 to 1999-2000 have already been successfully completed with a total outlay of ₹53.57 crores covering 42,090 hec. Watersheds sanctioned during 1999-2000 and 2001-02 will be continued during Tenth Plan period. In addition it is expected that 700 more watershed projects will be taken up during Tenth plan period.

The outlay proposed under DPAP would be ₹210 crores during Tenth plan out of which the State's share will be ₹52.50 crores. The total outlay towards Special Programme for Rural Development is ₹3500 crores.

Table. Proposed outlay for Special Programmes for Rural Development (₹in crores)

Sl. No.	Name of the scheme/Programme	Outlay for Tenth Plan (State share)
1	Member of Legislative Assembly Constituency Development scheme (MLACD)	1059.85
2	Village Self-sufficiency scheme	120.00
3	Capital Programme of Infrastructure Development by Rural Local bodies	100.00
4	Rural Sanitary Complex for Women	284.00
5	Construction of building for VAO's Office	19.80
6	Villlage Fair Development scheme	5.00
7	SGSY	131.45
8	SGRY	303.79
9	IAY under Special Component Programme	292.89
10	Special Component Plan for rural shelter	111.14
11	District Reform facility	225.00
12	Finance Commission Grants to Local bodies	659.47
13	DRDA Administration cost	20.07
14	Other Rural Development Programme	113.14
	Area Development Programme	
15	Western Ghats Development Programme	1.90
16	Drought Prone Area Programme	52.50
	Total	**3500.00**

COMMUNITY DEVELOPMENT

Formation of rural roads, construction of small bridges and culverts, provision of water supply and sanitation facilities, improvement and maintenance of minor irrigation tanks constitute Community Development activities.

RURAL SANITATION

To provide more and more sanitation facilities to rural population, generate awareness about health education and eradicate manual scavenging, the Total Sanitation Campaign scheme under RCRSP will be continued during the Tenth Five Year Plan period.

The Total Sanitation Campaign envisages a demand driven approach with greater public participation and more emphasis given for IEC activities to create awareness among the rural masses.

The project would be implemented in 24 months spread over 3 years in select districts with the ultimate objective of covering 80% rural population under sanitation. The expenditure on this scheme is shared by the Central and State Government on 80:20 basis. An outlay of ₹19.15 crores has been provided under the Tenth plan.

INTEGRATED RURAL SANITATION AND WATER SUPPLY PROJECT WITH DANIDA ASSISTANCE

This scheme aims to improve the health and sanitary condition in the project area villages through integrated approach to provide safe drinking water and sanitation through participatory and demand driven approach. This programme is being implemented with DANIDA assistance. Water supply works, individual household latrines and institutional latrines are taken up in the project area. The outlay provided is ₹16.27 crores.

IMPROVEMENT OF RURAL ROADS, BRIDGES AND DRAINAGE STRUCTURES

At present panchayats and panchayat unions are maintaining 52% of the total length of the roads in the state. The road transport has emerged as the most eminent mode of transport in the light of its inherent advantages of lower cost of travel and flexibility in operation. The rural roads also provide outlet to market centres, taluk headquarters and other main roads.

Hence, it is essential to improve village roads to all

weather roads *i.e.,* by black topping. The improvement of road works has been taken up under Rural Infrastructure Development Fund (RIDF) under NABARD. An outlay of ₹93.75 crores has been proposed under this head during Tenth plan. It has also been proposed to avail a loan amount of ₹93.76 crores under RIDF-V.

PROVISION OF INFRASTRUCTURAL FACILITIES IN TRIBAL BLOCKS

The objectives of the schemes are:

- To assist the ST families to cross the poverty line with special emphasis on improving agriculture, irrigation and education in tribal areas and
- To provide basic infrastructure facilities for better living conditions. An outlay of ₹2.39 crores has been proposed during the Tenth Plan.

PROVISION OF INFRASTRUCTURE FACILITIES FOR RURAL LOCAL BODIES

With a view to provide basic infrastructure facilities such as drinking water, street lights, link roads, construction of school buildings, health subcentres etc., an outlay of ₹294.68 crores has been proposed during the Tenth Plan.

LOCAL BODIES INCENTIVE SCHEME

An outlay of ₹80 crores has been proposed during the Tenth Plan. Thus the total outlay for Community Development for the Tenth Plan is ₹600 crores.

Table. Proposed outlay for Community Development (₹in crores)

Sl. No.	Name of the scheme/Programme	Outlay (State share)
1	Improvement of rural roads, bridges and drainage structures under RIDF	93.75
2	Loans for improvement of rural roads, bridges and drainage structures under RIDF-V	93.76
3	Integrated Rural sanitation and water supply project with DANIDA assistance	16.27

4	Central Rural Sanitation Programme	19.15
5	Local Bodies incentive scheme	80.00
6	Formation of Tribal blocks in Hill areas	2.39
7	Provision of infrastructure facilities for rural local bodies	294.68
	Total	**600.00**

3

Urbanisation in India

INTRODUCTION

The United Nations estimates indicate that at mid 1990s, about 43 per cent of the world population lived in urban areas. With the urban population growing two and a half times faster than its rural counterpart, the level of urbanisation is projected to cross the 50 per cent mark in 2005. United Nations projections further show that by 2025, more than three-fifth of the world population will live in urban areas. The growth rate of urban population of developing regions has been declining recently. It was estimated to be 3.9 per cent per annum during 1980-85, which declined to 3.79 per cent per annum during 1980-85, 3.62, and 3.43 during 1990-95 and 1995-2000 respectively.

The decline in the rate of urbanisation is also continuing in developed regions of the world. As a result, some of the European countries have experienced negative urbanisation during 80s. However, the continued absence, namely, adequate data on rural to urban migration in most developing countries as well as on natural increase in rural and urban areas separately precludes attribution of the slowing down of urban growth in most of the countries to any single demographic process. It reflects the effects the host of factors like the relatively week expansion of urban industries and price shifts unfavourable to manufactured goods, population aging, policies to alter migration and spatial distribution patterns in some countries, and no doubt other forces. The arguments of Kelly and William that the slow growth of agricultural land stock and high growth of population of labour force in developing countries are factors that presumably push rural population towards urban areas are not correct for the recent past. The sluggish performance of manufacturing remains largely responsible for the observed slower pace of urban growth in developing countries, and may have decelerated urban growth from what other wise would have been higher rates in the 1980s and 19990s by curbing net rural to urban migration. Even though manufacturing is performing well but can not generate adequate employment being capital intensive is unlikely to accelerate rural to urban migration. The likely deceleration of rural to urban migration could be the important reason for the slowing down of urbanisation in the developing countries in recent times. The fertility decline could also be the another important factor for lower urban growth in several parts of the developing world particularly in Latin America where total fertility rate declined from 6 in the early 1960s to 3 in the early 1990s. The push factors like population growth and unemployment etc. and pull factors like opportunities in the urban areas are debated in the studies of India's urbanization. The National Commission on Urbanisation has termed them as factors of demographic and economic momentum respectively.

The main objectives of the study are as follows:

- To study the level, trend and regional pattern of urbanization.
- To examine the relative contribution of natural increase as well as rural to urban migration in urban growth in the recent past.
- To examinee India's future urbanisation in the light of new economic policy.

SOURCES OF DATA AND METHOD

Census is the main source of data on urban population for not only India but also most of the countries of the world. Census defines urban areas based on certain criteria.

In India since 1961, two important criteria namely:

- Statutory administration and

- Economic and demographic aspects have been adopted to declare certain settlements as towns.

The former includes civic status of towns such as municipal corporations, municipality, cantonment board, notified area committee, etc., and the later includes criteria like population size, density of population and percentage of work force in non-agricultural sector. The former is also known as statutory town and the latter as census town. These two types of town based on two different criteria have added complexity to the urbanisation process in India.

For example, the predominance of non-agricultural activities is expected to be found in urban areas, but surprisingly we have significant number of towns in the country which are predominantly agriculture oriented. Such paradoxical development creates doubts about the quality of urbanisation in India. Further, the definition of urban had changed from time to time. Although, the definition of urban areas of 1961 census continued in later censuses, but it has been slightly modified in constituents of non-agricultural activities since 1981 census. In 1981 census, 75 per cent of male workers in non-agricultural activities is required for a settlement to be declared as urban. In addition to it, at a town level the change in boundary has been frequent, and in several cases adjustment for it is impossible due to lack of relevant information.

The sources of urban growth comprise natural increase in urban areas, migration, reclassification of rural areas into urban areas and the change in the boundaries of existing towns. The migration data and the information on reclassification of rural areas into urban areas are available from the census. But the information on emigration is not available in the country, although its effect is likely to be negligible. The data on natural increase are available from Sample Registration System published by Registrar General of India annually. The contribution of migration in the urban growth could be estimated directly from the data available in Migration Tables. However, it underestimates the contribution of migration due to several inadequacies. Alternatively, therefore, the residual method could be preferred in case of India.

INDICATORS

In order to understand the demographic and geographical dimension of urbanisation in the country, the following indicators of urbanisation have been considered in this study:

- *Percentage of urban population to total population*: This shows the level of urbanisation in an area.
- *Decadal growth rate*: This provides the change in urban population in percentage related to base year.
- *No. of towns per ten-lakh rural population*: This indicator shows the extent to which rural areas are served by urban centres.
- *Percentage of population in Class I cities/towns*: This indicates about the dominance of large towns in the process of urbanisation compared to medium and small towns.

The indicators of urbanisation have been analysed at the state level for the period 1981-1991. Smaller states and union territories are excluded from the study. Socio-economic variables like per capita net domestic product, literacy, work force in non-agricultural activities and infant mortality rate have been taken to examine their association with different indicators of urbanisation.

INDIA'S PLACE IN WORLD URBANISATION

The urban population of the world was estimated to be 2.96 billion in 2000

Table. Percentage of Population Residing in Urban Areas by Region, 1980-2010

World/Region	1980		1985		1990		2000		2010	
	%	,000	%	,000	%	000	%	000	%	000
World	39.4	1752	41.2	1997	43.1	2282	47.6	2962	52.8	3779
More Developed Region	70.2	797	71.5	838	72.7	880	75.8	968	79.1	1060
Less Developed Region	28.8	954	31.5	1159	34.3	1401	40.3	1993	46.8	2717
Africa	27.3	130	29.6	164	32.0	205	37.6	322	44.2	493
Asia	26.2	678	28.6	813	31.2	974	37.1	1369	43.8	1845
Latin America	65.0	233	68.4	273	71.5	315	76.6	400	80.4	482

It was estimated that nearly 50 million people are added to the world's urban population and about 35 million to the rural population each year. The share of world's population living in urban centres has increased from 39 per cent in 1980 to 48 per cent in 2000. The developed countries have higher urbanisation level compared with the developing countries. The urbanisation level has almost stabilised in the developed countries.

There was about 3 per cent increase in the level of urbanisation in the developed countries during 1990-2000. On the other hand the increase in the level of urbanisation was faster in developing countries. Table shows that the level of urbanisation in India was 25.7 per cent in 1991 which was lower than the average level of urbanisation in the developing countries.

Table. India: Indicators of Urbanisation

Census Year	No. of UA/ Towns	Urban Population in Million	% Urban Population	Number of Towns/UA per 10 lakh Rural Population	Decennial Growth Rate of Population (%)
1901	1827	25.85	10.84	8.6	–
1911	1815	25.94	10.29	8.0	0.35
1921	1949	28.08	11.18	8.7	8.27
1931	2072	33.45	11.99	8.4	19.12
1941	2250	44.15	13.86	8.2	31.97
1951	2843	62.44	17.29	9.5	41.42
1961	2365	78.93	17.97	6.6	26.41
1971	2590	109.11	19.91	5.9	38.23
1981	3387	159.46	23.34	6.4	46.14
1991	3768	217.17	25.72	6.0	36.10
2000	–	286.20	28.54	–	31.50

In south Asia, India has an edge over some of the neighbours in urbanisation. The countries like Bangladesh (18 per cent) Sri Lanka (21 per cent), Bhutan (16 per cent) and Nepal (10 per cent) have lower level of urbanisation than India. But Pakistan has higher level of urbanisation (32 per cent) than

India. It is however important to note that the comparison of the level of urbanisation at the world level is affected by definition of urban areas in each countries.

For example, in Bangladesh places having a municipality, a town committee or cantonment board are defined as urban; in Nepal, all localities of 9000 or more inhabitants are declared urban; in Pakistan places with municipal corporation, town committee or cantonment are declared urban; in Sri Lanka also Municipalities, urban councils and town are treated as urban. On the other hand in India both civic status as well as demographic aspect are taken as criteria for declaring a settlement as urban.

The recent census of India defined the urban places on the basis of the following criteria:

- All places with a municipality, corporation, cantonment board or notified town area committee etc.
- All other places which satisfy the following criteria:
  - Minimum population of 5000
  - At least 75% of male working population engaged in non-agricultural pursuits and
  - A density of population of at least 400 persons per square Km. Besides, the directors of census operations in states/union territories were allowed to include in consultation with the concerned with state Governments, union territory administration and the census commissioner of India, some places having distinct urban characteristics as urban even if such places did not strictly satisfy.

CORRELATES OF INDIA'S URBANISATION

The correlation co-efficient for the indicators presented in Table shows that the decennial growth rate is positively associated with literacy and non-agricultural work force and negatively associated with infant mortality, although the correlation co-efficient are low and insignificant.

Table. Correlation Matrix of Different Indicators of Urbanisation and Socio-economic Variables, India, (N = 15)

S. N.	% Urban (1)	Urban growth (%) (2)	No. of towns Per 10 Lakh Rural (3)	% Urban in class I cities (4)	Per capita Income (5)	% literacy (6)	IMR (7)	% work force in nonagricultural sector (8)
1	1.0							
2	–0.13	1.0						
3	0.53	–0.01	1.0					
4	0.78	–0.07	–0.02	1.0				
5	0.51	–0.24	0.47	0.24	1.0			
6	0.48	0.32	0.096	0.46	0.25	1.0		
7	–0.49	–0.29	0.06	–0.56	–0.35	–0.78	1.0	
8	0.63	0.11	0.23	0.54	0.68	0.84	–.88	1.0

The percentage of urban population is significantly positively related with non-agricultural work force, per capita income, and literacy and negatively related with infant mortality. The positive association between percentage urban population and percentage of urban population living in class I cities shows that urban population is highly concentrated in class I cities. The correlation matrix also shows that higher is the per capita net domestic product higher is the number of towns per 10 lakh rural population.

Literacy, infant mortality rate and percentage of work force in nonagricultural sector are significantly related with each of the indicators of urbanisation. While literacy and infant mortality have relatively weak relationship with indicators of urbanisation, non-agricultural work force is significantly positively related with percentage of urban population and concentration of population in class I cities.

TREND IN NATURAL INCREASE AND MIGRATION

There are three components of urban growth *viz.*, the natural increase, net migration and the areal classification *i.e.*, addition of new towns minus declassification of existing towns.

Besides the extension of boundaries of towns also tend to influence the urban growth. However, sometimes it could of small magnitude.

The natural increase reflects the role of demographic momentum, on the other hand migration is sensitive to economic growth. Table presents natural increase per thousand population at all India level for the years 1971 to 1999.

Table. Trend in Natural Increase in Rural and Urban Areas, India,1971-1999

Year	Rural Natural Increase	Urban Natural Increase
1971-80	19.99	19.27
1981-90	21.64	19.49
1991-99	19.57	15.75

Although the rural and urban difference in birth rate has remained significantly large in the early years of 1970s which narrowed down in the later 80s, the difference in natural increase between rural and urban areas was not significantly large and remains almost constant both in 1970s and 1980s. This is due to the fact that level of decline in death rate in both rural and urban areas were not uniform. The urban areas have advantages than the rural areas. The average natural increase was 19.99 per thousand during 1971-1980 for rural areas compared to 19.27 in the urban areas.

The natural increase has increased during 1981-90 in the rural areas and remained constant in the urban areas during the same period. This shows that natural increase is not responsible for the slowing down of India's urbanization during 1980s.

Therefore, the share of natural increase in the decadal growth has increased and the share of migration has declined substantially. In the decade of 1990s, the natural increase in urban areas has declined substantially from the level of 19.49 during 1980s to 15.75. The could lead to further slowing down of India's urbanization during the 1990s. As it has been noted that urban growth at all India level has declined during the last decade, this trend is also visible for most of the states of India for the period 1981-1991. Further, it has declined both in better off as well as poorer states. The poorer states like Bihar, Orissa, Uttar Pradesh and Rajasthan have shown very high growth rate during 1971-81 which declined to below 40 per cent in these states.

It has also declined in better off states like Maharasthra and Gujarat which are industrially advanced and agriculturally developed states like Punjab and Haryana also have registered decline in urban growth during 1981-91. The natural share of increase is very high in the urban growth in relatively poor as well as relatively rich states of India.

This clearly shows that the urbanisation in India in recent times is predominantly led by demographic momentum. On the other hand, the role of economic momentum in terms of pull factors are largely restricted to the large cities only where also the new entrants are finding difficult due to over increasing size of informal sector and growing nativism.

EVIDENCES OF DECLINING TREND OF MIGRATION

There are several ways to examine the contribution of migration to the urban areas depending upon the availability of data. One of the ways could be to examine the share of net decadal migration to urban areas to urban growth, but the census data have some limitations in estimating the net decadal migration to urban areas directly from Migration Tables as separate information in the wake of change in the area and population due to extension of municipal boundaries during the inter-censal period is not available either for the total or for the migrant population.

Secondly, the migration data for new and declassified towns are not available separately and this could introduce error m in estimating the contribution of migration in the share of urban growth over a period of time. It is found that share of migration estimated directly from Migration Tables underestimates the contribution of migration grossly. For example, Premi estimated 33.6 per cent contribution of net rural to urban migration along with increase due to changes in municipal boundaries compared with 39.4 per cent estimated by Jain and 36.1 peer cent by Pathak and Mehta for the year 1971-81 using the residual method. Table presents share of migration in urban growth along with natural increase and reclassification of towns for the census year 1971 to 1991 based on residual method.

Table. India: Components of Urban Growth 1971-1991

Per cent Share	1971-81	1981-91
Natural Increase	41.7 (45.1)	59.9 (58.7)
Net Migration + Changes in Municipal Boundaries	39.4 (36.1)	22.6 (23.7)
Reclassification	18.8 (18.8)	17.4 (17.5)

It may be seen that the share of migration along with changes in municipal boundaries was around one-third of the urban growth during 1971-81 which had declined to about one-fifth during 1981-91.

Table. Urban Growth and Share of Natural Increase in Selected States of India

States	Urban Growth (%)			Share of Natural Increase
	1961-1971	1971-1981	1981-1991	1981-91
Relatively Rich States				
Industrial				
Maharasthra	40.8	40.0	38.7	57.0
Gujarat	41.0	41.4	33.6	69.9
Agricultural Punjab	25.3	44.5	29.1	81.5
Haryana	35.6	59.5	43.1	62.1
Relatively Poor States				
Bihar	43.9	54.8	30.4	85.5
Rajasthan	38.5	58.7	39.2	65.3
Orissa	66.3	68.5	36.1	60.7
Uttar Pradesh	30.1	60.6	38.9	62.8

The share of new towns adjusted for declassified towns was estimated to be around 19 per cent during 1971-81 compared to nearly 18 per cent during 1981-91. The estimates clearly show that migration to urban areas had drastically declined during the 1980s. This is also reflected in the share of migrants in the total urban population as well as the share of decadal migrants to total migrants at the all India level as well as for the different states of India. Table shows that the percentage of migrants to total urban population as well as decal (0-9 years) to total urban migrants for the census year 1981 and 1991.

Table. India: Trend in Migration into the Urban Areas, 1981-1991

State/Country	Percentage of Migrants to Total urban Population		Percentage of inter -censal urban migrants to total urban migrants 1981			Percentage of inter-censal urban migrants to total urban migrants 1991		
	1981	1991	M	F	Total	M	F	Total
India	38.8	32.2	48.7	45.2	46.9	43.1	40.2	41.6
Andhra Pradesh	38.6	34.5	57.3	54.1	54.9	49.3	46.0	47.5
Assam	–	38.6	–	–	–	44.1	42.2	43.2
Bihar	38.5	31.8	53.1	42.3	47.1	42.1	32.3	35.9
Gujarat	39.6	38.1	42.1	44.7	43.5	42.6	41.8	42.2
J&K	–	–	–	–	–	–	–	–
Harlan	46.8	43.6	51.5	46.7	48.9	46.3	42.0	43.9
Himachal Pradesh	58.8	58.9	63.6	57.4	60.8	58.1	50.9	54.6
Karnataka	37.9	32.8	52.6	47.1	49.7	48.6	44.7	46.6
Kerala	25.0	25.5	53.9	48.0	50.4	48.3	43.7	45.5
Madhya Pradesh	41.8	39.1	53.6	46.8	49.9	45.5	41.5	43.2
Maharashthra	48.3	33.8	44.3	44.4	44.3	40.3	41.0	40.7
Orissa	47.7	37.0	59.9	52.6	56.4	49.4	43.4	46.3
Punjab	42.6	40.1	42.4	53.3	41.7	41.0	38.9	39.8
Rajasthan	32.9	30.0	55.9	43.2	48.5	49.3	39.	43.1
Tamil Nadu	35.8	28.2	51.9	49.9	50.8	40.9	40.8	40.8
Uttar Pradesh	28.8	22.3	49.9	36.4	41.6	44.1	35.5	38.6
West Bengal	39.4	28.5	31.3	33.4	32.3	28.3	32.1	30.3

It may be seen that share of migrants to total urban population was nearly 39 per cent in 1981 which declined to 32 per cent in 1991. Similarly, the share of decal migrants to total urban migrants declined from 49 per cent in 1981 to 42 per cent in 1991. The decline was observed for males as well as females separately. This shows the increasing nativity in the urban areas confirming the role of increasing role of natural increase in India's urbanization.

The increasing nativity was observed for most of the states of India except Gujarat, Kerala and Himachal Pradesh where the percentage of migrants to total urban population remained static between the 1981 and 1991 censuses. The increasing nativity was more pronounced in the states of Maharasthra, Orissa, Tamil Nadu, Uttar Pradesh and West Bengal. The decline in the share of migrant population to total urban population was highest in Maharasthra where the share had declined to 34 per cent in 1991 compared to 48 per cent in 1981 followed by West Bengal and Orissa where decline was nearly 10 percentage points between the censuses 1981 and 1991. The share of decadal migrants (0-9 years) had also declined sharply in most of the states of India indicating that the pace of migration has slowed down in the 1980s compared to 1970s.

Table. India: Trend in Inter-censal Rural to Urban Migration (0-9 Years) to Total Rural to Urban Migration, 1981-1991

State/Country	1981		1991	
	Male	Female	Male	Female
India	49.7	44.3	44.2	40.1
Andhra Pradesh	56.4	50.9	49.0	44.8
Bihar	52.7	40.7	41.6	31.4
Gujarat	47.1	43.3	43.4	41.8
Haryana	61.5	51.0	50.7	43.5
Himachal Pradesh	64.4	55.0	59.6	45.5
Kerala	51.4	45.7	46.8	42.3
Karnataka	50.9	44.1	49.2	49.8
Madhya Pradesh	55.3	45.9	46.4	41.0
Maharasthra	59.0	58.8	40.0	40.6
Orissa	58.5	50.0	48.1	41.5

Punjab	49.8	50.7	46.4	40.6
Rajasthan	58.3	41.2	51.6	38.5
Tamil Nadu	48.7	46.2	40.1	39.3
Uttar Pradesh	51.0	37.8	45.1	34.9
West Bengal	34.4	38.7	32.2	34.9

The share of intercensal rural to urban migrants (0-9 years) in the total rural to urban migration was around 50 per cent for males and 44 per cent for females in 1981 which declined to 44 and 40 per cent respectively in 1991. The decline in the recent rural to urban migration was very sharp for males and females in Maharasthra where decline was more than 15 per cent for both the sexes between the censuses 1981 and 1991. In Punjab, the female migration was much more affected in the 1980s compared with male migration.

As such the share of intercensal (0-9) female migrants to total rural to urban female migration has sharply declined from 51 per cent in 1981 to 41 per cent in 1991 whereas the figures for male was 50 per cent in 1981 compared to 46 per cent in 1991.

The unemployment data available from National Sample Survey show that unemployment was more in urban areas than rural areas and also the unemployment had increased in urban areas during the period 1983 to 1987. The metro cities show higher level of unemployment and females were more unemployed and unemployment among them had increased faster than males in urban areas.

Table. Unemployment Rates as Percentage of Labour Force in Urban Areas, India, 1983-1992

Year	Usual Principal Status		Current Weekly Status		Current Daily Status	
	Male	Female	Male	Female	Male	Female
1983	5.8	6.9	6.7	7.5	9.2	11.0
1987-88	6.1	8.8	6.7	8.9	8.8	12.8
1989-90	4.4	3.9	4.5	4.0	–	–
1990-91	4.5	5.4	5.1	5.3	–	–
1992	4.6	6.7	4.6	6.2	–	–

This shows that educated and uneducated females also increasingly competing for skilled as well as unskilled jobs with their male counter parts due to rising cost of living in the urban areas. This is another factor dampening the rate of rural to urban migration in the country during the 1980s. The more recent data on the growth of employment in organized sector shows that the average growth in employment was only 0.87 per cent per annum during 1991 to 1999 in spite of impressive growth in national income during the said period (over 6 per cent per annum).

This is because if economic growth becomes capital intensive it is likely to generate lesser employment. This has important implication so far India's urbanization is concerned. On the other hand the large metro cities which have a very dominating position in India's urbanisation stand as economic island where new entrants have to face greater difficulties in finding a foot hold, let alone jobs. The natives of the big cities have advantages in preparing themselves in terms of opportunities for skill formation. In spite of that it is difficult for the cities even to accommodate its labour force on the account of natural increase, let alone the migrants.

The likely impact in future will be reduced migration to urban areas and also to metropolitan cities. The slowing down of migration to urban areas was due to rising parochialism in cornering jobs for the natives. In recent years, due to shrinkage of jobs and increasing unemployment among youth the concept of sons of the soil is very much appealing to the natives of even in states where such campaign were little invoked by the political parties in the past. In a recent study in Ahmedabad by Desai (1999) found that local people feel that 80 per cent of jobs should be reserved for sons of the soil, a feeling or attitude repulsing the migration to urban areas in the wake of growing urban crisis.

THE FUTURE URBANISATION

India has launched the programmes of economic liberalization since 1991. Some of the proponents of this strategy of linking the country with the global economy would accelerate rural to urban migration and boost urban growth in 1990s and the following decade. The expectation is evidently based on the assumption that there will be a massive inflow of capital both from within and out side the country resulting in rapid development of infrastructure and industrial growth.

This is likely to give impetus to the process of urbanisation in the country since much of the industrial growth and consequent growth in employment would be within or around the existing urban centres. This enthusiasm is not correct. The benefits of liberalisation will accrue to only those who could acquire new skills commensurate with the demands of liberalisation of the economy. In view of sluggish growth in employment that too of skilled nature, it impossible for the common man and the poor to benefit from the liberalisation. Secondly, foreign investments are coming only in selected sectors concentrated only few pockets of the country in around metro cities.

And the magnitude of foreign investment is low in India compared to China. For example, in spite of several allurements only approximately 3.5 billion ₹ of the foreign direct investment (FDI) reached to India in 1998 compared with 43.8 billion ₹ (7 per cent) in China. Moreover, it is not likely to benefit the urban centres of non-metropolitan nature. Therefore, it will not be correct to think that urban growth and rural to urban migration will accelerate in future. On the other hand, critics of new development strategy have pointed out that the opening of the economy will destabilise the agrarian economy, resulting in high unemployment and massive exodus from rural areas.

This would lead to rapid growth of population in urban centres. This view is also not correct because it is uphill task for the poor people to survive in a situation of rising cost of living and increasing difficulty to accommodate themselves in the bloated informal sector. There is an increasing casualisation of work in the post liberalisation period also. It has further strained the informal sector-a refuge for poor migrants from rural areas. Thus in view of sluggish growth in employment and increasing casualisation of work in the 1990s, and the persistence of the under currents of sons of the soil factor backed by regional-linguistic political parties in different states of India, it is difficult to believe that the pace of urbanization or rural to urban migration will likely to accelerate in near future. On the contrary, the liberalisation as such by benefiting the people and urban centres selectively is potentially loaded for likely increase in intra-urban and urban-rural inequality.

4

Politics and Religion

After the tragic events in November 2008 in Mumbai media and the BJP and its Hindu militant allies have presented a simplistic understanding of the issues of terrorism. One religion encourages terrorism and Muslims conspire to undermine India emerging as a superpower. They suggest that military action must be taken to stop terror. I consider this approach to be wrong and would have long term consequences to the region. Hence, the BJP seeks once again to replicate the myth that "terrorism" is an exclusively Muslim phenomenon.

Therefore, I find important to discuss objectively on the use of religion and politics, particularly by the Hindu militant organisations. Hindu militancy is led by religious-cum-political groups such as RSS, VHP, Bajrang Dal and Shiv Sena. All these Hindu extremist organisations closely work together on political issues. I will focus on Hindu extremists here because somehow it is ignored by the West. The BJP is their largest political group, which right from its inception has been multi-faceted phenomenon.

During the last 15 years communalism has made major inroads into the civil society and as a result the nature of public discourse has undergone substantial changes. This is reflected in the legitimacy and acceptance gained by communal assumptions about society and polity in mass media. The idea of "Hindu Rastra" even those, for example, who believe in secularism, tend to concede the right of Hindus to the nation on majority grounds. The Indian civilization has come to be accepted as 'Hindu civilization'. Consequently the Muslims and Christians are identified as outsiders. The Hindu militants have promoted religiosity, which led to foment communal consciousness. The Hindu extremist organisations have presented past history in communal colour in order to seek legitimacy from the past for redefining the nation as Hindu.

Hindu extremists argue that Indian Muslims and Christians converted from Hinduism, should reconvert to Hindu religion. Their movement is "at the core very anti-Muslim". Although Hindu extremist played a minority role in India's parliament in decades after independence, they experienced rising popularity only after the 1980. The BJP held government at the Centre from 1998 to 2004. Now BJP is India's main opposition party politically important in populous states like Gujarat, Maharastra, UP, MP and Rajasthan. In the late 1980s the party campaigned on the issue that the '16th century Babri mosque was built on the site of a Hindu temple'. In 1992 Hindu militants led by BJP leader Mr. Advani stormed the Babri mosque and demolished it. About four thousand people died in the following riots in north India.

An important new phenomenon has taken place which will help us to understand the communalism in India. There has been a large migration of caste Hindus, especially from Gujarat to Europe and North America. These nonresidential Indians suffer from identity crisis and feel rootless in their host countries. They adopt to more religious outlook into their personal lives *i.e.* more Hindus than Hindus in India. These overseas Hindus are financing the Hindu militant organisations in India.

The Shiv Sena, another anti Muslim organisation based in Maharastra state, was formed with the active support by then S. K. Patil, the state Congress Party leader. In the 1970 Bhivandi riots killed more than 250 people, again mostly Muslims. The Justice Madon was appointed to inquire causes of the riots. He submitted his report implicating Shiv Sena leaders taking parts in the attacks and also the police for inaction to control the attacks against Muslim community. However, despite the clear evidence the government failed again to punish the culprits. The Congress Party, although spoke about secularism, but was never adopted secularism as core policy and some of its party activists subscribed to communal outlook. Also the party made several compromises with communal forces. After independence the Indian ruling elites were as much interested in the communal-divide as the British rulers.

The Indian ruling elites in post-independence manipulated the people on communal lines to get votes, which worsened the communal problem. Communalism in India is a modern phenomenon in the sense that with the advent of British-rule the socioeconomic structure and in consequence, the political relationship between Muslims and Hindus began to change. Pluralist society undergoing changes are rarely totally free from communal or ethnic tensions.

This change began to deepen further when socio-economic transformation began to accelerate after independence. New forces and new relationships gradually emerged. However, these changes again need to be looked with great care and complexities rather than resorting to oversimplifications. It is important to briefly look nature of communalism, as it is often thought by some is not the product of religion. It is in fact, the product of politics of elite of a religious community. Communalism was not product of medieval ages but of modern period. Medieval polity was not competitive.

The competitive politics between the elites of various communities that gives rise to communalism, especially under colonial administration, it assumes grave proportions. It is incorrect to solely blame the British colonial authorities to be responsible for the genesis of communalism. However, they did play a vital role in promoting it as well as its genesis. Right from 1857 onwards the British colonial rulers realised that the damage Hindu-Muslim unity could cause to their imperial rule and domination. They systematically began dividing the two communities.

Imperial scholars and officials were encouraged to distort historical records and Muslim rulers were always portrayed as destroying temples and oppressing Hindus. For example, selective 19th century translations from some of the pre-colonial historical records notably by imperial academics such as Elliot and Dowson had greatly contributed to communalisation.

After independence, the first Hindu-Muslim riots took in Jabalpur in 1962 when Nehru was prime minister and his own Congressmen were involved in attacking the Muslims along with RSS. The RSS was set up in 1925 on the basis of hate against minorities particularly Muslims. But Nehru could take no action to isolate those in his own party. During the 1970s and 1980s religious violence continued with increased intensity. However, during the 1980s it had a new twist when Indira Gandhi return back to power she did not support the secularism with any deeper conviction but a strategy to gain support. She used religion to increase her support and in fact seen competing BJP to win Hindu extremists. In 1984, after Indira Gandhi's assassination the BJP only got 2 seats in the parliamentary election. The Supreme Court decided the case of maintenance for divorced wife in her favour.

This was seen by Muslim religious leaders as interference in their religion. They did this without realising the wider consequences. Rajiv Gandhi's Muslim Women Act was passed by parliament which made the Supreme Court decision not applicable to Muslims. This was done to win over Muslim men. With this BJP got new opportunity to launch tirade against Muslims which is known as Shah Bano case. The BJP termed this issue as government 'appeasement of Muslims' and vigourously campaigned against it. Rajiv Gandhi in a balancing act to appease Hindu militants opened the door of the Babri mosque in Ayodhya for Hindus to worship.

It thus unleashed another controversy, which was exploited by the BJP for increasing its vote base. All these years the state remained soft towards communalism, and religion was used to win votes. The Congress regime never sincerely did anything practically to undermine communalism and never punished the guilty in communal riots. It remains an ugly fact that the security forces in the northern states invariably to reserve its subliminal brutal antipathy for Muslims a reality that has been repeatedly recorded whenever Hindu-Muslim riots take place. For example, riots in Meerut in 1987 and Bhagalpur in 1989. In both these riots, police collusion with the Hindu militants was observed.

The PAC security dragged young Muslim boys from Hashimpura in Meerut, UP state shot in the head some 45 Muslim young men in cold blood and dumped their bodies into a nearby canal. No action yet had been taken against these murderers. Also in Bhagalpur, Bihar state, police directly took part in the looting and attacking the minority. In fact a police sub-inspector in one village killed many Muslims and buried their bodies in a field. Once again, the culprits were never persecuted. After the Gujarat riots in 2002, there was no national campaign against the forces of Hindu extremists jointly by secular parties, which would have isolated them at least on the issue of mass murder of Muslims in Gujarat by Mr. Modi.

He used to be an activist of the RSS and currently leading the BJP state government. In 2002, the communal violence in Gujarat broke claimed 3 000 mostly Muslim lives. It was also reported that widespread allegations of "state government complicity in anti-Muslim attacks". The violence continued for months unchecked by the both BJP led governments in state and at the Centre. The media do not want to talk about the genocidal slaughter of Muslims in Gujarat in 2002 or the brutal repression in Kashmir by Indian security forces. For example, in Kashmir the shameless rigging of the 1987 state elections led to wide spread resentment. Soon after, bombings and assassination began. India responded with great brutality to the insurgency. More than a three-quarter million army were dispatched to the valley.

There were mass arrests, violence and rape against defenceless civilians, nothing was ever independently investigated. A large number of people known to have disappeared and some 65 000 people have been killed in this conflict since 1987 in Kashmir. William Dalrymple, a British writer, has summarised recently in The Observer Sunday 30th November 2008 as, "India meanwhile continues to make matters worse by its ill treatment of the people of Kashmir, which has handed to the Jehadis as entire generation of educated, angry middle-class Muslims... The boys in the operation wore jeans and Nike and were described by eyewitness as chikna or well off. These were not poor, madarsah-educated Pakistanis from the villages, brain washed by Mullahs, but angry and well educated middle class kids furious at the gross injustice they perceive being done to Muslims by Israel, the US, the UK and India".

Recently in Jamia Nagar, Delhi, where two young Muslims were killed at the hands of police in their rented flats claiming that they were responsible for serial bombings. There were protests by local community leaders, academics, lawyers and social activists who demanded judicial inquiry into the incident. During the same month a report submitted to the court admitted that Special Cell of Delhi police had abducted two innocent Muslim men Irshad Ali and Moarif Qamar in 2005, planted 2 kg. RDX and pistols on them and then arrested them as "terrorists". There are hundreds of Muslims who have been similarly jailed, tortured and killed on false charges. The recent investigation of September 2008 into Malegaon bomb explosion case, the police arrested a Hindu preacher Mr. Pragya and Lt. Col. Purohit, a serving officer of the Indian army. All arrested belong to Hindu militant organisations. A well known Mumbai based Islamic scholar Asghar Ali Engineer commented on the situation as, "It is deeply worrying that Army personnel are involved in such terror activities. It just goes to show how deep the infiltration is involved in such terror activities. It just goes to show how deep the infiltration is in this country.... Constant indoctrination over decades by the RSS, VHP, Bajrang Dal, Shiv Sena and BJP has resulted in this kind of violence, which will be disastrous for India". Hence, there are multiple sources of terrorism in India. India has a Muslim population of more than 150 million, making the state with the second-largest Muslim population in the world after Indonesia. Justice Sachar Commission reported in 2006 on the conditions of India's Muslims that "the community had sunk to the bottom of the heap, below even the untouchables, when it comes to benefits flowing from the government-run welfare schemes, access to education, employment, bank credits etc. Poverty and insecurity have driven them into ghettos where they are open to exploitation".

Muslims make up about 13.8% of India's population yet hold fewer than 4% of government posts and make up only 4% of the undergraduate student body in India's elite universities. About 25% of the Muslim children in the 6-14 age groups either never went to school or dropped out before completing primary school. The Sachar report, Muslims were now worse off then untouchable caste. Some 52% Muslims men were unemployed compared to 47% of untouchable men. Almost half of Muslims over the age of 46 could not read or write. Only one out of 25 under graduate students and one out of 50 post-graduate students in 'premier college' are Muslims. The percentage of graduates in poor households pursuing postgraduate studies is significantly lower for Muslims *e.g.* Hindus general 29%, untouchables 28%, while Muslims only 16%. In post independent India, the successive governments including secular ones have tended to leave Muslim's grievances unresolved.

Many Indian Muslims believe that for long-justice have been denied to them and also it is institutionalised discrimination. The media often identifies Muslim with terrorism. We may recall the terror method adopted by the Zionist organisations. The detail records are now available of the modus operandi of the Zionist terror Hagana, Irgun and Stern terror groups were led by western favourite people like Menahem Begin, Yatzak Shamir, and Ariel Sharon. One has never heard the RSS, Shiv Sena, Bajrang Dal or LTT Tamil terrorism as Hindu terrorism. Muslims in India in the words of one analyst "suffer double discrimination, by virtue of being Muslims and poor". Finally, the religious extremists whether Hindus or Muslims are reactionary and dangerous because they do not present radical alternative but rather accept, de facto, existing exploitative system and fully support imperialist economic policies. They rather split the masses by creating an internal enemy. An important question is why the entire South Asian region has become increasingly prone to terrorist attacks. Besides discrimination and repression of the Muslims, and recent years the new phenomena namely globalisation and economic liberalisation has further exacerbated the situation. This had led the growing of inequalities in the region which is fuelling resentments amongst parts of the population.

Moreover, India's affinity to the US and Israel is inviting terrorists attacks in the country. In 1991, the Congress government established diplomatic relations and it reached new heights under BJP government. Today Israel is India's largest supplier of defence equipment. India helped Israel to launch spy satellite in January 2008, primarily to monitor Iran. Furthermore, there are signs that parts of Indian ruling elites are eagerly waiting close military cooperation with the US under new President Obama with the hope that India would be the sole beneficiary of new war in south Asian against terrorism.

The recent violent attack on Mumbai must open our eyes that more violence is not the most effective way to deal with violence that exist. I find that further extension of US led war against Islamic militancy to the South Asia seems to be no good news for the people because that policy can redefine Pakistan-India relationship just as to priorities of the US imperialists. It appears such development would lead towards greater disaster. It would be naive to think that further extension of the failed US aggressive military policy can benefit the people of South Asia. India and Pakistan seem to be getting deeper into dual trap as well worsening inter-state conflict and continuing internal militarization, which will certainly further deteriorate the already appalling living conditions of the large number of their inhabitants.

5

Science and Spirituality

Modern science was introduced to India under the shadow of colonialism. This neither means that its progress in India was simply a matter of European discovery and imperial dissemination, nor that there was no "science" in India prior to the British conquest of India. However, what is important to observe is that between modern science and traditional science there was a marked disjunction as there was between traditional knowledge and "English education. " Because these gaps have still not been properly studied, let alone bridged, the history of modern science in India is inextricably linked with the history of colonialism as well. All the same, the trajectories of the two are neither coextensive or coterminous.

While colonialism rose, reached its peak, then declined, and officially ended, modern science has enjoyed a steady and incremental rise since its inception. In fact, after independence its claims to an exalted social, political, and cultural status have risen dramatically, especially with the heavy investment and continuous monitoring of the Nehruvian state in its growth and development. Today, science is very much a part of how the Indian state seeks to see or project itself, deriving legitimation and political advantage from it.

When we look, instead, at the development of modern Indian spirituality, we see that though it is also inextricably linked with the history of colonialism and, later, nationalism, its causal connections with the two are not all that direct or determinate. Under colonialism, traditional Indian spirituality encountered modern Western ideas, including modern science. Indian spirituality, though not necessarily as challenged as religious practices and dogmas were, had, nevertheless to reinvent itself, a process that still continues. One way by which it coped was by identifying a distinct real for its own functioning that had little to do either with colonialism or with modernity.

Yet, several Indian spiritual leaders, starting with Rammohun Roy, took an active interest in Western science. Sri Ramkrishna's disciple, Swami Vivekananda, best exemplifies not just the curiosity of Indian spirituality in respect of modern science, but its first wellarticulated enthusiasm, even endorsement of science. From time to time, other spiritual masters such as Sri Aurobindo and Paramhansa Yogananda also continued this interest in and partial approval of modern science. While India's national struggle for independence, especially the majoritarian thrust of it, had a distinctly spiritual colouring to it. Not only was the Indian National Congress founded by Alan Octavian Hume, a Theosophist, but many of its prominent leaders, especially Sri Aurobindo, and later, Mahatma Gandhi, had an overt interest in spirituality. Yet, India as a secular state, kept itself aloof officially from matters religious. Unlike science, which was a part of the state policy, spirituality, though a political force, was never official recognized by the state. Therefore, when we come to the relationship between modern science and spirituality in India, we see not so much causal or direct connections, but subtle and covert connections between them. Much of this seminar will be devoted to understanding these interrelationships.

One starting point for such an inquiry is to ask what relationship modern science in India bears to, what is now called traditional or indigenous science, and then ask the same question of Indian spirituality. We notice at once vital traces of continuity rather than disjunction between traditional and modern spirituality in India. In fact, the holistic, nondualistic orientation of traditional Indian knowledge systems does not allow us even to separate science and spirituality too clearly in premodern India. One might argue that this was also the case in pre-enlightenment Europe. The fragmentation of knowledge and the ensuing proliferation of specialization is thus relatively new even to the West. In fact, this fragmentation is itself one of the constituents of modernity.

We thus have our first contrast between science and spirituality as systems of social construction and cultural authority in India. While modern science was seen as being alien and superior to traditional science, modern spirituality was seen as a natural outgrown and flowering of traditional Indian spirituality. What is, perhaps, even more interesting is that traditional Indian science and traditional Indian spirituality were closely, even intrinsically linked. For instance, while Ayurveda, as its name suggests, was described as the fifth Veda, thus not only linked to the Vedas but sharing its worldview and notions of wellness, modern Western medicine was seen as whole secular, if more effective in some cases. It is not that Indians in the 19th century dispensed with traditional medicine in favour of Western medicine.

Both systems coexisted, but it was thought that when the disease worsened, the patients turned to Western medicine. The coexistence of multiple, incommensurable systems of medicine persists even today in India, though the dominance of Western medicine is far greater. But this plurality of knowledge systems is also characteristic of the metaphysical and epistemological multiplicity of modern India, a location in which we see the unresolved coexistence of contending systems of signification and meaning. Though not primary to their relationship, the issue of power cannot be ignored while exploring the sciences pirituality dialogue.

As David Arnold observes, because traditional Indian sciences were heterogenous and plural, it becomes difficult not only "to characterise Indian science as a whole but also to determine the precise nature of its interaction with the forms of science and technology emanating from the West by the late eighteenth and early nineteenth century". One might extend this argument to contend that Western or modern science, though ostensibly unified by one, universal "methodology," is actually heterogenous and culturally conditioned as well. Thus, British imperial science, as Deepak Kumar and others have shown, had its own peculiarities and identifying traits that made it different not only from science practised in Britain, but also from science in other European countries. For instance, colonial science was more descriptive and enumerative, than theoretical or experimental. It was also more heavily invested in fields such as geology, plant biology.

The other factor that complicates the story of the growth of modern science in India is the debate over whether it was a case of impact and reception as was largely thought of earlier, or of continuous interaction and exchange as the more recent and considered opinions declare. There is also the allied question of how to model the historiography of tradition Indian sciences.

The earlier view in this regard, which followed the Orientalist construction, was one of high achievement, followed by decline and stagnation, ending with a new rejuvenation under the Western stimulus. We now tend to disagree with such a view, seeing instead remarkable progress and interaction between Muslim and Hindu ideas and sciences during the medieval period of Muslim rule in India.

The decentred nature of India's polity and the lack of sustained research to reconstruct its history of science make it impossible to offer a coherent account, but it should be clear that any simplistic, reductive, or unidirectional model will be misleading. This applies as much to the advent of modernity in India, in which science played an important role, as it does to the development and growth of modern Indian spirituality. George Basalla, "The Spread of Western Science" offers a threephase "diffusions" model. In the first phase of colonial discovery, expansion, and conquest, the nonEuropean areas served as sources of scientific data.

This may be termed the "contact phase." In consonance with the colonial interest in exploiting the natural resources of conquered territories, botany, zoology, and later, astronomy, geology and geography were emphasized. While modern science was disseminated in various parts of the world during this phase, Basalla believes that only the advanced countries of Europe were able to assimilate this new information and knowledge, thereby transforming science in metropolitan centres in Britain, France, and Holland.

In the second phase, which he calls "colonial science," local scientific institutions start to appear, with the participation of local born scientists. Basalla calls this a "dependent" science because it was controlled and directed by colonial authorities and imitated metropolitan models. This applied not only to countries like India directly colonized by the British but also to China, Japan, and the United States. Extra European societies in phase three strove to establish national or independent scientific traditions.

Political independence, but more significantly, institutions of national importance, awards, state funding and infrastructure brought scientific research to critical thresholds in a number of countries, in fact, enabling them, in some cases to overtake European science. Both America and Russia achieved this stage during the world wars, while Canada, Australia, and Japan were lower down. The rest of the world in Asia, Africa, and Latin America lagged far behind. Basalla has been universally criticised for being simplistic, unidirectional, reductive, but after all, he was only offering a preliminary schema in a short document.

The categories he proposed, however, including "colonial science" have proved to be extremely influential and persistent. As Arnold sums up, "In Basalla's Eurocentric model, dynamism belongs to an homogenous West, leaving the rest of the world to participate only passively in the process of diffusion, unable to make any original contribution of its own or even to negotiate with an ascendant Western science". Dhruv Raina has tried to upturn this notion by suggesting that the ideology of science has been "actively redefined" by the "recipient culture": the receiving culture "subverts, contaminates, and reorganises the ideology of science as introduced by Europe".

The problem with such a counter argument which Arnold does not notice is that in accepting the originary Europe and the recipient India, all Raina and Habib do is to give more agency to the recipient, reducing the power of the diffuser.

Their model of scientific production remains not only diffusionist and Eurocentric, but also dualistic. Arnold asks the fundamental question of what we can do if we reject this diffusionist approach. If "distinctions between centre and periphery, between 'metropolitan' and 'colonial' science, fundamentally misrepresent the way in which science evolved internationally" how can one ignore the differential power relations between the metropolitan centre and the colonial peripheries, with their still persisting hierarchies and dependencies. Science and technology "were, and surely remain, aspects of a global hegemony".

The other point that Arnold takes up is the role of science in the creation and spread of modernity in India. As Gyan Prakash puts it, "scientific reasoning became the organizing metaphor in the discourse" of Indian modernity, promoted not only by the colonial administration but by an increasingly participatory native elite. Scientific evangelism, along with Christian evangelism, became the battering ram that tried to destroy the traditional cultures of India. But just as modernity was not unproblematic to Indians, modern science too was not. As Partha Chatterjee shows, Indian nationalism attempted to mediate between the rejecting of colonial authority and the acceptance of Western modernity thus becoming for Indians a way to effect what Sri Aurobindo called a "selective assimilation" of the West:

- "Nationalism provided a discourse ... which, even as it challenged the colonial claim to political domination... also accepted the very intellectual premises of 'modernity' on which colonial domination was based".

But what this really means is that neither modern science nor modernity itself are homogenous. The diffusionist model needs to be questioned in both spheres. At the same time we need to recognize the hierarchies of power, inequality, and hegemony that mark both domains. One might argue that Indian scientists sought to forge their own brand of science as Indian intellectuals did their own brand of modernity. That this story has not been told does not mean that it cannot be told. It is just that both science and scientists are reticent if not resistant to such a proposition, undermining as it does the very fundamental, constitutive, and selfdefining characteristic of science as objective, valueneutral, universal, rational, and so on. Arnold acknowledges that this was possible for Indian modernity:

- "Indian scientists and intellectuals tried to construct their own brand of Indian modernity, particularly through the selective incorporation of Hindu ideas and traditions, through a mix of elements, the degree of 'hybridity' involved in the process, varied widely from one individual to another, even with the emergent scientific community."

He doesn't take this so far as to suggest that India had the capacity and indeed demonstrated the ability to devise its own culturally unique brand of science, a sort of neo-Hindu science, if you will. I think this is one of the key questions for any serious study of science and spirituality in India. Is there a distinctly Indian science? If so what are its defining characteristics? And what is the role of spirituality in the constitution of Indian science? David L. Gosling argues that the distinctive contribution of Indian science is its holistic and integrative approach: "what has always been the most distinctive feature of Indian science is a form of integral thought, a kind of intuitive ability to hold together ideas which have elsewhere remained unrelated". Quoting the work of Jagadish Chandra Bose, Gosling observes, "From the point of view of Indian scientists the progress of science in the West seemed to be a fulfillment of an important Hindu insight—the fundamental unity of all existence". Gosling, Bose's work proceeded from the fundamental principal that "In the multiplicity of phenomena, we should never miss their underlying unity".

The foregoing discussion suggests that the interrelationship between science and spirituality in India is a historically evolving one. In its earlier. phase in the late nineteenth century the relationship was possibly closer, partly because both science and spirituality in India contributed to the creation of Indian modernity and, what is perhaps, more significant, both also became central to the process of consolidation of Indian nationalism. Many of the early scientists were also nationalists. However, the relationship between the two has changed in more recent times to one of the independence of the two domains.

If we revert to Ian Barbour's classic formulation of a fourfold typology of conflict, independence, dialogue, and integration, we notice that in India all four types of relationships have been present both in the past and in the present, but that conflict has never been predominant unlike in the West. Moreover, while a number of practicing scientists stress the independence of the two domains, a number of spiritual leaders have advocated both dialogue and integration. Indeed, His Holiness, the Dalai Lama, who is present with us today, has often stressed the need to dialogue. Dialogue, of course, is the precondition to a possible integration.

Despite the shift from a scientific universalism during high modernity to a sort of cultural relativism engendered by postmodernist philosophy, science in the sense of a welldefined, commonly accepted, multicultural enterprise continues to inform and determine constructions of truth and reality in our contemporary world. While tradition may be the repository of values, beliefs, and ways of relating to each other and the world, we need not, as V.V. Raman suggests in the conclusion to Glimpses of Indian Science, cling to premodern explanatory models just because they are culturally significant.

To do so would make us cultural fundamentalists if not outright reactionaries. On the other hand, dogmatic scientific materialism may also result in the closure of the mind and of the possibilities of experiencing and explaining phenomena. As suggested, have to admit that there are areas of knowledge and truth which are simply outside the parametres of science as it is understood today.

Those who believe in the evolutionary possibilities of human futures aver that we are on the brink of a global renaissance which requires the integration of not just Western and Eastern cultural and civilizational resources, but the coming together of science and spirituality. On the ground such a convergence seems as yet only a distant dream. Even so, the unexplored possibilities of dialogue between these two domains affords us challenges and opportunities hitherto unexplored. India, I believe, has a crucial role to play in such a dialogue, positioned as it is. Custodian of an ancient civilization which is also the home of unique experiments in a plethora of spiritual endeavours, it is at the same time positioning itself as one of the leaders in the IT revolution that is sweeping across the globe. This makes India not just a fertile ground for such an enquiry but the bearer of a special responsibility towards the future of such a dialogue.

6

Population Dynamics

AN OVERVIEW

India is often described as a collection of many countries held together by a common destiny and a successful democracy. Its diverse ethnic, linguistic, geographic, religious, and demographic features reflect its rich history and shape its present and future.

No fewer than 16 languages are featured on Indian rupee notes. It is also only the second country to achieve a population of 1 billion. While it is an emerging economic power, life remains largely rooted in its villages. Only a small fraction of Indians are benefiting from the country's expanding industrial and information sectors.

India has more people than Europe, more than Africa, more than the entire Western Hemisphere. India's population will exceed that of China before 2030 to become the world's most populous country, a distinction it will almost certainly never lose. Just one group, Indian boys below age 5, numbers 62 million—more than the total population of France. India's annual increase of nearly 19 million contributes far more to annual world population growth than any other country. This Population Bulletin presents a demographic portrait of the diverse country of India in the early years of the 21st century and offers insight into some of the forces driving continued growth.

A RICH HISTORY

Although the region has a rich and ancient history,

present-day India is a relatively new nation. India gained independence from British rule in 1947, after decades of struggle against the former colonial power. The country was then partitioned into primarily Hindu India and Muslim Pakistan. The eastern part of Pakistan is today's Bangladesh. In the largest mass migration ever recorded, millions of Hindus left Pakistan to resettle in India, as millions of Muslims moved from India to Pakistan.

The upheaval of the partition also unleashed a period of horrific violence between Hindus and Muslims, and sporadic conflicts between Hindus and Muslims and between India and Pakistan continue to this day. At independence, India consisted of provinces defined by the British, along with more than 500 princely states whose territory was ultimately taken over by the new Indian government. Boundaries for today's states were largely drawn along language lines after independence. In the 21st century, India is a federal republic comprised of 28 states and seven union territories.

States and union territories are split into 593 districts and 5,564 subdistricts. New states are created periodically to ease the burden of governing as their populations grow or to provide separate states for ethnic and tribal groups. Three new states were created in 2000 when Jharkhand was split from Bihar, Chhattisgarh was cut from Madhya Pradesh, and a few mountain districts were carved out of Uttar Pradesh to form the state of Uttaranchal.

Part of Kashmir, along the northwestern border with Pakistan, is occupied by Pakistan, although India considers it Indian territory. Disputes over this territory have spawned intense political battles and terrorism. India's 1.2 million square miles equals about one-third the land area of the United States.

In the far north, India is dominated by the grand sweep of the Himalayas, Hindu Kush, and Patkai mountain ranges, which soon give way to the vast and fertile Indo-Gangetic plain of the north, fed by such major rivers as the Ganges and Yamuna. Here are located many of India's most populous states such as Haryana, Delhi, Uttaranchal, Uttar Pradesh,

Bihar, Jharkhand, and West Bengal. Moghuls invaded from Afghanistan in the 16th century, leaving a mark on the architecture, food, and dress of northern India still discernable today. Hindi, India's official language of government, is spoken in much of the north, and the area from Rajasthan to Bihar is often referred to as the "Hindi Belt." This region, which contains just over 40 per cent of the national population, is known for high birth and death rates, low literacy levels, and endemic rural poverty.

Mountain ranges divide north from south, marking the beginning of the Deccan Plateau that makes up much of southern India. The north/south division also marks enormous socioeconomic differences.

In contrast to high illiteracy, rapid population growth, and poor health common in the north, the southern states of Kerala, Karnataka, and Tamil Nadu are known for high literacy levels, long life expectancy, and low birth rates. Throughout history, the south had more contact with an outside world attracted by its profitable spice trade. Trade and interaction with foreign people encouraged literacy and introduced a diversity of religions.

Although Hinduism predominates throughout the region, Kerala, on the southwestern coast, has one of the highest proportions of both Christians and Muslims in India. That state has also historically been one of India's most advanced in terms of women's rights and education levels. Northeast India, barely connected to the rest of the country by a narrow strip of land known as the Siliguri, or "Chicken's Neck," consists of seven smaller states, some carved out of the state of Assam, which are ethnically closer to Southeast Asia than to the rest of India.

POPULATION CHANGE

The Indian subcontinent has long been one of the world's most populous regions, but as in many of today's developing countries, population growth took off in the 20th century. India began the century with a population of about 238 million and ended it with 1 billion.

Table. Population Size and Growth, India, 1901–2001

Census year	Population	Number	Per cent	Multiple of 1901 population
1901	238,396,327	—	—	1.0
1911	252,093,390	1,3697,063	5.7	1.1
1921	251,321,213	–772,177	–0.3	1.1
1931	278,977,238	27,656,025	11.0	1.2
1941	318,660,580	39,683,342	14.2	1.3
1951	361,088,090	42,427,510	13.3	1.5
1961	439,234,771	78,146,681	21.6	1.8
1971	548,159,652	108,924,881	24.8	2.3
1981	683,329,097	135,169,445	24.7	2.9
1991	846,421,039	163,091,942	23.9	3.6
2001	1,028,737,436	182,316,397	21.5	4.3

India added another 100 million by 2006, when its population reached an estimated 1.1 billion. This phenomenal growth followed a century of relatively stable population size, just as to most historical estimates. Scholars differ in the historical estimates of the region's population, but many assume that the population was roughly 200 million in the early 1800s. India's population total remained more or less static during the 19th century, reflecting a slender balance of births over deaths. Growth slowly accelerated in the late 1800s. By 1871, India's population had reached 255 million.

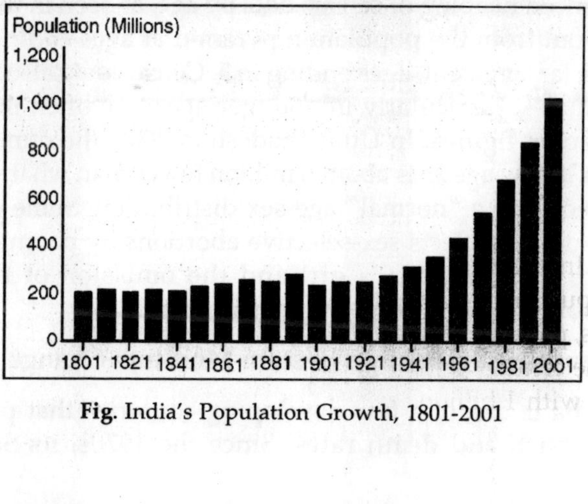

Fig. India's Population Growth, 1801-2001

The first population census was conducted in 1872, and a census has been taken every decade since.

POPULATION STATISTICS IN INDIA

The Census of India—Counting 1 Billion People

Often called the largest administrative exercise in the world, India's census is a truly monumental exercise that involves 2 million enumerators and supervisors. In the year before the census, enumerators canvass the entire country listing every dwelling—whether a house or temporary structure. This list serves as a basis for planning enumerator assignments and other organizational needs.

The 2001 Census population questionnaire featured 23 questions for people in households, including a new question on women's work as an economic activity. In 2001, provisional population totals were released only three weeks after the census date—March 1—an amazing feat considering the size of the country. The Indian censuses have very good coverage by global standards. After the 1991 Census, the Registrar General's office estimated that the census undercount was about 1.8 per cent of the population.

Detailed data from the census highlight the fact that many Indians do not know their exact birth year and often report an approximate age rounded to a "0" or "5." This rounding causes pronounced heaping of census data by age, as seen in the bars jutting out from the population pyramid at ages ending in 0, and to a lesser extent, ages ending in 5. Census data also reveal that females, particularly in younger ages, are often missing from census figures. In Uttar Pradesh in 2001, the number of females below age 25 is about 6 million fewer than what would be expected in a "normal" age-sex distribution. Some of this female deficit reflects sex-selective abortions by parents who want to avoid having a girl and the omission of female household members from the census count.

The Sample Registration System Monitors Change

India is one of a few developing countries that publish annual birth and death rates. Since the 1970s, its Sample

Registration System has collected data on births and deaths from sample villages and from sample census blocks in urban areas. India publishes annual estimates of birth, death, and infant mortality rates; life expectancy; and other key measures for the nation and most states. Less detail is provided for smaller states because of insufficient sample sizes. The quality of SRS estimates has improved over the years, and the SRS provides valuable data for officials and planners who rely on population data. In 2004, the SRS covered 7,597 sample units comprising 1.3 million households and 6.7 million people.

National Family Health Surveys Enrich India's Demographic Data

The National Family Health Surveys, a part of the global Demographic and Health Survey programme, have provided a wealth of information on a wide variety of socio demographic topics. The NFHS produce measures of fertility, contraceptive use, childbearing desires, the status of women, infant mortality, immunization coverage, use of iodized salt, reproductive health, knowledge of HIV and AIDS, housing, and other valuable data.

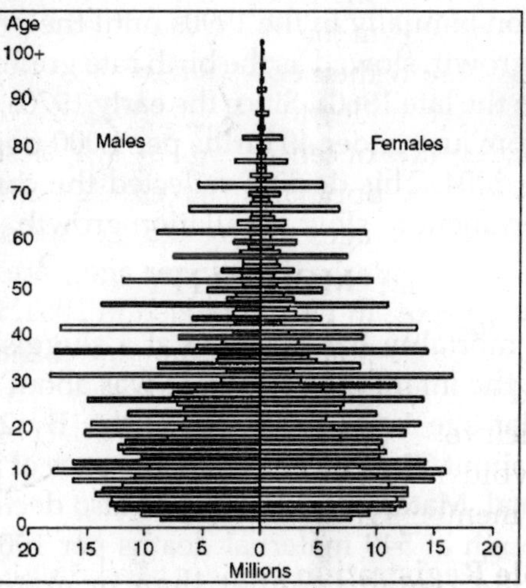

Fig. India's Population by Sex and Single Years of age, 2001 Census.

The first two surveys were taken in 1992–1993 and 1998–1999. With a sample size of nearly 90,000 women of childbearing age, the NFHS provides detailed analyses down to the state level. A third NFHS being conducted in 2006 has an even larger sample size, will include men, and will test participants for HIV infection. India's population growth pattern is typical for a high-fertility and high-mortality country in that population grew quite slowly, even declining in the early 20th century. High birth rates were counterbalanced by high death rates, along with periodic famines, outbreaks of lethal diseases such as cholera and smallpox, and endemic parasitic diseases such as malaria. But epidemics and famines receded in the first half of the 20th century. The year 1921 is often referred to as the "Year of the Great Divide," because it marked the shift from a pattern of relatively static population size to one of steady and often rapid increase.

As the mid-20th century approached, growth began to accelerate as the more serious threats to public health waned: Death rates fell but birth rates remained high. India's population growth rate peaked between the 1971 and 1981 censuses, but growth in absolute numbers has not yet peaked. The country added 16 million people annually in the 1980s and 18 million annually in the 1990s until the present. India's population growth slowed as the birth rate gradually declined beginning in the late 1960s. Since the early 1970s, the birth rate has fallen from just under 40 births per 1,000 population to 24 per 1,000 in 2004. This decline reflected the concerted effort by the government to slow population growth.

MORTALITY

India's mortality has declined at a sluggish rate. In the early 1970s, the infant mortality rate was about 130 deaths to infants under age 1 per 1,000 live births. By 2004, the IMR declined to about 58. In recent years, the pace of improvement has quickened. Maternal mortality has also declined since the 1970s, although at 540 maternal deaths per 100,000 births in 2000, the rate remains higher than in many other less-developed countries, and nearly 10 times higher than in China.

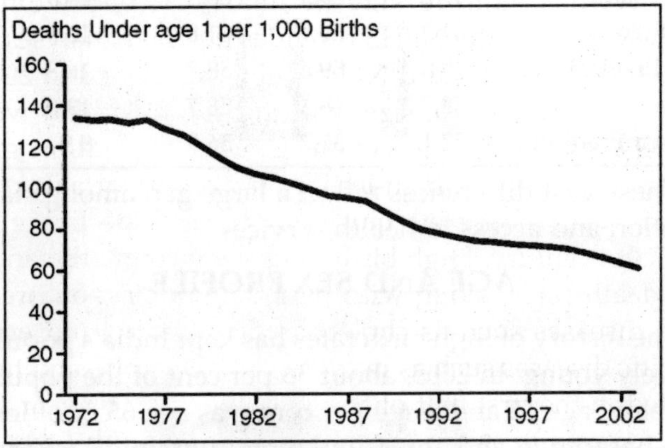

Fig. Infant Mortality Rate in India, 1971-1973 to 2002-2004

Declining death rates, especially among infants and young children, boosted the average life expectancy for Indians from about 50 years in the early 1970s to 63 years for the 1999–2003 period. The national average is similar to levels in neighbouring Bangladesh, Nepal, and Pakistan. Yet, life expectancies are above 70 years in some Indian states such as Kerala, and other Asian countries, including Sri Lanka and Thailand, and are 80 or above in Singapore and Japan, suggesting there is considerable room for improvement in India. A substantial fall in mortality could boost population growth unless accompanied by further declines in the birth rate. Life expectancy at birth varies by nearly 20 years among Indian states, ranging from 57 years in Madhya Pradesh to 74 in Kerala.

Table. Life Expectancy at Birth in Years, India and Selected States, 1999–2003

State	Both sexes	Male	Female	Change since 1970–1975 Both sexes
India	62.7	61.8	63.5	13.0
Kerala	73.6	70.9	76.0	11.6
Punjab	68.6	67.6	69.6	10.7
Maharashtra	66.4	65.2	67.6	12.6

Tamil Nadu	65.4	64.3	66.5	15.8
Rajasthan	61.3	60.7	61.8	12.9
Uttar Pradesh	59.3	59.6	58.7	16.3
Orissa	58.7	58.6	58.7	13.0
Madhya Pradesh	57.1	57.2	56.9	9.9

These vast differences reflect a large gap among states in education and access to health services.

AGE AND SEX PROFILE

The history of high birth rates has kept India's population relatively young: In 2005, about 36 per cent of the population was below age 15 and just 4 per cent was age 65 or older. The broad-based age and sex population "pyramid" taken from United Nations projections shows this youthfulness clearly. More than half the population is below age 25. The young population virtually guarantees further growth, as these young people produce their own families, who will also require additional schools, jobs, and housing.

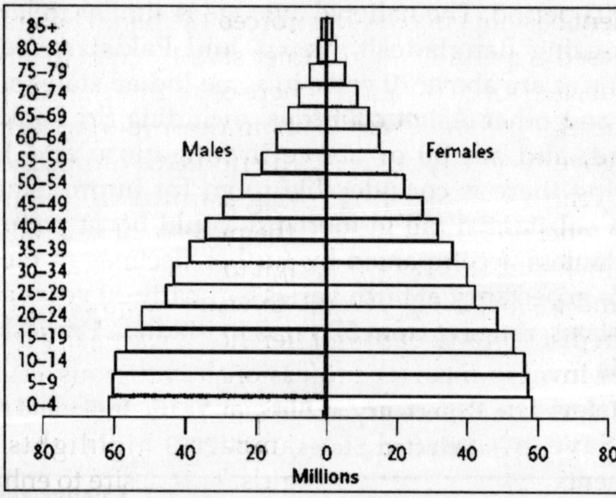

SEX RATIO AT BIRTH

One of the most striking features of India's population profile is its abnormally high ratio of males to females, particularly at young ages. While about 105 boys are born for every 100 girls in most countries, the ratio is about 113 per

100 in India, and it ranges up to 129 per 100 in some states. This skewed ratio has been increasing.

Table. Ratio of Boys per 100 Girls at Birth, India and Selected States, 2001–2003

State	Total	Urban	Rural
India	113	115	113
Tamil Nadu	105	110	103
Karnataka	106	105	106
Assam	111	109	111
Kerala	112	107	114
Haryana	124	131	123
Punjab	129	131	128

Note: Globally, the average sex ratio at birth is 105 boys to 100 girls.

The overriding explanation is the abortion of female fetuses. While abortion has been legal in India since 1972, sex-selective abortion has been illegal since 1994. However, the government has not effectively enforced the ban. The practice has increased, especially in wealthier states, such as Haryana and Punjab, and in urban areas, where couples are more likely to have access to the prenatal tests to determine their fetus' sex. The government has redoubled efforts to enforce the ban in recent years in the face of growing alarm at the frequency of female feticide. Efforts to stem the practice of sex-selective abortion include a broader campaign to improve the status of women and to encourage parents to value daughters as well as sons. In districts where son preference is especially strong, initiatives involve medical professionals, religious leaders, schools, television shows, and politicians.

A "Save a Girl Child" campaign highlights the achievements and value of young girls. This desire to enhance the value of daughters was behind the government's decision to choose a baby girl as India's official "billionth baby," born in Safdarjung Hospital in New Delhi on May 11, 2000. Some states are initiating their own campaigns. Delhi is launching a "Girl Child Protection Scheme" campaign under which 5,000 rupees will be deposited in the name of every girl born in a government hospital or maternity home. The money and accrued interest will be given to the girl when she reaches 18 and completes a specified level of education. The Punjab government will give a reward of 250,000 rupees to communities that achieve a target sex ratio among recorded births. Jalahmazra village in Nawashahr, Punjab, received this reward in 2006.

GEOGRAPHIC DIVERSITY

The Indian population is heavily concentrated in the broad fertile northern plains. Historically higher birth rates in the northern states continue to shift a larger share of India's population growth northward. Four northern states—Bihar, Madhya Pradesh, Rajasthan, and Uttar Pradesh—often referred to as the "BIMARU" states, accounted for 40 per cent of India's population, but 47 per cent of the country's population growth between 1991 and 2001. Uttar Pradesh, with 166 million people in 2001, is by far India's most populous state and is larger than Pakistan and Bangladesh.

Table. Population Size and Growth of States and Union Territories, 1991–2001

State/union territory	Total population 1991	Total population 2001	Per cent change 1991–2001	Per cent of national population 2001
India	846,421,039	1,028,737,436	21.5	100.00
Uttar Pradesh	132,061,653	166,197,921	25.9	16.2
Maharashtra	78,937,187	96,878,627	22.7	9.4
Bihar	64,530,554	82,998,509	28.6	8.1
West Bengal	68,077,965	80,176,197	17.8	7.8
Andhra Pradesh	66,508,008	76,210,007	14.6	7.4
Tamil Nadu	55,858,946	62,405,679	11.7	6.1
Madhya Pradesh	48,566,242	60,348,023	24.3	5.9
Rajasthan	44,005,990	56,507,188	28.4	5.5
Karnataka	44,977,201	52,850,562	17.5	5.1
Gujarat	41,309,582	50,671,017	22.7	4.9
Orissa	31,659,736	36,804,660	16.3	3.6

Kerala	29,098,518	31,841,374	9.4	3.1
Jharkhand	21,843,911	26,945,829	23.4	2.6
Assam	22,414,322	26,655,528	18.9	2.6
Punjab	20,281,969	24,358,999	20.1	2.4
Haryana	16,463,648	21,144,564	28.4	2.1
Chhattisgarh	17,614,928	20,833,803	18.3	2.0
Delhi	9,420,644	13,850,507	47.0	1.4
Jammu and Kashmir	7,837,051	10,143,700	29.4	1.0
Uttaranchal	7,050,634	8,489,349	20.4	0.8
Himachal Pradesh	5,170,877	6,077,900	17.5	0.6
Tripura	2,757,205	3,199,203	16.0	0.3
Meghalaya	1,774,778	2,318,822	30.7	0.2
Manipur	1,837,149	2,293,896	24.9	0.2
Nagaland	1,209,546	1,990,036	64.5	0.2
Goa	1,169,793	1,347,668	15.2	0.1
Arunachal Pradesh	864,558	1,097,968	27.0	0.1
Pondicherry	807,785	974,345	20.6	0.1
Chandigarh	642,015	900,635	40.3	0.1
Mizoram	689,756	888,573	28.8	0.1
Sikkim	406,457	540,851	33.1	0.1
Andaman and Nicobar Islands	280,661	356,152	26.9	–
Dadra and Nagar Haveli	138,477	220,490	59.2	–
Daman and Diu	101,586	158,204	55.7	–
Lakshadweep	51,707	60,650	17.3	–

Fertility decline has been most dramatic in southern states, and those states contribute less and less to India's annual population growth. Andhra Pradesh, Karnataka, Kerala, and Tamil Nadu accounted for 22 per cent of the country's population in 2001, but contributed only 14 per cent of its population growth. This disparity is certain to increase.

INDIA LIVES IN ITS VILLAGES

Although many Westerners associate Indian life with teeming megacities, as the country's registrar general said in 2005, "India lives in its villages." A large majority of Indians live in relatively small localities and are engaged in farming or some activity related to farming. In 2001, the average Indian lived in a village of about 4,200 people; 72 per cent of India's total population was classified as rural, and 58 per cent of workers were engaged in agriculture.

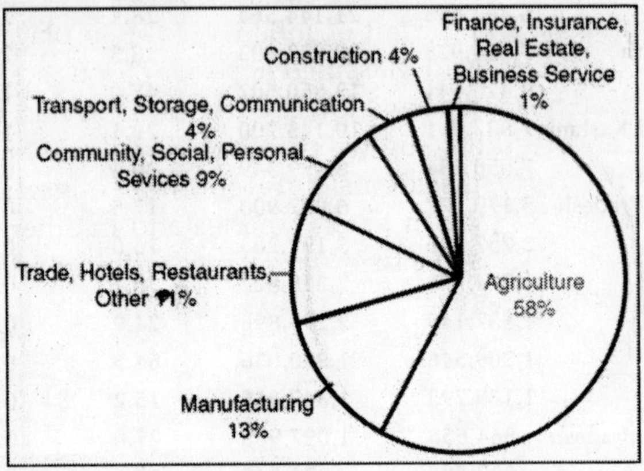

Fig. Indian Workers by Sector, 2001

Just 11 per cent of Indians lived in large cities of 1 million or more residents.

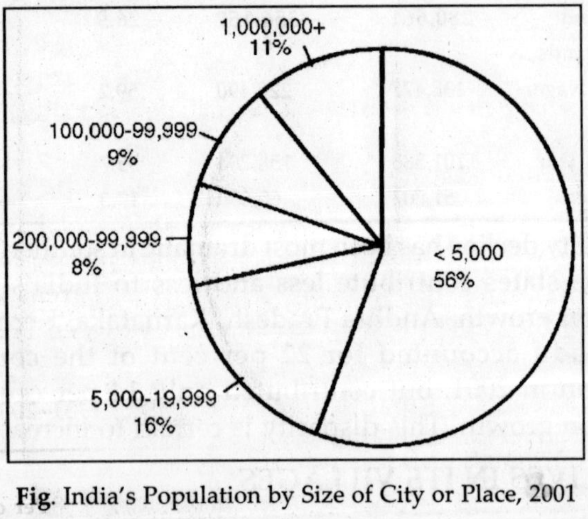

Fig. India's Population by Size of City or Place, 2001

Many Indians who live in relatively populated areas are classified as rural because their communities are highly dependent on agriculture and lack the population density required for the official urban designation. In general, India classifies communities as urban if they have at least 5,000 people; a population density of at least 400 people per square kilometre; and less than 25 per cent of the male labour force engaged in agriculture.

Many of the 16 per cent of Indians living in places with 5,000 to 19,999 people are classified as rural. Throughout most of India, rural residents have lower educational levels, higher mortality and fertility, higher poverty, and fewer modern amenities than urban residents. Rural-to-urban migration has been much slower than in Latin America and in other world regions. Most Indians live their entire lives within a relatively limited geographic area.

URBAN INDIA

Before 1951, defining an urban area was left entirely to the discretion of local authorities, leading some demographers to joke that "in the pre-independence era, some princely states of India, in order to lay a claim to respectability, were inclined to treat any habitation with a lamppost as an urban centre." The definition of an urban place in India has varied, but now is similar to that used in most other developing countries. Some places—centres of government, for example—are officially designated as urban regardless of their other characteristics.

As in other countries of South Asia, India's urban population has grown relatively slowly for the last century. The percentage of Indians living in urban areas rose from 11 per cent in 1901 to 28 per cent in 2001. Rural areas added significantly more people than urban areas between 1991 and 2001: 114 million compared with 69 million.

Table. Urban and Rural Population in India, 1901–2001

Census	Population in thousands		Change over decade (thousands)		Per cent
year	Urban	Rural	Urban	Rural	urban
1901	25,855	212,541	—	—	10.8
1911	25,948	226,145	93	13,604	10.3
1921	28,091	223,230	2,143	–2,915	11.2

1931	33,463	245,515	5,371	22,285	12.0
1941	44,162	274,498	10,700	28,984	13.9
1951	62,444	298,644	18,282	24,146	17.3
1961	78,937	360,298	16,493	61,654	18.0
1971	109,114	439,046	30,177	78,748	19.9
1981	159,463	523,867	50,349	84,821	23.3
1991	217,611	628,810	58,148	104,943	25.7
2001	286,120	742,618	68,509	113,808	27.8

INDIAN MEGACITIES

The world has about 20 megacities—urban areas with 10 million or more people. Three are in India: Delhi, Kolkata, and Mumbai.

Table. Indian Urban Areas with 2 Million or More Residents, 2001

Urban Population agglomeration (U. A.)/city	State	Population (Millions)
Greater Mumbai U. A.	Maharashtra	16.4
Kolkata U. A.	West Bengal	13.2
Delhi U. A.	Delhi	12.9
Chennai U. A.	Tamil Nadu	6.6
Hyderabad U. A.	Andhra Pradesh	5.7
Bangalore U. A.	Karnataka	5.7
Ahmedabad U. A.	Gujarat	4.5
Pune U. A.	Maharashtra	3.8
Surat U. A.	Gujarat	2.8
Kanpur U. A.	Uttar Pradesh	2.7
Jaipur Municipal Corporation	Rajasthan	2.3
Luchnow U. A.	Uttar Pradesh	2.2
Nagpur U. A.	Maharashtra	2.1

Delhi is one of the world's oldest cities and has been India's capital since 1911. Kolkata, Mumbai, and Chennai (Madras) were established under colonial rule. Kolkata was founded as a port for the British East India Company while Mumbai was founded by Portuguese colonialists. India's fourth-largest city, Chennai, in the southern state of Tamil

Nadu, was another British creation, beginning as Ft. George. Delhi is the world's fastest-growing megacity, adding nearly one-half million people per year. Although the city has long since expanded beyond the original inhabited area, it still has room to grow both within its borders and in adjacent suburbs. Mumbai, located on a long peninsula in Maharashtra state, has had to build up rather than out and available land is now virtually nonexistent.

Large cities have sprung up across the bay on the mainland, expanding the greater Mumbai area. With its tall buildings and status as a financial capital, downtown Mumbai gives some visitors the feel of a Manhattan. At partition, Kolkata became the capital of the Indian state of West Bengal, while the eastern half of Bengal became East Pakistan and, in 1971, Bangladesh.

When Kolkata—the commercial centre of Bengal province—was cut off from the rest of its population, Bangladesh was left largely dependent on subsistence agriculture, and remains one of the world's poorest countries today.

Other major cities include Bangalore, the capital of Karnataka state with its gleaming Indian headquarters of such companies as IBM and Intel; and Hyderabad, capital of Andhra Pradesh state and another important centre of India's growing computer industry.

SLUM POPULATIONS

More than 40 million urban Indians live in areas classified as slums—a number roughly equal to the population of Spain. Slums are defined as any area designated as such by a state or local government or any "compact area of at least 300 population or about 60 to 70 households of poorly built, congested tenements in unhygienic environment usually with inadequate infrastructure and lacking in proper sanitary and drinking water facilities." India conducted a systematic enumeration of the urban slum population for the first time during the 2001 Census, pegging the slum population at 42.6 million, or about 14.9 per cent of the national urban population.

The largest slum populations are in major cities, Mumbai (6.5 million slum dwellers), Delhi (1.9 million), Kolkata (1.5 million), Chennai (0.8 million), and Nagpur (0.7 million). Even the "hi-tech" cities of Bangalore and Hyderabad have 1 million slum residents between them.

By far the largest percentage of population living in slums is in Mumbai, a shocking 54 per cent. Next are Faridabad (46 per cent slum dwellers) and Meerut (44 per cent), both in the Delhi National Capital Region, followed by Kolkata at 32 per cent. Six million children under age 7 lived in slums in 2001, with 1.6 million in Maharashtra state alone. Most inhabitants of slums came to the city in hopes of earning some income, no matter how meager.

Other slum dwellers may, in fact, have paying jobs but live in the slums because of a severe shortage of other housing. Nearly three-fourths of slum residents are literate (73 per cent), just below the 81 per cent literacy reported among the general population in states reporting slums. Slightly more than one-half of men living in slums were reported as working, about the same as among the general population. Yet women who live in slums are less likely than the average to be working: just 12 per cent of women compared with 26 per cent among women in the total population of those states in 2001. Slums are by definition illegal, usually rising on a piece of empty government or private land in less desirable places near railway lines or drainage canals.

They may obtain some services, such as electricity and sanitation. In other cases, city governments may remove the slums, relocating residents to the city fringe and allocating them about 250 square feet (20 to 25 square metres) of land per household. These relocated slums often develop into full-scale towns with brick houses and shops. Some slums simply become too large to move and become permanent parts of the city.

SOCIO-ECONOMIC CHARACTERISTICS

India's society is deeply rooted in religion, language, and tradition. Religion and conflicts among religious and cultural groups are fundamental forces in Indian life that bear on economic and educational disparities, the division of political power, the traditional role of women, and on the demographic profile of the country. At the 2001 Census, just over 80 per cent of Indians practiced Hinduism, one of the world's oldest religions. Muslims are second, with 13 per cent. The balance consists of Christians, Sikhs, Buddhists, Jains, and others, such as Parsis.

The ongoing conflicts between the Hindu majority and Muslim minority—which occasionally erupt in violence—fuel fears about the long-term effects of demographic changes that could shift the balance of the two groups in some states. Muslims have higher fertility and are growing at a slightly faster rate than Hindus. While a relatively small minority nationally, Muslims make up one-quarter or more of the population in Kerala, West Bengal, Assam, and Jammu and Kashmir, as shown by 2001 Census results.

With higher fertility and a more rapid growth rate, the Muslim percentage is slowly increasing nationally. Between 1991 and 2001, the Muslim percentage in India increased from 12 per cent to 13 per cent. The Muslim percentage increased slightly more in many states, for example, it rose from 23 per cent to 25 per cent in Kerala, from 28 per cent to 31 per cent in Assam, and from 18 per cent to 19 per cent in Uttar Pradesh. Hinduism has been a unifying force throughout India's history. With its many holy days, festivals, and caste system, it defines life for the great majority of Indians.

Several other religions, although with much smaller percentages of the population, have also had an important influence in some regions. Sikhs, for example, whose religion branched off from Hinduism, are native to Punjab state. They are generally credited with turning that region's marginal crop land into "India's granary." The importance of Hindu traditions is manifested in India's deeply rooted caste system, which continues to play a key role in the organization and stratification of Indian society. The system, which was largely based upon occupation, has four main divisions: Brahmin (priests, teachers), Kshatriya (kings, warriors), Vaishya (merchants, landowners, craftsmen), and Shudra (laborers, artisans).

The "Untouchables" are the lowest caste, who usually performed menial jobs. Mahatma Gandhi attempted to remove discrimination against this group by referring to them as Harijans or Children of God. Today, Untouchables are called by the label they themselves prefer, Dalits, or the oppressed.

The discriminatory aspects of the caste system have been under assault since India's independence in 1947, but the system has been difficult to dislodge, particularly because of its deep roots in ancient texts at the basis of Hinduism, such as the Vedas, and the belief that the creator of the universe, Brahma, also created the four main divisions.

Still, the Indian government has attempted to lower caste boundaries and to redress the effects of discrimination against the Dalits. In 1947, well before the landmark civil rights laws in the United States, India established a system whereby a percentage of public-sector jobs and university slots were reserved for certain castes of Dalits. The castes identified were known as Scheduled Castes (SCs) and recognized only among Hindus and Sikhs.

The reservation of jobs and university seats was also extended to specific tribal groups that had suffered from discrimination. STs were not necessarily Hindu or associated with a caste, but had a long history of poverty and low educational attainment. In 2006, 15 per cent of job vacancies and university seats were reserved for SCs and nearly 8 per cent for STs.

The reservation policy is not without controversy, in part because of concerns that STs and SCs are not adequately prepared for these positions, and that they prevent morequalified candidates from getting jobs or university seats. Many ST and SC youths grow up in poverty, with limited educational resources, and find it hard to compete with more-educated students in the university setting. In Times of India, 2,000 of the 9,000 places reserved for SC/STs in prestigious Delhi University remained unfilled at a time when India is trying to expand the number of qualified graduates.

But the significance of these groups is apparent when we consider that they represent one-fourth of the country's population. In addition to SCs and STs, a large group of lower castes who had not previously benefited from the scheduled caste system, other backward classes are now seeking similar accommodation.

While the caste system has not been eliminated, it plays a somewhat reduced role among the educated elite. It is quite common to see the phrase "caste no bar" in advertisements in the matrimonial part of newspapers placed by the parents of prospective brides and grooms.

LITERACY AND EDUCATION

Mass education and literacy are a hallmark of modern society. In India, the goal of free and compulsory education through age 14 is provided for under Article 45 of the Constitution. Literacy is defined as the ability to read and write any language, regardless of level of education. In the census, literacy is based on the response of whoever answers the enumerator's questions, nearly always a male household head. Thus, the census figures may overstate the functional literacy levels of the population.

In 1999, there was a network of more than 1.1 million educational institutions, from primary through preuniversity level, with more than 5.4 million teachers and a student enrollment of 186 million. Still, the national literacy rate at the time of the 2001 Census had reached only 65 per cent—75 per cent for males and 54 per cent for females—a gender gap of 22 percentage points.

Among the states, literacy for both sexes in 2001 was highest in Kerala at 91 per cent of the population above age 6 and lowest in Bihar at 47 per cent. For females, the highest literacy was also in Kerala, 88 per cent, and the lowest in Bihar, 33 per cent.

Given the low literacy among Indians at independence, the government has made great progress in educating the population, particularly in the past two decades. The percentage of the population who were literate rose from 16 per cent to 65 per cent between 1951 and 2001, but this total belies the substantial and persistent gap between men and women.

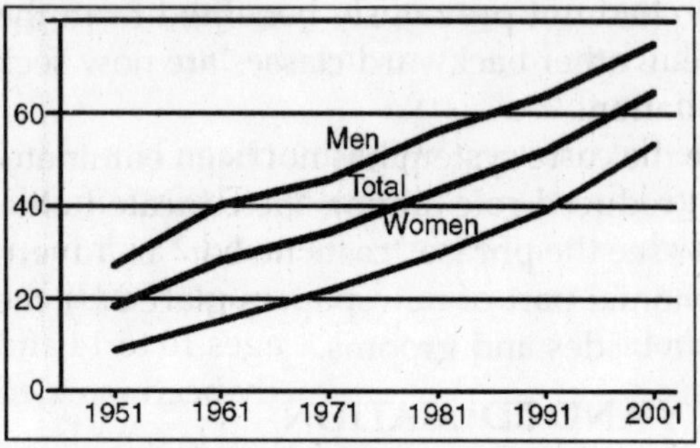

Fig. Per cent of Indians who are Literate, by Sex, 1951-2001

Between 1981 and 1991 the number of illiterate Indians declined, and they were outnumbered by literates for the first time in India's history.

WOMEN'S ROLES AND MARRIAGE

The gender gap in literacy highlights another important aspect of Indian society and tradition: the generally low status of women. Within a family, girls receive less nutrition and medical care than boys, undermining their health and sometimes leading to premature death. Surveys show that girls are less likely than boys to be immunized against major childhood diseases. And girls were traditionally less likely to go to school. Marriage is universal in India. Most Indian marriages are arranged by parents, leaving little choice to the couples themselves.

Unlike contemporary Western cultures, marriage is seen as more of a family or social duty than a romantic liaison, and the selection of mate and marriage ceremonies are important social and religious events. The practice of dowry was outlawed in 1961, yet it remains widespread and appears to be gaining importance as a status symbol among wealthier Indians. The amount of the dowry can become a contentious issue for a new bride when her in laws feel it was insufficient and pressure the bride to secure more from her parents. Dowry-related violence is a major problem in India and is grossly under reported. In extreme cases, brides are hounded until they commit suicide; or young wives are murdered in suspect "kitchen fires," freeing the husband to seek another bride with another dowry.

While the universality of marriage has not changed, age at marriage has risen significantly. The minimum legal age at marriage was set at 18 for women and 21 for men in 1929, but most Indian women married before age 17 until fairly recently. In 1961, about 20 per cent of girls ages 10 to 14 and 71 per cent of women ages 15 to 19 had already been married. By 2001, a remarkable social transformation had taken place. The rate for 10-to-14-year-olds had dropped to near zero and the rate for the 15-to-19 group had fallen by nearly two-thirds. The age at marriage affects fertility, because it affects the number of years a woman is at risk of getting pregnant. A rising age at marriage is associated with lower fertility, because women spend fewer years exposed to the risk of pregnancy.

The shift in marriage patterns of recent decades favours further decline in India's birth rate. The decline in adult mortality can have the opposite effect on fertility rates. With increased longevity for both men and women, fewer women die or are widowed at younger ages, exposing them to the risk of pregnancy for longer periods.

The major factor in India's fertility decline in recent decades, however, has been an increase in the use of family planning. Indians have been slow to adopt family planning, and the issue has been fraught with political and social controversy. But contraceptive use and family planning are gaining wider acceptance, especially among more-educated women.

POPULATION POLICIES

India justifiably claims to be the first country to adopt an official policy to slow population growth, beginning with the country's first Five Year Plan in 1952. In the 1950s, the country was experiencing accelerated population growth created by declining death rates and high birth rates—a situation shared by many developing countries in that period. Death rates had fallen as these countries gained better public sanitation, widespread immunization of children, and expanded medical care. But birth rates remained high, pushing population growth to unprecedented heights. Initial efforts to implement a family planning programme were rather limited.

The programme began by setting up family planning clinics with the expectation that people would seek out the clinics on their own. But the goal of reducing birth rates through family planning was hampered both by deep-seated traditions that favoured larger families and by the enormous challenge of bringing services to a vast, largely rural population.

In the second Five Year Plan, expenditures for family planning were increased and the idea of incorporating family planning into community-based development programmes were introduced.

Home visits by family planning workers was expanded in the 1960s to reach even more people. The population programme gained status when it was brought under the new Ministry of Health and Family Planning in 1966. The government's concern about the country's population growth was heightened in the 1970s when successive censuses had shown that the rate was rising, despite the policies and investments in family planning. This concern set the stage for the family planning program's most controversial period. This took place during the National Emergency declared by Prime Minister Indira Gandhi in 1975, partly to thwart her political opposition.

With financial support from the central government and the political backing of Mrs. Gandhi's popular son Sanjay, many states adopted coercive measures along with quota systems that resulted in the establishment of the infamous sterilization camps. In the 1976–1977 programme year, 8.3 million sterilizations, primarily vasectomies, were performed, up from 2.7 million the year before. The abuses and negative publicity generated by the Emergency compromised the reputation of the government family planning programme, and family planning services were suspended. By the 1977–1978 programme year, the number of sterilizations had plummeted to 0.9 million. The slow decline in India's fertility rate of the previous decade stopped.

To distance itself from the negative image of the Emergency, the name of the ministry responsible for family planning was changed to the Ministry of Health and Family Welfare, and remains so to this day. The backlash against the involuntary sterilizations was partly responsible for the defeat of Mrs. Gandhi's party in the next elections. Successive governments—including Mrs. Gandhi herself, who returned to power in 1980 and served until her assassination in 1984—have been careful to emphasize the voluntary nature of the programme.

Following the 1994 International Conference on Population and Development in Cairo, India announced that it was adopting a "target-free" approach in its population policy. This change reflected the spirit of the Cairo conference, which called for greater emphasis on a full programme of reproductive health that would be less concerned with specific demographic goals.

In reality, this new approach has been applied differently in different areas of the country. In some cases, local clinics found it hard to operate without specific quotas, such as the number of women accepting family planning or for condoms distributed.

Some states, such as Andhra Pradesh, continued to offer incentives such as cash or goods such as transistor radios, for women to agree to sterilization. In the 1998-1999 period, 67 per cent of women ages 25 to 29 in Andhra Pradesh had been sterilized, a remarkably high percentage for women under age 30. The failure of some states to lower their birth rates also has undermined their political clout in the national legislature.

Seats in India's parliament are apportioned among the states just as to population size. But giving the rapidly growing northern states more seats was viewed as rewarding them for poor performance in lowering birth rates and contradicting the government's policy to reduce population growth. The Indian Supreme Court has repeatedly frozen the allocation of seats to the population distribution as of 1971. In 2000, the year population reached 1 billion, the government promulgated its first National Population Policy, NPP 2000.

This policy contained a comprehensive socio demographic programme covering 14 topics such as reducing infant and maternal mortality, promoting later marriage, universal immunization of children, and preventing the spread of HIV.

The policy maintains a commitment to couples' "voluntary and informed choice" of reproductive health services so that replacement level fertility of two children per woman could be achieved by 2010.

The need for a separate national population policy had been identified as early as 1983, but was not realised for 17 years. This long delay at least partly reflected fears of a political backlash against family planning, as there had been after the Emergency.

More recently, a debate has been underway regarding elected officials leading by example, willingly or unwillingly, in the practice of family planning. In a number of states, including Maharashtra, people with more than two children are banned from any elective office from state assemblies to five-member village councils.

There has been an outcry against this policy as inequitable and too strict, and charges that it will increase, not reduce, female feticide. In the wake of the controversy, Himachal Pradesh state withdrew its two child limit for elected officials in 2005.

FAMILY PLANNING AND FERTILITY

Despite the obstacles, family planning use did slowly rise in India, from 13 per cent of couples in 1970 to 53 per cent for the 2002–2004 period.

Given the logistical problems of supplying information and services to more than 250 million women of reproductive age, this increase is a remarkable achievement. Women's knowledge of contraception is nearly universal, although knowledge of traditional methods such as rhythm and withdrawal is less common. Most Indian women know about female sterilization, but other modern methods, such as intrauterine devices or the pill, are much less well known. Female sterilization remains the most common method of family planning.

Table. Contraceptive Methods Used in India, 1992–1993 to 2002–2004

	Per cent of married women ages 15–49 using contraception		
	1992–93	1998–99	2002–04
Any method	40.6	48.2	53.0
Any modern method	36.3	42.8	45.7
Pill	1.2	2.1	3.5
IUD	1.9	1.6	1.9
Condom	2.4	3.1	4.8
Female sterilization	27.3	34.2	34.3
Male sterilization	3.4	1.9	0.9
Any traditional method	4.3	5.0	7.3
Periodic abstinence	2.6	3.0	4.1
Withdrawal	1.4	2.0	2.7
Other	0.2	0.4	0.5
Not using a method	59.4	51.8	47.0

Female sterilization rose from 27 per cent to 34 per cent of contraceptive methods used between NFHS-1 and the Reproductive and Child Health Survey of 2002–2004. Among women familiar with them, "spacing" methods such as the pill and IUD are widely mistrusted for fear of side effects, and female sterilization is often viewed as the best alternative.

Male sterilization is unpopular; prevalence recorded in the NFHS and other surveys has been declining as older husbands who had been sterilized in the 1970s during the Emergency age out of the sample of women ages 15 to 49. In NFHS-2, for example, 8 per cent of husbands ages 45 to 49 had been sterilized, compared with only 1 per cent of those ages 30 to 34. Contraceptive use is higher in urban than rural areas and increases with a woman's educational attainment.

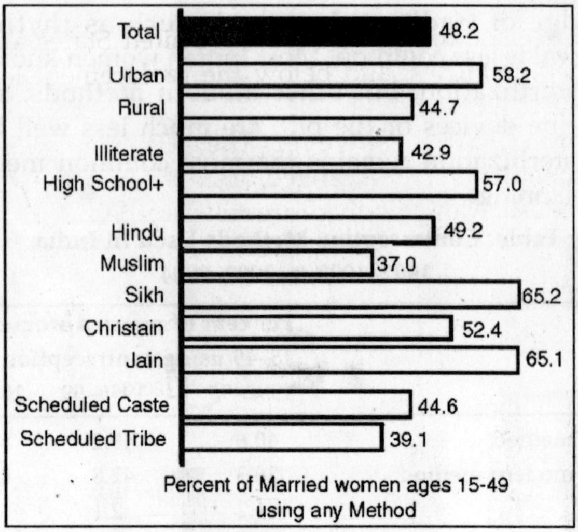

Fig. Contraceptive Use by Selected Indicators, 1998-1999

Among religious groups surveyed in NFHS-2, Sikhs and Jains had the highest use, 65 per cent, followed by Christians at 52 per cent and Hindus at 49 per cent. Muslims have the lowest rate of contraceptive use at 37 per cent. Contraceptive use was also well below the national average among women from the scheduled tribes in 1999, but not for women in scheduled castes. Contraceptive prevalence varies widely among the states.

The RCH survey reported the highest level of use in West Bengal, Himachal Pradesh, and Kerala, with between 69 per cent and 74 per cent of married women ages 15 to 49 using a family planning method. The three lowest states were Jharkhand, Uttar Pradesh, and Bihar, with between 31 per cent and 38 per cent of women using family planning.

FERTILITY TRENDS

Since 1950, fertility in India has decreased by about half, from just under six children per woman to about three. The total fertility rate or average total number of children a woman would have given current birth rates, was 2.3 or fewer in seven states in 2003. Two states, Kerala and Tamil Nadu, had TFRs below 2.0, close to the level of the United States and other developed countries, and below the replacement level of 2 children per woman.

In most states, however, the TFR was well above replacement level, and it ranged up to 4.2 in Bihar and 4.4 in Uttar Pradesh. Although there are still considerable differences in state-level TFRs, the rate has declined by just over 2 children per woman in most of the states.

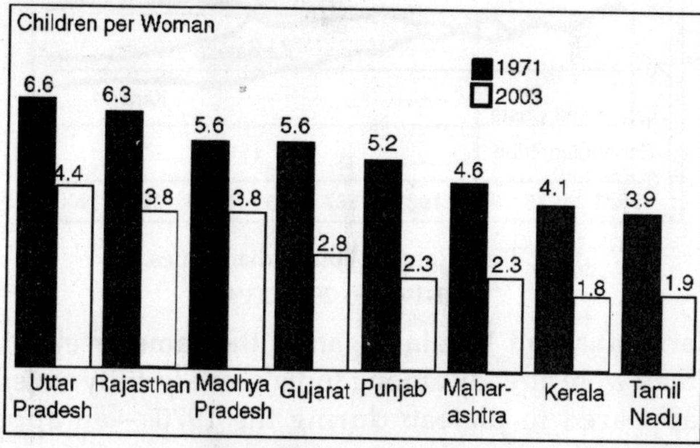

Fig. Total Fertility Rate, Selected States, 1971 and 2003

In percentage terms, however, the declines were greatest in Kerala and other lower-fertility states. The TFR was a full child higher among rural than urban women in 2003, 3.2 to 2.2. In the NFHS-2 survey, the TFR was highest for Muslim women (3.6), followed by Hindus (2.8), Christians (2.4), Sikhs (2.3), and Jains (1.9). Probably reflecting their lower educational and income levels, scheduled classes and tribes had relatively high TFRs: 3.2 among SCs and 3.1 for STs in 1998-1999. Fertility decline in the 1990s was greater among older than younger women, a typical pattern for a population with declining fertility.

Past trends in birth rates can offer some insight into the future, an important issue given that fertility trends are the primary factor determining India's future population size. As a population transitions from high to low fertility, fertility often declines rapidly to a moderately low rate, then the pace of decline slows as the TFR approaches the replacement level of two children per woman. But the pattern of decline can vary significantly within countries, as showed by the trends in the birth rate for two low-fertility states and two high-fertility states between 1971 and 2004.

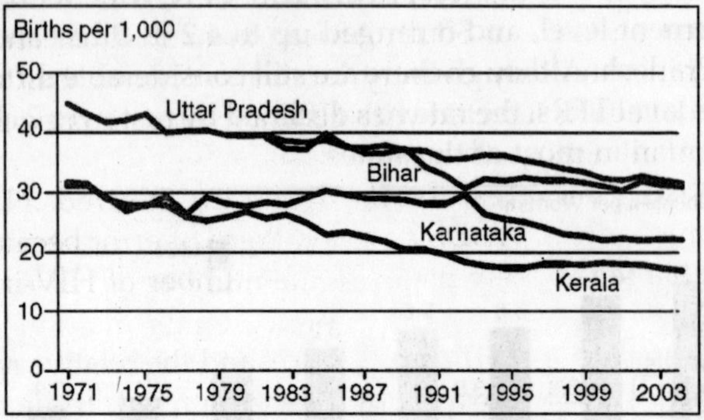

Fig. Birth Rates in Four Indian States, 1971-1973 to 2002-2004

Karnataka and Kerala began at the same level in 1971, when they were already among India's low-fertility states. The rates appeared to plateau during the 1970s—an apparent rejection of family planning after the excesses of the Emergency. But Karnataka's birth rate was stagnant through the 1980s, while Kerala's plummeted. The gap between the two states has narrowed during the early 1990s, but both have plateaued, with no sign that Karnataka's birth rate will fall as low as Kerala's.

The TFR in Kerala was down to 2.0 as early as 1988, and fell to 1.8 in 2003, while Karnataka's was still 2.3 in 2001. The two high-fertility states shown, Bihar and Uttar Pradesh, also exhibit somewhat different patterns. Fertility declined fairly steadily but slowly in Uttar Pradesh, but it is difficult to guess how much further it will fall. There has been no significant fertility decrease since the early 1990s in Bihar.

HIV AND AIDS

India is a low-prevalence HIV/AIDS country, with an estimated 0.9 per cent of the adult population ages 15 to 49 infected with HIV. While the rate is relatively low, India has the world's largest number of people of all ages with HIV: 5.7 million in 2005. South Africa is estimated to have a similar, but slightly lower number of HIV-infected people: 5.5 million. South Africa's population is much smaller than India's but an estimated one-fifth of South African adults are infected with HIV. China, the only country larger than India, has just 0.1 per cent of adults infected with HIV, and an estimated 650,000 people of all ages.

These estimates, from the Joint United Nations Programme on HIV/AIDS have a margin of error because it is impossible to precisely measure the number of HIV-infected people.

The estimates of HIV prevalence, and the relative ranking of countries, have always been controversial. India uses a network of "sentinel sites" to evaluate the extent of HIV-infection, a practice followed in most developing countries that lack accurate data on disease. Most sites are at sexually transmitted disease and antenatal care clinics in government hospitals. People visiting sexually transmitted disease clinics are considered a high-risk group, while those visiting ANCs are considered low-risk.

Often, HIV prevalence among women at ANCs is used as a surrogate for overall HIV prevalence in a country. But the women visiting ANC clinics are not statistically representative of the entire population, and coverage is fairly thin in many Indian states. More accurate estimates of HIV infection among the general population are expected when the results of the 2005–2006 NFHS-3 become available. HIV-testing of respondents was an important component of NFHS-3, and will provide the first nationally representative prevalence estimates for India and for some severely affected states.

COMBATING HIV AND AIDS

India reacted to the earliest cases of HIV, discovered in 1986 in the port cities of Chennai and Mumbai, by establishing the National AIDS Control Programme. The initial budget was insufficient for the task and the programme did not gain momentum until about 1992. State AIDS Cells set up to manage the programme at the local level proved cumbersome, and the programme languished. But an experimental programme established in 1994—the Tamil Nadu State AIDS Control Society—was so successful that it has become the model for other states. State AIDS Control Societies based on the Tamil Nadu programme—which drew members from all government departments and from nongovernmental organizations—have been established in 32 states and union territories.

HIV is spreading largely through sexual activity, although intravenous drug use plays a major role in the two high-prevalence northeastern states of Nagaland and Manipur. Four other states—Andhra Pradesh, Karnataka, Maharashtra, and Tamil Nadu—are considered to be high-prevalence states because the prevalence measured at ANC sites has been 1.0 or above. HIV-prevention campaigns are often aimed at truckers—who spend long periods away from home and on the road. The prevalence is higher along major highways. Commercial sex workers, another high-risk group, are more difficult to locate because so many do not operate from fixed locations.

HIV programmes in India have been expanding geographically, and include more testing and counseling centres, a new anti-retroviral treatment programme, and expanded publicity. TV spots with popular sports figures and actors, as well as newspaper advertisements and billboards, are attempting to spread information about how to avoid HIV infection and to reduce the intense discrimination faced by HIV-positive people in India. More people know about HIV/AIDS than in the past. In the 2001 Behavioural Surveillance Survey, about 82 per cent of men and 70 per cent of women had heard of HIV/AIDS—a figure that has undoubtedly increased over the past five years because of widespread publicity campaigns. But the knowledge gap between urban and rural populations is probably still substantial, even if it has narrowed. In Bihar, for example, just 22 per cent of rural women had heard of HIV/AIDS in 2001, compared with 63 per cent of urban women.

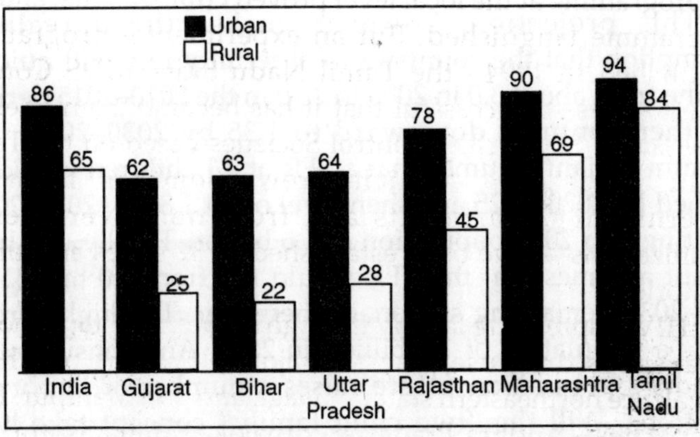

Fig. Per cent of Women Ages 15-49 who Have Heard of Hiv/AIDS, India and Selected States, 2001

The government's campaign, assisted by major support from foreign governments and foundations, has continued to expand, but given the size and diversity of India's population, few countries face a bigger challenge in fighting HIV.

INDIA'S FUTURE POPULATION

India's future population size will largely depend upon the future course of the birth rate, particularly in the heavily populated north. UN projections offer one view of India's population future. The low variant sees India growing from 1.1 billion in 2006 to 1.3 billion in 2050.

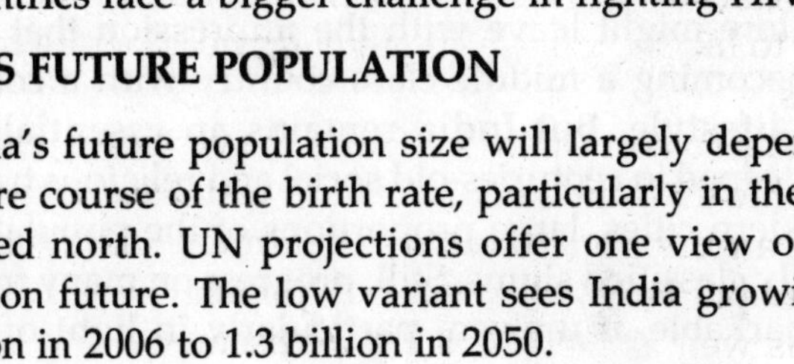

Fig. India's Population Projected to 2050: Three Scenarios

This projection, however, makes the unrealistic assumption that the country's total fertility rate will quickly decline from about 3.0 in 2005 to 2.10 in the 2010–2015 period, and then continue downward to 1.35 by 2030–2035. The medium variant assumes that a TFR of 2.1 children would be reached by 2020–2025 and then level off at 1.85 by 2030–2035, resulting in a 2050 population of 1.6 billion. Finally, the high variant assumes that the TFR would fall from 3.0 to 2.35 by 2030–2035, remaining stationary thereafter. The high variant yields a population of 1.9 billion in 2050. Any consideration of India's population future raises a number of important questions. Will the "two child family" concept take hold throughout the entire country Or will other factors such as the preference for sons and deeply rooted family traditions counter the notion in many parts of the country?

CONCLUSION

Few countries are as complex as India. A visitor to Delhi or Bangalore might leave with the impression that India is rapidly becoming a middle-class country with a consumer-oriented lifestyle. But India remains an essentially rural country steeped in centuries-old social and religious traditions. In its modern cities, large proportions of the population live in officially classified slums. Still, progress on many fronts has been remarkable, if uneven, particularly in light of its vast population.

Agricultural production quadrupled during a remarkable transformation of its agricultural sector in the 1960s and 1970s, which, along with expanded transportation and communications networks, have made famines nearly obsolete. Nonetheless, almost 50 per cent of Indian children are malnourished. The expansion of the health care system has raised life expectancy at birth to 63 years from less than 40 years in 1950. But less than half of births are attended by skilled health personnel, and maternal mortality is still high. During the 20th century, India's population growth awoke from the doldrums as real progress was made against disease and hunger.

The quarter-billion of 1900 became the 1 billion of 2000. Slowing such unheard-of growth became a national priority from the nation's beginning, and India can count many successes in that effort. But India's wide social diversity has resulted in very different demographic situations—persistently high fertility in the Hindi Belt compared with below-replacement fertility in Kerala, for example. Success in one area has not been matched by success in others. India's future population size will depend upon what happens in the heavily populated north. In 2000, India's population reached 1 billion. Now the question of 2 billion arises. Will India become the world's first population "double billionaire?" Such a development is well within mathematical possibility. That is one of India's most compelling future issues.

7

Industrialization in India

AN OVERVIEW

India has made considerable economic progress since its Independence. Most noticeable are the expansion and diversification of production both in industry and agriculture. New technologies were introduced in many industries. Industrial investment took place in a large variety of new industries. Modern management techniques were introduced. An entirely new class of entrepreneurs have come up with the support system from the Government, and a large number of new industrial centres have developed in almost all parts of the country.

Over the years, the Government has built the infrastructure required by the industry and made massive investments to provide the much-needed facilities of power, communications; roads etc. A good number of institutions were promoted to help entrepreneurship development, provide finance for industry and to facilitate development of a variety of skills required by the industry as well as agriculture. The Government also followed a policy of encouraging indigenous industries and provide them all facilities and encouragement.

As a result, we have now a widely diversified base of industry and an increased domestic production of a wide range of goods and services. The index of industrial production has gone up from 7.9 in 1950-51 to 154.7 in 1999-2000. Electricity generation went up from 5.1 billion Kwh to 480.7 billion Kwh in the same period. Particularly significant achievement has taken place in the field of agriculture. Between 1950-2000, the index of agricultural production increased more than four-fold. Between 1960 and 2000, wheat production went up from 11 to 75 million tonnes, and the production of rice increased from 35 to 89.5 million tonnes.

We are now having a problem of plenty, with Government godowns overflowing with wheat stocks. This is not a mean achievement for a country that relied on imported food aid until the early 1960s. The credit for this green revolution goes to Indian scientists as well as to millions of Indian farmers, who wholeheartedly cooperated with the Government, to make India self-sufficient in the matter of its food requirements. This economic expansion contributed to a steady and impressive growth in India's GNP. With the exception of 4 years, India experienced a positive rate of growth. As a result, India's per capita Net National Product (NNP) in 1999-2000 was 2.75 times higher than that of 1951. The rate of growth before 1980 was 1.2% per capita. Thereafter, it grew at the rate of 2.4%, and between 1950-90, by 3.2% on average every year. Between 1993-94 and 1999-2000, it registered an average rate of growth of 4.8% per year.

A variety of promotional policies were followed by the Government to achieve this success. In the early years, Indian industry thrived within protective tariff walls. The policy was to encourage Indian industries and though foreign technical collaborations were encouraged, direct foreign investment in any corporate body was restricted to 40%. In 1991, this policy was changed completely and foreign majority investment was encouraged in a variety of industries, import restrictions were removed, customs tariff was brought down and the doors of the Indian economy were opened for foreign competition. As suggested, briefly trace the developments that took place in the field of industrial economic policy of India during these years. The year 1991 will now be regarded as a landmark in the economic history of India.

INDUSTRIAL POLICY AND INCENTIVES SINCE 1947

After India became independent in 1947, the country

embarked upon an ambitious plan of industrial development and encouraged the setting up of new industries and the expansion of existing industries. We may briefly recapitulate some of the steps that were taken to achieve these objectives.

PROTECTION TO INDIAN INDUSTRIES

India is probably one of the few countries in the world which used its import policy for the healthy development of local industries. Barring the first few years after Independence, the country was facing a shortage of foreign exchange, and because of this shortage, imports had to be restricted. Imports of consumer goods were, therefore, disallowed. A good number of restrictions were put on the import of industrial goods, and the effort of the Government was to encourage the production of these goods indigenously. Local industries were encouraged to have foreign collaborations and to import the technical know-how needed to produce what was being imported into the country.

Levying higher tariffs restricted imports, and there was also a total or partial physical ban on the imports of such products. This gave a muchneeded sheltered market for Indian goods, and many industries thrived within these protective walls. Initially, products produced by Indian industries were not of good quality. But as years went by, industries acquired experience in manufacturing and turned out quality products comparable with imported products. There was a continuous effort to improve quality. During the Second and Third plans, the emphasis was on the development of capital goods industries. India wanted to make machines that helped to produce other machines.

Therefore, greater emphasis was given to the development of machine tools, textile machinery, power equipment and so on. We were importing these mother machines, and the new effort was to produce them in India, to achieve self-sufficiency. As a result of this policy, encouragement was given to import technical know-how and to enter into foreign collaborations to undertake manufacture of capital equipment locally. This gave further fillip to industrial development. Protection from imports encouraged Indian industry to undertake the manufacture of a variety of products. There was a ready market for all these products. The Government also gave encouragement to industries to import parts and components that were required for indigenous production. The import policy was meant to serve two categories of importers -actual users and established importers. Actual users of imported raw materials or products were given preference over the category of established importers *i.e.* traders. Certain items that were scarce and not available were channelised through the State Trading Corporation, Mines and Minerals Trading Corporation and such other Government bodies. They arranged for the import of such products and distributed them to indigenous industries just as to requirements. Thus, imports were strictly controlled by the import policy announced every year by the Government of India.

HIGH CUSTOMS TARIFFS

Apart from strict control over imports and the physical ban on the imports of many products, customs tariffs were raised in some cases to 200 to 300% on imported products. This gave protection to local industries. The price of local products was comparatively cheaper than those of imported goods. The Government also followed a policy of low tariffs on the import of raw materials, parts and components compared to those on finished products. This encouraged Indian industries to import parts and components, and to manufacture or assemble final products in India.

FINANCIAL INFRASTRUCTURE

To provide the financial infrastructure necessary for industry, the Government set up a number of development banks. The principal function of a development bank is to provide medium and long-term investments. They have to also play a major role in promoting the growth of enterprise. With this objective, the Government of India established the Industrial Finance Corporation of India (IFCI) (1948), Industrial Credit and Investment Corporation of India (ICICI)

(1955), Industrial Development Bank of India (IDBI) (1964), Industrial Reconstruction Corporation of India (1971), Unit Trust of India (UTI) (1963), and the Life Insurance Corporation of India (LIC) (1956). For financial assistance to small entrepreneurs, Finance Corporations were established in all states on the basis of an Act that was passed by Parliament in 1951. In addition to this, the National Small Industries Corporation was also established at the Centre and a Small Industries Development Bank of India was established in 1989.

CONTROL OF INDIAN BUSINESS

As a consequence of the restrictions on imports, those who were importing products entered into collaboration with their principals and entered the field of manufacturing. Thus, what was once a trading community, gradually transformed into a community of industrialists. Regulations under the Foreign Exchange and Regulation Act (FERA) restricted foreign investment in a company to 40%. This ensured that much of the control in companies with foreign collaboration remained in the hands of Indians. To succeed, Indian businessmen had to learn and apply modern management and production techniques.

ENCOURAGEMENT TO SMALL INDUSTRIES

Though some of the policies of the Government resulted in inhibiting the growth of large-scale industries, they gave encouragement to small-scale industries by providing a number of support measures for growth. Policy measures undertaken by the Central and State Governments addressed the basic requirements of the SSI like credit, marketing, technology, entrepreneurship development, and fiscal, financial and infrastructural support.

These promotional measures covered:

- Industrial extension services through small industries service institutes and other organisations.
- Factory space in industrial estates through cooperative and other industrial estates, ready built shades and developed industrial plots made available through State Government agencies.

- Credit facilities at concessional rates of interest and credit guarantees through commercial banks and State Finance Corporations.
- Special financial assistance schemes at concessional rates of interest and low margins for technician entrepreneurs.
- Availability of indigenous scarce raw materials through special quotas and imported materials through import licenses.
- Provision of training facilities.
- Subsidised power tariffs and exemption of electricity duties.
- Supply of local and imported machinery on hire purchase basis.
- Assistance for domestic as well as export marketing.
- Special incentives for setting up units in backward areas.
- Differential central excise levies for the small-scale sector.
- Preference for products produced in small-scale industries and 15% price preference to them in State Government purchases.
- Reservation of products for exclusive manufacture in the small-scale sector.
- Creation of a large number of institutions both by the State Governments and the Central Government to help small enterprises.
- Special effort to promote new entrepreneurs by providing them training in entrepreneurship development.

While most of the institutional support services and some incentives were provided by the Central Government, the State Governments offered others in varying degrees to attract investments and to promote small industries.

INVESTMENT IN INFRASTRUCTURE

Energy-Transport-Communications facilities are extremely essential for smooth and accelerated industrial growth. The Government made huge investments in providing such infrastructure facilities to industries. The Central Government, as well as the State Governments invested huge funds in power generation and distribution, and many new power projects were undertaken and completed. Similarly, investments were made in road building, communications, creation of port facilities etc.

Apart from this, various State Governments made developed plots of land or industrial estates with power, water, roads, and communications available to entrepreneurs who wanted to set up industries. This helped considerably in the growth of industries. Changes in the production of primary commercial energy since 1950- 51 are summarised in the following table:

Table. Production of Commercial Energy

Form of energy	Unit	1950-51	1990-91
Coal	Million tonnes	33.00	211.73
Lignite	Million tonnes	–	14.07
Crude oil	Million tonnes	0.26	33.02
Natural gas	Million cubic mets	–	17,998.00
Thermal power	Billion Kwh	3.00	186.45
Hydro power	Billion Kwh	2.52	71.54
Nuclear power	Billion Kwh	–	6.24

Oil and natural gas emerged as significant sources of energy since the eighties. The pattern of sectoral consumption has also undergone noticeable changes over the years as can be seen from the following table:

Table. Shares Percentage in Final Energy Consumption

Sector	1953-54	1990-91
Industry	39.8	50.4
Transport	46.2	24.5
Domestic	9.9	13.8
Agriculture	1.7	9.0
Others	2.4	2.3
Total	100.0	100.0

Power shortages caused by substantial shortfalls in achieving power targets have been a recurring theme from plan to plan.

OIL AND NATURAL GAS

The Oil and Petroleum industry must be considered a gift of the planning era. The indigenous oil exploration programme gained credibility in the seventies. New sources of oil were discovered, and considerable refining capacity was created. The Oil and Natural Gas Commission was set up for oil exploration. Additional refining capacity was created through the expansion of some of the existing plants, and the commissioning of new refineries.

TRAINING AND SKILLS DEVELOPMENT

Trained manpower is necessary for industrial growth. To cater to the growing needs of industries during the last fifty years, the Government set up a large number of industrial training institutes, all over the country to train skilled workers. It also set up Indian Institutes of Technology, Management Institutes and Engineering Colleges to train persons with higher management and technical skills. Our youth have been quick at learning skills. We have therefore had no shortage of skilled manpower to cater to the growing requirements of industry.

SCIENTIFIC RESEARCH

Research in science and applied technology is very much needed in order to sustain technological development in industries.

The Government of India set up 48 national laboratories to undertake applied research in chemistry, physics, electronics, botany, etc., and these research institutes developed a number of new processes which are commercially exploited by industries.

Indian scientists and technologists also ushered in the Green Revolution, and the White Revolution, and developed space technologies on their own.

BACKWARD AREA DEVELOPMENT

Before Independence, industries were mostly located in and around port cities like Mumbai, Kolkata or Chennai. After Independence, new centres of industries were developed as a result of the infrastructural facilities that were made available by the State Governments. Baroda, Coimbatore, Bangalore, Pune, Hyderabad, Faridabad, Rajkot, and many others, grew up as new industrial cities.

Both the Central Government and the State Governments followed a deliberate policy of encouraging industries in backward areas. The Central Government selected a few backward districts and offered 25% capital subsidy for industries set up in these areas.

Various State Governments also offered similar capital incentives, exemption from sales tax levy, subsidies on power rates, cheap developed land, sales tax, loans and other facilities for the growth of industries in these areas. This considerably helped the growth of under developed or backward areas in the different states.

EMPHASIS ON PUBLIC SECTOR

Right from the beginning, the planners attached great importance to the public sector. It was expected that the sector would control the 'Commanding heights of the Indian economy. ' In the Industrial Policy Resolutions of 1948 and 1950, a very important role was assigned to the public sector. Power, telephones, communications, atomic energy, defence industries and some areas were reserved for the public sector. Certain industries like life insurance, civil aviation, banks were nationalised and were included in public sector. Thereafter, whenever there was a shortage, the Government stepped in to bail out, as it did with the cement and document industries. The Government took over sick industries to provide employment. That is how a large number of textile industries came into the public sector. Upto the year 1999, there were 235 public sector undertakings and the Government had invested an amount of ₹273700 crores in such undertakings. In 1998-99, they made a gross profit of ₹397.7 crores.

EVOLUTION OF INDUSTRIAL POLICY IN INDIA

Before Independence, the policy of the British Government was against encouraging industrial development in India. No incentives were offered to Indian industries for their growth. There were many desired and undesired hurdles placed in the way of the growth of Indian industry. Whatever industrial development took place in India was in spite of the negative and hostile attitude of the British Government. Credit must be given to pioneers like Jamshedji Tata, Walchand Hirachand, Lala Sriram, G. D. Birla and others, who laid the foundations of modern industry in India.

AFTER INDEPENDENCE

Immediately after Independence, the Government of India announced its industrial policy in 1948 and laid down the plan for future industrial growth in the country. It also declared its policy on foreign capital in 1949, and invited foreign capital for investment in the country. The Government was keen to dispel the apprehension that foreign enterprises may be taken over.

INDUSTRIAL POLICY RESOLUTION, 1948

The first Industrial Policy Resolution, announced in 1948, broadly laid down the objectives of the Government's policy in the industrial field and clarified industries and enterprises into four categories, namely:

- Those exclusively owned by the Government, *e.g.* arms and ammunition, atomic energy, railways, etc.; and in emergencies, any industry vital for national defence.
- Key or basic industries, *e.g.* coal, iron and steel, aircraft manufacture, ship building, telephone, telegraphs and communications equipment except radio receivers, mineral oils, etc. The undertakings already existing in this group were promised facilities for efficient working and 'reasonable' expansion for a period of ten years, at the end of which, the State could exercise the option to nationalise them.

- The third category of 18 specified industries were to be subject to the Government's control and regulation in consultation with the then provincial (now State) Governments.
- The rest of the industrial field was, more or less, left open to the private sector.

INDUSTRIAL (DEVELOPMENT AND REGULATION) ACT, 1951

The Industrial Policy Resolution of 1948 was followed by a Government of India (GOI) Resolution on 2nd September 1948, constituting a Central Advisory Council of Industries under the chairmanship of the Minister for Industry. In 1951, the Industrial (Development and Regulation) Act was passed by the Parliament.

The main provisions of the Act were:

- All existing undertakings at the commencement of the Act, except those owned by the Central Government were compulsorily required to register with the designated authority.
- No one except the central Government would be permitted to set up any new industrial undertaking "except under and in accordance with a licence issued in that behalf by the Central Government."
- Such a licence or permission prescribed a variety of conditions, such as, location, minimum standards in respect of size and techniques to be used, which the Central Government may approve.
- Such licenses and clearances were also required in cases of 'substantial expansion' of an existing industrial undertaking.
- The industries to be brought under regulation were divided into two parts, Part I and II in the Schedule to the Act.

In regard to the industries listed in Part I of the Schedule, the Central Government could issue necessary directions in respect of quality of its products, falling production, rise in prices etc.

- Government could transfer industries specified in one part to another.

IMPLEMENTATION OF THE INDUSTRIAL DEVELOPMENT AND REGULATION ACT, 1951 (IDR)

The IDR Act gave very wide powers to the Government. This resulted in more or less complete control by the bureaucracy on the industrial development of the country.

They had full control over:

- Approval of any proposal on capacity, location, expansion, manufacture of new products etc;
- Approval of foreign exchange expenditure on the import of plant and machinery;
- Approval for the terms of foreign collaboration.

INDUSTRIAL POLICY RESOLUTION, 1956

After 1948, India adopted a democratic constitution, guaranteed fundamental rights and also enunciated certain directives of state policy. The Parliament accepted the socialistic pattern of society as the objective of social and economic policy. A new Industrial policy was therefore announced in 1956. This Industrial Policy divided industries into three categories. All basic and strategic industries were to be set up in the public sector, and were called category A type of industries. In category B industries were private enterprises who could participate along with public enterprises.

This sector was called the joint sector. All remaining industries falling in category C, were left to be developed by the private sector. The Industrial Policy of 1956, for the first time, emphasised the role of small-scale industries in the development of the national economy. The statement pointed out the importance of the SSI Sector in providing employment. It also laid emphasis on the equitable distribution of national income and the effective mobilisation of resources. The industrial policy, therefore, recommended the development of ancillary industries in areas where large industries were to be set up.

MONOPOLIES COMMISSION

In April 1964, the Government of India appointed a Monopolies Inquiry Commission "to inquire into the existence and effect of concentration of economic power in private hands. " The Commission was requested to look at the prevalence of monopolistic and restrictive practices in important sectors of economic activity, the factors responsible for these and the legal solutions for them. The Commission looked at concentration of economic power in the area of industry, and examined industry wise and product-wise concentration. The Commission also examined the concentration ratio. This Commission drafted a law to control monopolies and recommended the setting up of a permanent Monopolies and Restrictive Trade Practices Commission. On this basis, an Act was passed and a Monopolies Commission was appointed by the Government in 1969.

INDUSTRIAL LICENSING POLICY INQUIRY COMMITTEE

In July 1969, an Industrial Licensing Inquiry Committee was appointed to examine the shortcomings in licensing policy. The Committee felt that the licensing policy had not succeeded in preventing the practice of pre-empting capacity by large houses; it had not ensured development of industries just as to announced licensing policies; it did not prevent investment in non-priority industries etc. In 1969, the Monopolies and Restrictive Trade Practices Act (MRTP) Act was passed by the Government and following the report of Industrial Licensing Policy Inquiry Committee (ILPIC), a number of new restrictions were put on the large industrial houses in the industrial licensing policy announced in February 1970.

FERA AMENDMENT, 1973

The Foreign Exchange and Regulation Act (FERA) was amended in 1973. This brought a great change in the foreign investment policy of the Government of India. Foreign firms were not allowed more than 40% of equity. Only certain industries in the area of sophisticated technology were allowed

51% foreign capital. FERA companies were subject to many restrictions, and were not allowed to participate in certain industries. They were also not allowed to expand and take up production of new products.

INDUSTRIAL POLICY STATEMENT, 1973

The Policy Statement of 1973 drew up a list of industries to be started by large business houses so that the competitive effort of small industries was not affected. Large industries were permitted to start operations in rural and backward areas with a view to developing those areas and enabling the growth of small industries around. A Secretariat for Industrial Approvals (SIA) was set up in November 1973, and all industrial licenses, capital goods, import licenses, terms of foreign collaboration were brought under the SIA.

INDUSTRIAL POLICY STATEMENT, 1977

The thrust of the Industrial Policy Statement of December 1977 was on effective promotion of Cottage and Small Industries widely dispersed in rural areas and small towns. It emphasised that "whatever can be produced by small and cottage industries must only be so produced." The focal point of development of small-scale industries was taken away from the big cities to districts. The concept of District Industries Centres was introduced for the first time.

Each district would have such a district centre which would provide all the support and services required by small entrepreneurs. These included economic investigation of the districts, supply of machinery and equipment, raw material and other resources, arrangement for credit facilities, call for quality control, research and extension etc. Within the SSI sector, a new concept of tiny sector was introduced. It was defined as an industrial unit with investment in machinery and equipment upto Rupees one lakh, and situated in towns with a population of less than 50,000 just as to the 1971 census. This tiny sector was to be given special attention and extended help, by way of provision for margin money assistance. The policy statement considerably expanded the list of reserved items for exclusive manufacture in the small-scale sector. This concept was recommended by the Karve Committee and was introduced in 1967 with 47 products. The list of such reserved items was 504 till 1977. The new policy expanded this list to 807.

ERA OF LIBERALISATION

After 1980, an era of liberalisation started, and the trend was gradually to dilute the strict licensing system and allow more freedom to the entrepreneurs.

The steps that were taken in accordance with the policy included:

- *Re-endorsement of licenses*: The capacity indicated in the licenses could be re-endorsed, provided it was 25% more than the licensed capacity (1984).
- Automatic re-endorsement of licensed capacities (1988).
- Broad banding and selective delicensing (1985-86) extended to 25 industries.
- Liberalisation of 31 May 1990. This policy included:
  - Exemption from licensing for all new units and those having an investment of ₹2.5 crores in fixed assets, and an entitlement to import upto 30% of the total value of plant and machinery.
  - Investment of foreign equity up to 40% was freely allowed.
  - Location restrictions were removed.
  - Investment ceiling for small industries were removed.

Though the Government policies and procedures were aimed at industrial development of the country, the enactment of the IDR Act, procedures laid down for obtaining industrial licensing and various rules made under the Act acted as a great deterrent to the growth of industries in the country. The bureaucracy acquired unprecedented powers and authority over all kinds of industrial activities and industrial entrepreneurs felt that they were placed at the mercy of these bureaucrats. Apart from the IDR Act, there were a number of other Acts which were enacted and which acted as obstacles and retarded the industrial development of the country.

Despite industrial licensing, an entrepreneur had to obtain clearance from many Agencies, like:

- Secretariat for Industrial Approvals (SIA)
- Department of Industrial Development
- Chief Inspector of Factories
- Pollution Control Board
- Director of Town Planning
- Department of Company Affairs
- Registrar of Companies
- Exchange Control Department of RBI
- Chief Controller of Explosives
- Chief Inspector of Boilers
- Commissioner, Food and Drug Administration
- Director of Mines
- Controller of Capital Issues
- Chief Controller of Imports and Exports etc.

Thus, when the Government of India announced the new economic policy in July 1991, Indian industries were not competitive in the world market. Our industries were suddenly required to face international competition. It is no wonder that many of these industries allowed their foreign collaborators to take over, sold their interests or preferred to close down. Those who remained in the field are trying to downsize and reduce their operations. For the existing ones, it is becoming increasingly difficult not only to face competition in the world, but also competition at home with the products of multinationals, either produced in the country or imported from abroad.

8

Changes in Dalit Culture and Civilization

THE MAHAR MOVEMENT'S MILITARY COMPONENT

Dr. Bhimrao Ramji Ambedkar, is famous for being "the most highly educated Untouchable in India." His education, encouraged and financed largely by the Gaikwad of Baroda, led to his role as the Untouchable's chief spokesman, the founder of a political party for Untouchables, and the moving spirit behind organizations, schools, and colleges established for their uplift. One of Ambedkar's final acts was the initiation of a Buddhist conversion movement that ultimately attracted more than 3 million Untouchable adherents.

This part of Ambedkar's story is well-known. However, his family's military service in the British Raj is not widely acknowledged for creating an environment that laid the foundation for his later success. Eleanor Zelliot, an expert on Dr. Ambedkar and the Mahar movement, maintains, "The hundred year period of Mahar recruitment into British armies may well have been the single most important factor, aside from economic reasons, in producing the Mahar movement."

This object examines the importance of military service in improving the social status of Ambedkar's caste, the Mahars of Maharashtra. The focus is on their relationship with the British. The Mahars benefited from their participation in the British Army in a number of ways. First, military service became "a significant part of caste élan and mythology." The first part provides the historical evidence they use to establish their credentials as a caste with martial traditions. The advantage especially education, that accrued from military service and discusses their access to the government that otherwise was unavailable to Untouchables. The final part discusses the British decision to recruit only "martial races," in which the Mahars were not included, for the British Indian Army and the Mahars' efforts to gain reinstatement in the Army.

EARLY MILITARY PARTICIPATION

Eleanor Zelliot explains that the British gave Mahars the opportunity to seek different occupations from their traditional role as a village servant. She explains that before the arrival of the British,

- Mahars had no special skill or craft, but performed necessary duties for the village as watchmen, wall-menders, street-sweepers, removers of cattle carcasses, caretakers of the burning ground, servants of any passing governmental official.... Mahar service was essential for the village; his status was low, his work menial, but his place was secure. With the coming of the British and the spread of new ways of administration and communication, the Mahar place in the village grew less important.

Military service provided Mahars with the opportunity to move beyond their traditional social position in the village. In fact, the Mahar tradition of being in armies precedes the British Raj. The recorded history of the Mahars' military achievements dates back to Shivaji's Army in the 1600s. Cynthia Enloe, a noted sociologist who has written extensively on ethnic-military relationships, states, "The best of all militaries in the eyes of a state elite is one in which the most competent soldiers are also the most politically reliable, because they have the greatest stake in the continuation of the current system. " The Mahars met this condition just as to descriptions of their loyalty. Colonel V. Longer, author of Forefront Forever: The History of the Mahar Regiment, states:

- There were a number of useful functions which the Mahars performed. Their Argus eye; their daring tenacity and determination; their faithfulness, loyalty and honesty; their courage and candour, were inestimable qualities which were always held in respect and were for ever utilized to advantage by the village.... In course of time, their voice carried great weight when there were disputes over property as their evidence was considered most accurate, intimate, and trustworthy.

This sense of loyalty and trustworthiness led Shivaji to include Mahars as a vital component of his army. Shivaji, leader of the Maratha nation, fought for a Hindu empire, but using Untouchables did not bother him. He "found the Mahars useful, for the wily Maratha chief realised that the best way of obtaining the maximum results was to mix up various castes in his garrison forces. " He used the Mahars "to watch the jungles at the foot of the hill forts, act as scouts and [they] kept the forts supplied with wood and fodder. " This was the first exposure of the Mahars to an organized army that provided its soldiers with steady pay and benefits.

After Shivaji's death, Mahar units continued to serve his descendants throughout the 1700s. Their experience with Shivaji and others encouraged them to seek similar employment as sepoys of the British East India Company. Ardythe Basham, in her detailed examination of the Mahars and the military, found the perceived early martial history to be an important part of Mahar identity. She concludes, "Whether or not these incidents are historically true, they are widely accepted by the Mahars as part of their tradition, and now form part of the official history of [today's] Mahar Regiment. "

The Mahars have often used this martial identity, rooted in the 1600s, to legitimate their continued presence in the military. Mahars began their service with the British in the 1750s. Stephen P. Cohen, an expert on the Indian Army, discusses the importance of Mahars in the Bombay Army in his seminal work, The Indian Army: Contribution to the

Development of a Nation. He writes that Mahars were a sizeable portion of the armies of the Mahratta chieftain Shivaji, served as hereditary local policeman, and were thus a "natural" martial class. Heavily recruited in the premutiny years, the Mahars constituted a fifth to a quarter of the entire Bombay Army. In addition to the size of the Mahar contingent, they were also praised for their conduct as soldiers. The Mahars rewarded the British with the same loyalty that Shivaji had enjoyed. The Bombay Army fought in several battles, and in most, the Mahars were recognized for their skills.

Longer proclaims:

- Much praise was showered on the Mahar Sepoys of the Bombay Army who endured the rigours of difficult marches when rations were low and disease was high among men and animals. Whether they were charging ahead or were besieged or taken prisoner-of-war, whether they were storming fortresses or making tactical withdrawals, they always stood steadfast by their officers and comrades, never letting down the honour of their Regiments.

The recorded history of their exploits, especially prior to the mutiny of 1857, supports this effusive adoration. Basham located evidence of Mahar participation in the Second and "Third Anglo-Maratha War, the Second Anglo-Sikh War and the Second Afghan War. " The Mahars' exploits in these conflicts form an important part of their military lore. The Mahar participation in the battle of Koregaon on 1 January 1818 is the most famous, and also the best documented, action involving Mahar soldiers. This battle gave the British the advantage in the Third Anglo-Maratha War.

The successful defence of Koregaon by a small force of 500 men... under the command of Capt. F. F. Staunton fought without rest or respite, food or water continuously for twelve hours against a large force of 20,000 Horse and 8,000 Infantry of Peshwa Baji Rao II who was threatening the British garrisons at Kirkee and Poona. Mahars dominated Staunton's unit. The Peshwa's troops inexplicably withdrew that evening, despite their overwhelming numbers, giving the British an important victory. The men of the 2/1st Regiment Bombay Native Infantry, including many Mahars, who fought in this battle, were honoured for their bravery. The official report to the British Resident at Poona recalls the "heroic valour and enduring fortitude" of the soldiers, the "disciplined intrepidity" and "devoted courage and admirable consistency" of their actions. Further, the action is commemorated by a monument, with the names of twenty-two Mahars killed there, erected at the site of the battle and by a medal issued in 1851.

Today, the monument still "serves as a focal point of Mahar heroism. " Similar anecdotes are recorded in the written histories of the Mahar Regiment and Bombay Army. All demonstrate that most Mahars soldiers were dedicated and courageous. In addition to Army units on land, the Mahars formed a vital component of the Bombay Army's Marine Battalion. This unit's history is well documented and provides numerous examples of Mahar actions, including several acts of bravery by Mahars in the battalion. In September 1810, during the Second Maratha War, several Mahars proved their loyalty when captured by the French Navy. The French tried to induce their prisoners to enter their own service, a practice which enjoyed some success with Irish, Madrassi and Bengali troops. On this occasion, the Bombay sepoys were shown the captured Bengal and Madras Sepoys dressed in French uniforms and enjoying considerable privileges and luxuries, whereupon the Bombay Detachment started abusing them as being dead to all shame that they could forget the oath and desert their colours. The upshot was that they were very roughly treated and some were severely wounded. To the seventeen survivors who reached Bombay a special medal was given and of this number twelve were Mahars.

This is just one of many cases where Mahars distinguished themselves as a part of the Marine Battalion and is another part of the martial history that the Mahars used to legitimize their important role in the British Indian Army. But, in the wake of the 1857 mutiny and threats from Russia, the British reexamined their recruitment policies. The Mahars were a casualty of this new thinking.

THE MAHARS DELISTMENT

Despite the Mahars' long martial history, the British ceased recruiting them in 1893. The Bombay and the other Presidency Armies were reevaluated following the 1857 mutiny. The Peel Commission first examined class composition of the armies in 1858. One report to the Commission "emphasized that `we cannot practically ignore it, so long as the natives socially maintain it. " This led to the discrimination against the Mahars and other low-caste groups as well as some Brahman castes which were considered unreliable. General Lord Roberts, while not originating the concept of martial races, was instrumental in implementing a strategy of building "class regiments. " Recruiting policies were rewritten, and the Bombay Army "was notified that the Mahars, together with a number of other classes of the Bombay Army, would no longer be recruited to the Army. " Lord Roberts recorded his rational in his autobiography, Forty-One Years in India.

He writes:

- I have no doubt whatever of the fighting powers of our best Indian troops; I have a thorough belief in, and admiration for, Gurkhas, Sikhs, Dogras, Rajputs, Jats and, selected Mahomadans; I thoroughly appreciate their soldierly qualities; brigaded with British troops, I would be proud to lead them against any European enemy.

Roberts thought that the first step to making the Indian Army was "to substitute men of the more warlike and hardy races for the Hindustani sepoys of Bengal, the Tamils and Telagus of Madras, and the so-called Mahrattas of Bombay." He was convinced that

- In the British Army the superiority of one regiment over another is mainly a matter of training; the same courage and military instinct are inherent in English, Scotch, and Irish alike, but no comparison can be made between the martial value of a regiment recruited amongst the Gurkhas of Nepal or the warlike races of Northern India, and of one recruited from the effeminate peoples of the south.

The Mahars believed that their martial history demonstrated their abilities as warriors, but the British had made their decision. Mahars could only enlist as bandsmen or clerks. This would not provide the same opportunities for promotion, and allow little change in their social status. As expected, the Mahars felt the British had betrayed them after over 100 years of loyal service to the British Raj. Throughout India, there was controversy about which groups should remain in the Army.

The Mahars had support from some British soldiers, including three commanders who recommended their continued service. The commander of the 2nd Grenadiers argued that "the Parwari is of far better fighting material than the Deccani Mussulman," and suggested that the Marine Battalion might be made a class regiment of Parwaries. The commanding officer of the 9th Bombay Infantry thought that a regiment of Parwaries, especially from the Deccan, would "give a very good account of itself." The Commanding officer of the 19th Bombay Infantry stated that:

- "They are possessed of as much soldierly quality as many

However, their assistance was not enough to overcome the sentiments of Lord Roberts and other senior officers of the British Indian Army. Longer provides an excellent commentary on the impact of the decision on the Mahars.

He writes:

- The excellent system with its cosmopolitan composition, which had worked out over the years, was dismantled and destroyed. The Mahars, who had proudly carried the Colours of various Regiments of the Bombay Army, were crestfallen and heartbroken. For years they had provided abundant evidence of their courage, resolution, perseverance, constancy, and fidelity. When they bade farewell to arms there were eight Subedar-Majors, 62 Subedars, 34 Jemadars, and a host of Non-Commissioned Officers and Sepoys of the Mahar community who had served with distinction in the Bombay Army.

The Mahars would continue to fight for the right to re-enlist in the Indian Army. They were loath to lose the benefits that the military provided. Furthermore, the education provided to the soldiers had created an educated cadre that would transfer their skills into political action. However, there were few Mahars left in the Army by the beginning of World War I.

BENEFITS OF MILITARY SERVICE

Eleanor Zelliot notes that the "emergence of Mahar leaders and a new spirit of militancy in the 19th century was due in large measure to the influence of education acquired in the military."

The result was that:

- During the 19th and 20th centuries, a substantial number of Mahars removed themselves from their traditional village servant role. The establishment of British rule in Bombay Presidency provided Mahars with the opportunity for service in the army, employment in cotton mills, ammunition factories, railroads, dockyards, construction work, and as servants in British homes. The 1921 Census records that only 13.5 per cent of the Mahar working force of nearly 300,000 were employed in their traditional occupation even though most Mahars maintained strong ties with their ancestorial village.

The Mahars' ability to work among the British exposed them to Western ways, and helped them to realise that their status as Untouchables did not keep them from working in successful and satisfying occupations. They aggressively used the advantages provided by their relationship with the British. Military service provided important benefits to its soldiers. The benefits include "pay and pensions, access to education and/or specialized training, preferential access to employment, enhanced social status, and personal satisfaction." For the Mahars, the access to education and increased social status was the most important benefits. The best example of their results was Dr. Ambedkar. Zelliot writes that Ambedkar's experiences were "[f]ree from the traditional village role, his early life was spent among educated ex-army men, imbued with the pride of soldiers and acquainted with a more sophisticated Hinduism than that found in the village." In fact, Ambedkar extends much of the credit for the start of the movement to improve the Untouchables' place in society to contact with the British Army.

He maintained:

- Until the advent of the British, the Untouchables were content to remain Untouchables.... In the army of the East India Company there prevailed the system of compulsory education for Indian soldiers and their children, both male and female. The education received by the Untouchables in the army... gave them a new vision and a new value. They became conscious that the low esteem in which they had been held was not an inescapable destiny but was a stigma imposed on their personality by the cunning contrivances of the priest. They felt the shame of it as they ever did before and were determined to get rid of it.

It is indisputable that this access to education was helpful to Ambedkar, and therefore, to all of India's Untouchable communities. Ambedkar's family had extensive links to the military. Additionally, his mother's "father and her six uncles were all Subedar Majors in the Army," the highest rank that Indians could hold. Ambedkar's father also was a Subhedar Major and

- A full-fledged teacher trained at the Normal School then established by Government for turning out teachers to impart education that was then compulsory for the children as well as both male and female relations of the military servants. For fourteen years Ramji Sakpal served as Headmaster in the military school.

Undoubtedly, the accomplishments of this family were exceptional. Nonetheless, the availability of education had a positive effect on all members of Mahars in the military, including women. Consequently, Basham concludes, "The loss of this education option with the loss of their right of enlistment was therefore a real blow, not merely the loss of a theoretical benefit which few actually received." The quality of life for soldiers and their families suffered because of the loss of educational opportunities available through participation in the military. Mahars joined the military with the intent of improving their social status. They were successful in this regard.

As Basham explains:

- Within the closed circle of the regiment, caste prejudice was, if not actually absent, at least officially discouraged. Army regulations no distinction was made between soldiers on the basis of their caste or community.... Mahar officers were able to command men of other castes apparently without difficulty.

After growing up in this environment of equality it was a shock for the Untouchables to travel and live in situations away from the military cantonments. Ambedkar's biographer, Dhananjay Keer, writes of young Ambedkar's shock the first time he travelled outside the military environment while he was in school. He and his brother were travelling to meet his father in a distant village. At the railway station, they hired a bullock cart to take them to the village, but

- Aardly had the cart gone a few yards when the god-fearing touchable Hindu cartman, to his wrath, came to know that the well-dressed boys in his cart were the accursed Untouchables! In a fit of rage he threw them out on the road as one overturns the dust bins;for he felt they had polluted his wooden cart and destroyed the purity of his domestic animals!

This was Ambedkar's first experience that forced him to confront his status as an Untouchable. Life in the military cantonment had sheltered him from the prejudice and discrimination for the early part of his life. After retirement, there was a period of adjustment for Mahars who lived outside the cantonment. Basham concludes:

- As nearly as can be deduced from rather limited

information, it would seem that while actually in the army, or after retired or taking other employment, while in contact with British employers and officials, the Mahar soldier was not treated in any way differently from a soldier of higher caste. Once retired and living in his native village, a Mahar soldier, although he might have a relatively high status among the Mahar community and even among caste Hindus, would nevertheless once again have to accept his untouchable status.

The important point is, even after retirement, Mahars with a military background still had access to the British government. The retired military officers were an effective lobby for Mahar rights. Retired officers also created a group of political leaders with access to the Indian government. This was especially true near military cantonments in Poona, Satara and Ahmednagar. Basham relates an incident where Mahar children were not being offered equal educational opportunities. Local caste Hindus and low-level British education officials refused the Mahar demands for Mahar boys to be integrated into classes with caste-Hindu boys.

The dispute was resolved in favour of the Mahars. Basham argues that this demonstrates they were seeking not just education for their sons, although this was obviously important, but also an improvement in their social status. The fact that many of these parents were retired officers, and therefore could legitimately make a claim on the attention to government officials, indicates the value of military service in this respect. Clearly, the type of access available to the soldiers, active or retired, was unavailable to most Untouchables All the benefits the Mahars received were the result of their ability to develop a link with the British. This helped them overcome the obstacles erected by the Hindu social system. Zelliot observes:

- [I]t was their entry into the British army which proved significant for the subsequent history of the Mahar movement. It is important to gauge this significance. It consists not in any automatic elevation

> in the social hierarchy through military service, which indeed is ruled out in a hierarchical system governed by considerations of ascriptive status and ritual purity. It rather consists in the fact that military service at such an early date exposed them to British institutions much before the dissemination of western culture took place on a large scale.

Such an exposure socialized them sufficiently early to the new political order so that when new opportunities and alternatives became available, they were found prepared to use them more effectively than those groups which did not have this opportunity. Following the delistment of 1893, the Mahars would need all the access and knowledge they had gained to overcome the impact of being refused service in the Army.

THE FIGHT FOR RE-ENLISTMENT

The Mahars did not give up their positions in the Army easily. The British decision of Mahar "[d]elistment in 1893 had been a severe blow to them as a community, not only threatening their economic status, but also giving official sanction to caste Hindu discrimination against them." Overcoming both of these threats was the focus of two different efforts to petition the Government of India to reconsider its decision between 1894 and the start of the first World War. The Mahars used two different strategies to influence the government; with both they tried to regain enlistment privileges in the army and an improved social status. Zelliot maintains that these efforts "show the importance of army service to the Mahars.

This was clearly the beginning of their efforts to induce government to intervene on their behalf, and their questioning of their traditional inferior status." In both instances, the movement was led by educated, former military officers. The first organized attempt was in April 1895. Some of the details of the petition drive presented by Zelliot and Basham are speculative. Basham, who has completed the most recent study, states it was originally presented to the Viceroy, but was later returned for resubmission through the Bombay Government. It appears that the petition was submitted by Gopal Baba Walangkar, a retired military officer, on behalf of the Anarya Doshpariharak Mandali, the non-Aryan committee for the rightings of wrongs, an Untouchable organization. Dr. Ambedkar, following the death of his father, found a copy of the petition in his documents.

Ambedkar "believed that his father had obtained the assistance of Justice M. B. Ranade in preparing the petition." The petition compares Mahar actions to those of the higher castes and requests reinstatement in the military. The petition's pleas were simple. The Mahars believed that, in 1859, the Government had declared that the castes who fought loyally for the British were to be given due preference for military enlistment.

Therefore, they demanded:

- In view of that promise, Government should employ in civil, military and police department without any discrimination these faithful and honest persons. They should also be given education and proper opportunity for suitable posts in the department.

The case they presented for reinstatement was more complicated than their demands. Much of their argument attempts to demonstrate that their identification as Untouchables was a mistake. The 1895 petition argues that the Mahars as a group who are actually of the Kshatriya caste. This represents the Mahars attempt to change their position in the caste structure by "Sanskritization."

The petition states:

- Our ancestors were Kshatriya. In about the year 1396 there was a great famine for about 12 years which was called Durhavedi famine. That time our ancestors survived by eating whatever they could find. Therefore, they were considered low case under the Peshwa rule.

It continues by attacking the legitimacy of the higher castes. It claims, "The so called high caste and pure people's ancestors were as degraded as our people and were used to eat flesh of cow and beef. They wrote their own religious scriptures." Finally, the petition provides a "creation myth" about the high castes.

It maintains:

- The high caste people of the South are progeny of Australian Semitic Anaryas and African Negroes whereas the high caste people from North are mixture of several castes.... Several castes of foreign origin became high caste Hindus by giving up beef-eating.
- The Chitpavan Brahmins of Konkan came from the Jewish race. They fled from Africa for fear of their lives by the invaders and their ship was wrecked nearby Malabar coast. Their children and women drown and died in the sea. Those men who survived, married the native low caste women.... [W]hen they became rulers, they called themselves Brahmins.

The document's tenor shows the importance of military service to the Mahars and the use of Sanskritization tactics to show they were at least equal to the alleged high castes. This campaign was unsuccessful. The Mahars were unaware of the debate "over recruitment policy or the acceptance of Lord Roberts views on martial races" which was the prime component in the British decision. However, Basham shows "the government of India took the petition seriously enough to request information about the Koregaon monument from the government of Bombay.

Eighteen months after the initial submission of the petition, the Indian government replied that it was "unable to rescind the orders which have been issued regarding the castes to be admitted to the Bombay Army." Shortly after the turn of the century, a second attempt was organized. The second major petition was submitted to the government three times between 1904 and 1910. The document's "signatories included forty-two military pensioners" including Dr. Ambedkar's father. Basham's research found that "several of the signatories had also written letters to newspapers or had signed at least one other petition, suggesting a long-term commitment and a willingness to agitate for change." This petition had a broader base of support than the one in 1895. This campaign was more sophisticated than the first.

The spokesman, Shivram Janba Kamble, spoke English. More importantly, the petition's "appeal for consideration was not on the basis of the Mahars' having been demoted from Kshatriyahood, but on the grounds of former service, English justice and human worth."

This pragmatic approach attracted greater support than the earlier petition, and used arguments that were later refined by Dr. Ambedkar. In fact, Ambedkar took over leadership of the Mahars from Kamble. The 1910 petition was more polite and less argumentative than the 1895 petition. The document states, "We do not aspire to high political privileges and positions, since we are not educationally qualified for them, but humbly seek employment in the lowest grades of the Public Service, in the ranks of Police Sepoys and of soldiers in the Indian Army."

It continued:

- We are making no new demands; we do not claim employment in services in which we have not been engaged before. Indeed, some few of our people do still hold positions in the Police Force, and have acquitted themselves most honourably. So also have our people been employed in the Indian Army from the very commencement of the British Raj in our country, and they have risen to the highest positions by their valour and good conduct.

Despite the reasoned arguments, this petition demands, like the first, were denied. The manpower demands of World War I had a greater effect, and beginning in 1914 Mahars, again, were recruited into the Army and given their own Regiment, the 111 Mahars. The Regiment's three battalions "were formed the towards the end of the war, but they did not see action and their martial qualities were untested." Shortly after the war, the Regiment was disbanded by the British "on the excuse of the economy." More important, however, is that the petition drives provided an organization for Dr. Ambedkar to use after the war to improve the social status of Untouchables.

Basham correctly concludes:

- Military service had been a significant factor for the Mahars in two respects. Education and skills acquired through military service created a class of community leaders, and the wish to retain the social and economic benefits derived from military service was a powerful incentive to organize behind these leaders and work for a common goal. A high level of organization and political activity in the Mahar community by the 1940s was therefore at least in part a consequence of their military past.

The long association with the military gave Mahars an issue to organize around and the movement then worked to achieve more substantial achievements than just military service.

The 120 years of service in the British military gave the Mahars excellent skills.

Basham concludes:

- Mahar soldiers were able to establish a link with the most powerful institution in India—the British Raj—and in some instances to use that link to bypass local authorities. Military service was also a way to sever the ties of village customary law which maintained the inferior status of the Mahars. Other forms of employment could take the Mahar out of the village, but none offered long-term financial security in the form of pensions.

This case study shows how military service has assisted the Mahars to fight the stigma of untouchability. Their positive experiences fighting with Shivaji encouraged them to seek similar opportunities from the British. It is clear, that in their service they received their most tangible benefits. Before delistment, Mahars in the Bombay Army received a steady wage, housing, and education. With this, many were able to retire with a pension, which, often, eliminated the need to return to the traditional Mahar occupations following their military service. These obvious benefits were eliminated following the 1893 decision. However, military service still influenced Mahar life following delistment.

As Basham argues:

- If the army system of education had produced no effects for the Mahars other than to provide an appropriate environment for Ambedkar's early life this in itself would be a significant impact on the Mahar community.

Furthermore, the petition drives provided political organizations to press for overcoming the stigma of Untouchability. There were other benefits that were accrued, even if their requests for reinstatement were refused until the beginning of the war. Kamble's work in Poona that formed the base for Ambedkar's later political movements is the best example of this. Therefore, even after military service was taken away from the Mahars, the traditions and accrued benefits continued to be an advantage to this Untouchable community.

UNDERSTAND BAHUJAN PHILOSOPHY INSTEAD OF PROLETYSING

INDIAN HISTORY

This is in response to letter from Dr. Choudhrie in DV of Sept.1-15. I am glad to know that he is trying to study Ancient Indian History. Not only it is illuminating, but it throws ample light on the happenings of today. One finds that from times immemorial, the struggle between the so called upper caste savarnas on one side and the rest of population on other side is going on. It had assumed different names, shapes and forms during the course of different periods of history, and the history of India is nothing but the history of conflict between these two ideologies, as is well demonstrated by Dr. Ambedkar. The present name for this is bahujan-vad and bahujan-virodh-vad. The present day protagonists of these are Phuley, Shahu and Ambedkar on one side and Tilak, Gandhi and Golwalkar on the other. All the leaders of christians and muslims need to understand this point and explain it to the gullible ignorant and illiterate christian and muslim masses, instead of thinking in lines of proletising Dalits. These are the only two ideologies in present day India, and sooner the people understand this, earlier they will be freed from their slavery.

UNCHRISTIAN SIDE OF THE INDIAN CHURCH

In his rejoinder to Dr. Chaudhrie's letter, VTR has very aptly described the situation. It is like feeding milk to the serpents' offsprings. He had also suggested that at least 50% of seats in all christian convents must be given only to SCs and STs at no charge, and the deficit be made good by charging double fees from the children of oppressors.

AMBEDKAR'S ADVICE TO CHRISTIANS

I like to make all conversant with one of the speeches of Dr. Ambedkar, during the period of active consideration of choice of religion to adopt. May be, this might clear doubts, if any. The speech delivered to Indian Christians of Sholapur. Published in 'Janata' of 5.2.1938, reproduced from 'Dnyanodaya' "From the available religions and personalities in the world, I consider only two-Buddha and Christ for conversion. We want a religion for me and my followers which will teach equality freedom among men, and how man must behave with men and God, how child should behave with father etc.

"Missionaries feel they have done their duty when they convert an untouchable to Christianity. They do not look after their political rights. I find this is a big fault in Christians. Because they have not entered into politics up till now. It is difficult for any institution to survive without political support. We, Untouchables, though are ignorant and illiterate, we are in movement. That is why we have 15 seats in the Legislative Assembly. Students are getting scholarships, there are government hostels. Such is not the case of Christian students. If an untouchable student getting scholarship get converted, his scholarship is stopped though his financial status remains same. If you were in politics, things would have been opposed.

"Your society is educated. Hundreds of boys and girls are matric. These people have not agitated against this injustice unlike the uneducated untouchables.

If any girl becomes a nurse or any boy becomes a teacher they are involved in their own affairs, they do not get involved in public affairs. Even clerks and officers are busy in their work, he ignores the social injustice. Your society is so much educated, how many are District judges or magistrates? I tell you, this is because of your neglect towards politics, because there in nobody to talk of and fight for your rights...."

BSP AND KANSHIRAM

To relieve the humanity from suffering, in India, the remedy is to develop the spirit of Bahujan Samaj. We cannot progress by merely "Dalit Unity", or by only "Dalit Muslim Unity", or by only "Dalit Christian Unity", we have to build a Bahujan Samaj, which is not an easy task. One has to understand the mechanics of Bahujan Samaj. There are many misconceptions about BSP, Kanshiram and Mayavati, purposefully spread by vested interests.

One has to understand Bahujan Philosophy with all its intricacies. It is pity that Dr. Choudhrie could not get time to understand BSP while he was in Punjab. I hope he will have ample opportunity to understand it in M. P., where there is remarkable influence of BSP. BSP is not merely a political party unlike many others; it is a movement. One must read Phuley, Shahu Ambedkar and follow it with reading about Kanshiram and BSP.

SOCIAL SERVICE AND SOCIAL TRANSFORMATION

This is the important point which one must understand. Medical ethics says, prevention is better than cure. Instead of curing a disease give more attention to its prevention. To mend a fracture is social service, to create environment so that fractures do not take place is social transformation. To give vitamin pills to malnourished Adivasi children is social service, to give their parents employment so that they can buy wholesome food for their children is social transformation. To give charity to a beggar is social service, to create social atmosphere so that nobody has to beg is social change. To give rice at ₹two per kilo when market price is ₹7/- is social service, to raise the income of the person so that he can buy the rice at market price is social change.

To feed the hungry is social service, to create situation where nobody remains hungry is social change. To teach an illiterate is social service, to destroy the social structure which made him illiterate is social change. To open a new school in thee vicinity of an illiterate poor colony of zopadpatti could be social service, to motivate the poor hungry and illiterate man to send his child to school walking five kilometres away even on an empty stomach is social transformation. To protect a weak person by giving him weapons is social service, to make him strong enough to let him manufacture and use his own weapons is social change.

To teach an egalitarian prayer to a school child may be social service, to dynamite the scriptures spreading inequality among human beings is a social change. To assure protection to scared minorities may be social justice, to give them power so that they can defend themselves is social transformation. I have great respect for missionaries who did a tremendous amount of good work.

If there were no missionaries, there would have been no Phuley, no Shahu and no Ambedkar, let alone Kanshiram and Mayawati. In my humble opinion, missionaries in India are doing social service, and are the very best at that but still it is not social transformation.

I think here lies the importance of BSP, which is not a political party alone but a movement which stands for not social service or social justice alone but for social transformation and economic emancipation.

THE NATURE OF DALIT MUSLIM UNITY

It was a great misfortune that Dr. Ambedkar and Br. Jinnah could not work together, Adv. Karim says. He says Azad was a stooge. He says the anti Muslim activities are a symptoms and not a disease. He says Muslims are not a minority. He believes that population of Muslims could be more than presumed 15 per cent. He also quotes authorities to show that Islam is an egalitarian religion.

All this need not refuted and any Bahujan can agree with all these points. He avers that Muslim masses in India are in a need of allies to fight the existing system under the guidance of Islam He advises his Muslim brothers to help the Dalits in all spheres, and keep good contacts for future interaction. This is quite correct. But the main point is, what kind of unity is sought for. He says: "The future of India lies in the unity of Dalits and Muslims-not under the banner of this party or that because no party is aiming at providing an alternative to the existing social, political and economic setup but under the in vigorating and revolutionary message of Islam..." Why no political party is thought to be neccesary?

Is it an invitation for the Bahujans to adopt Islam? Is it a proletising work? If it is, well and good; nothing wrong in that; only that perhaps DV is not a forum for it. Our experience of mixing religion with politics is always counter productive. The combination does neither promote the religion nor the politics. The political meetings of RPI used to start with Buddhist prayers, the non Buddhists in the party, gradually, faded away. The religious sermons to Budhists used to end with request for support to RPI work, the non-RPI Buddhists stopped comming. I feel the two must not be combined, the religion and politics. I hope Adv. Karim does not wish to propagate religion from political platform.

WHAT IS THE SPIRIT OF ISLAM

Do the Muslims consider Dalits as non-hindus? I think, it is the first neccesity that they must make a distinction between "Hindus" and Dalits. Dalit leaders have time and again declared that. Leaders of all Dalit parties, of all shades and colours. But Muslim leaders do not think about this. I think this is the main hurdle. No doubt, Islam is a great religion. Also it can not be gainsaid that meeting of Ambedkar and Jinnah could not bear fruits. If the unity has to bear any fruits, today, it has got to be based on secular points. The basis has to be non-religious. It should be purely on political ideology. What is that ideology? I believe, that ideology could only be Ambedkarism. Our Muslim brothers have got to get themselves aquainted with Spirit of Ambedkarism, which is different from Spirit of Buddhism

HINDU MUSLIM RIOTS AND DALITS

A letter by Dr. Ambedkar sent from England at the time of Third Round Table Conference published in "Janata" of 24.12.1932, "When Hindus and Muslims fight among themselves, the Untouchables tend to incline towards Muslims. They feel, they would be benefitted if they develope friendship with Muslims. But Untouchables should keep in mind that it is not all that true as it appears and so they should be very careful. What I experienced at the time of Sarada Act about the Muslim policy, can not called satisfactory.

I got first severe jolt when I found that almost all the Muslims got ready to oppose the essential Act like Sarda Act along with the obsolete and puranic, fundamentalists and revivalist orthodox Hindus. And at the time of Round Table Conference, I got second experience now that their attitude can be how narrow and retrograde, like that of sanatani orthodox Hindus. A special telegram from the Brahmin President of Varnashram Brahman Sangha was received recently by a Muslim delegate, Mr. Gazanavi. It was a message that Muslims should cooperate with orthodox Hindus in opposing the Untouchables temple entry movement.

It was also suggested that, if India gets freedom, it would be dangerous to the religion of both Hindus as well as Muslims, and so the religious Muslims should be careful about the swaraj like religious Hindus. The sanatani brahmins also requested Mr. Gaznabi to put forward the side of sanatani Hindus by the Muslim delegates in the RTC! Thus, it could be said that these arthodox brahmins have materialised the proverb that 'we are orhtodox brahmins and our relatives are muslims'. Mr. Gazanabi has published this telegram in 'Times' here. The fact, that the orthodox Bengali Muslim like Mr. Gaznabe should be entrusted the job of preserving the religion of Hindus, by the orthodox Hindus, and that he should accept it, should be borne in mind by all the reformists in India. It is an example of how an orthodox sanatani Hindu is ready to pray even an 'yavan' or a 'mlenchha' when he finds the life of his 'dharma' is in danger.

And the 'dharma' of Hindus is such a provokative one, that whenever any thing new happens, or due to time any change takes place in traditional customms, they shout that, dharm' is in danger. Just like a sanatani Hindu, the Indian Muslim also is a strange object. He is averse to all social reforms. His corelegionists outside India have turned to be social revolutionaries. A Muslim patriot like Kemal Pasha has quashed all customs and traditions which are hurdles against the progress of nation and human life. I have great respect and affinity for Kemal Pasha. But the Indian Muslims, even the patriots and nationalists like Shaukat Ali, do not like Kemal Pasha and Amanullah. Because they are reformists, and in the eyes of a Indian Muslim, reform is a sacrilege."

SUB-CASTES WITHIN THE SC/ST

This has reference to the object on rivalry of subcastes Madigas and Malas among the SCs, and a frank debate welcomed by our editor.. Our editor has welcomed the rivalry among the subcastes in these words: "There is nothing to be ashamed of or worried about the inter-Dalit bickering. Rather this should be welcomed." This attitude is quite in keeping with his old known notion that if you could strengthen each jati and make them strong enough to demand their rightful share just as to their population from the 'evil' jati people, then the system of jatis will crash.

Unfortunately I beg to defer with him. Some time back Bhoja Tarakkam from Hyderabad had argued that it is against Ambedkarite principles to think of strengthening any jatis. I fully agree and endorse his view. Dr. Ambedkar had specifically advocated that the process of abolition of castes must not start with abolition of subcastes. He averred that if the process stops at that level, as suggested, end up by strengthening the caste system. What applies to subcastes equally applies to castes within the SC/ST group. Annihilation of castes was what Dr. Ambedkar wanted. It could only be achieved through social amalgamation by inter caste marriages, and to promote that the sanction behind the sastras must end.

This was what was intended. Your contention is that, when castes, individually, become strong enough, will fight with BSO and get their rightful number of positions, and thereby reduce the power of BSO. Unfortunately this does not happen in practice. When Ambedkar said educate, agitate and organize, he meant agitate against BSO oppressors. We took it to mean struggle amongst ourselves. We fight amongst ourselves for every thing and we beg for favours from others. We have become subservient dummy stooges of others, popularly termed 'chamchas'. Though we do not have enough strength to get elected in Parliament, we rush to the feet of men in power, and that too individually and separately,ignoring the so called unity, and beg for a berth in ministry for self and get kicked out.

All our self respect vanishes that time. This is the state of affairs. How do you expect that such a people will be able to fight with the oppressors for the rights of masses, they can only beg for self prosperity. First we have to increase our strength, then and then alone we can bargain. Power is something that can not be obtained by begging, begging only budgets petty alms. Why some castes among the SC/ST could not progress? This is the question one must answer with some clear vision and self intro- spection. It must be agreed that, in spite of equal opportunity given by the reservations which started at the same time for all SC/STs, the progress made by different castes among the SC/ST is not uniform.

There are many reasons, which must be understood before we devise ways and means to bridge the gap of disparity among the SC/ST castes. The main point is that, Dr. Ambedkar had given a call to denounce old ways of earning a subsistence and embark on mass scale education. Some people followed his ways were Ambedkarites, and some followed Gandhi's ways and were called 'harijans'. They did not change. Those people who abandoned their ancestral calling and gave up the dirty means of livelihood, which they were ordained to follow by the Brahmnical social order for centuries, progressed faster and those who stuck to their old professions lingered behind. Why there is dissatisfaction?

The main reason is that there is supposed to be a restriction imposed by Supreme Court to limit reservations to 50 per cent. Under what circumstances Supreme Court has given this ruling and what are legal ways to counter it, must be debated by the legal luminaries from among the bahujans and people should take steps legal or legislative to amend the constitution, if needed, to ensure that every caste must get their rightful share in running of government, *i.e.* in legislature and executive, including judiciary, as Kanshiram says *"jisaki jitani sankhyaa bhaari, usaki utani bhaagidaari"*. I consider this is the only method, by which dissatisfaction among the various castes can be reduced.

When there is enough for everybody, nobody should grumble. There is now grumbling because share of 50 per cent people is appropriated by 15 per cent. Reservations must not be on economical grounds Shri T. P. Kamala- nathan has given, in the same issue of DV, the instances of people against caste based reservations. Everybody knows that manuvadis are behind this. Unfortunate part of this is that, even the OBC people, who are co-sufferers, are brain washed to support this argument. They are made to believe that the OBCs can't get jobs because of SC/ST reservations. They should be explained that 1.

Even after half a century, SC/ST strength is not complete as per their quota, and SC/ST are not responsible for grabbing OBC's share. OBC's share is grabbed by those from 15 per cent, who rightfully deserve only 15 per cent and are now holding about 70 per cent. We find even today it is not very difficult for higher caste people to obtain a certificate of being SC/ST by corrupt means. When they can obtain false caste certificates, how much easy it will be to obtain a false income certificate of low income for these people, and how much corruption will be there to prevent SC/ST poor people from obtaining their rightful share. The question of enlightenment of OBCs is rather crucial.

They have been brain washed by upper castes for centuries to be against Dalits. Their ignorance is phenomenal and their prejudice is outstanding. In spite of countrywide movement by BSP for Mandal Commission, there are many among OBCs who believe that it is something which is meant for upliftment of Dalits alone and not of OBCs. If we succeed in convincing the OBCs that caste based reservations are good for them, most of bahujan's problems will end and a strong bahujan samaj will emerge. What is our aim? Our editor is fighting for Dalit Muslim BC unity for a long time. This is same thing what Kanshiram calls bahujan samaj taking this word from old Buddhist literature. It is simple formula of 85 per cent versus 15 per cent.

But what is the meaning of unity. When different groups live in physical proximity, and have desire in them to come closer and unite, the ultimate step is social unity where whole society becomes one and there is full harmony and rapport with matrimonial relationships between groups which were differing to each other and may even be antagonistic. This is the ideal state and should be the ultimate aim. That is annihilation of castes, as Dr. Ambedkar envisaged. But it takes centuries to achieve and has to pass through various stages. Religious harmony is an earlier stage, and that also takes tremendous will power to unite and strong urge for it and is also a lengthy process.

The first stage is, of course, political unity, which must be achieved before there is any kind of dialogue possible within the groups. When we talk of unity, we only mean political unity at this early stage of understanding. If we can develop among all these groups goodwill and friendship even on only political lines, it will be a great achievement. At the movement these groups are warring groups, there is not even a dialogue, let alone sense of common belonging. On 14th October 1956, Dr. Ambedkar converted half a million Dalits to Buddhism. Next day there was a meeting of selected workers only in Hotel Shyam in Nagpur where Babasahib was staying, and I was fortunate to be present there as one of the three student workers. That was Babasahib's first speech in Hindi, I heard. He expressed his anguish for infighting among the workers and expressed his desire to launch a party which will have people from all castes.

He asked the workers to develop readiness to work in association with others. Also on his last day, he wrote some letters to leaders like Lohia and P. K. Atre etc. But we find that, the party of his vision, could not go beyond its scope of one single caste. Even whatever people from other castes were in the party, they gradually left and now it has an image of one caste party. Hopes and aspirations expressed by our saviour are shattered to make a united party. Only hope now seems to be Kanshiram, who has not only paved the way of political unity among the various groups but also started a campaign of *jati todo samaj jodo* and tried to assimilate people of different castes, an aim which was very dear to our beloved saviour Dr. Ambedkar.

What is to be done? One must accept that when schedules of castes and tribes were made to be incorporated in the constitution, there was a tremendous hurry. Many were left out and many were superfluous. This was known to the founding fathers of constitution, so an arrangement was made to review the schedule periodically. This should be taken in spirit of adjustment and not of antagonism. But at the same time we should prevent categorization within SC/ST. I endorse the view of D. Venkateswarlu that this will weaken the masses and perhaps that is what the BSO wants. We must not play in their hands.

We get only those reservations which are pleasing to BSO For decades RPI was demanding abolition of political reservations of SC/STs. But they are forced on us. Whereas nobody demanded reservations for women, but they are granted in a hurry and when some people wished to link caste based questions with it, the bill is shifted to select committee. We, thus get what is good for them, without any consideration for what we want. For last fifteen years or so Kanshiram has brought forward the theory of 15 per cent versus 85 per cent.

You yourself have sup- ported this theory many times. Now if you advocate different castes among these 85 per cent to get consolidated separately instead of together, then how are we going to struggle against the 15 per cent. After all, at this stage of our development we are not asking for social unity, we are not asking for religious unity, we are asking only for political unity.

BAHUJAN SAMAJ AND THE EUROPEAN KNOWLEDGE

India lost these Equality and fraternity also.

The learned author points out:

- "At a still later point of time, in the long meandering course of our history, the society got divided into innumerable castes and sub-castes. The evil of discrimination as high and low among men, on the basis of birth, hereditary avocations and other considerations raised its head and the pernicious practice of untouchability with all its degrading implications."

After the demise of Equality and fraternity in India it took its birth in Europe. The rights of citizens in the preamble of the Constitution are taken from the declaration of the rights of Man pronounced by the French Constituent Assembly. The concepts of three varieties of Justice, Liberty, etc were also foreign to the caste-ridden society of India. The principles of socialism were borrowed from the economic and political thoughts of the West and USSR. So much was the debt of the nation to European knowledge, not to speak of European Science and Technology.

How did India come in contact with the European Knowledge? As in other parts of the world enquiry in this part of the world was also speculative. The attempt was to explain the reasons for various occurrences in nature. It was observed that there were evil effects during solar and lunar eclipses. Why? It required an explanation. It was attributed to the emission of poison of the snakes, which was swallowing the Sun or the Moon. Similarly Aristotle wanted to explain why the fire when it was lit went up and the stones thrown up returned to the Earth. Aristotle every object had its natural resting-place and it desired to go to its resting-place, whenever it was displaced.

Heaven is the resting-place of fire and therefore whenever fire was lit it went up. The stones had the Earth as its resting-place. So whoever it is lifted returned to the earth. The intensity of the desire of an object to go back to its resting-place depended on its size. The greater is the size the stronger is its desire of an object to come to its resting-place. So bigger objects returned earlier than smaller object. Galelio wanted to know whether it was really so. He climbed Leaning Tower of Pisa and dropped from there two objects of the same material but of different size and observed whether it fell simultaneously on the ground or whether the bigger one due to its stronger desire to come to its returning place fell earlier than the other. He found that two objects fell simultaneously on the ground disproving the Aristotelian concept.

This type of activity led to the growth of a new branch of knowledge. The specialty of this type of knowledge was that it could be tested by anyone anywhere in the world and its truth could be established beyond any doubt. This knowledge attained universal acceptance. This type of experimental knowledge came to be known as science and it made rapid progress encompassing all departments of life and natural phenomena. Europe was the centre of this activity. It had its impact on India also.

During the first half of nineteenth century, in the field of education, there were two schools of thought in India; one wanted only the traditional education in Arabic. Persian and Sanskrit and the other advocated elementary education in vernacular and higher education in English. It was at that time MACAULAY reached the shore of India. It marked the turning point of India's intellectual progress. On 10th July 1833 speaking on the India Bill in the House of Commons MACAULAY said "It may be that the public mind of India may expand under our system till it has outgrown that system; that by good Government we may educate our subjects into a capacity for better Government; that having become instructed in European knowledge they may, in some future age, demand European Institutions.

Whether such a day will come, I know not. But never will I attempt to avert it. Whenever it comes, it will be the proudest day in English history." MACAULAY came to India as Law Member of the Executive Council of the Governor general of India. He in his celebrated minute dated 2-2-1835 placed before the Supreme Council strongly defended those who advocated English education.

His arguments were supported by the following two illustrations:

1. "The first instance is the great revival of letters among Western nations at the close of the 15th and the beginning of the 16th Century. At that time almost everything that was worth reading was contained in the writing of the ancient Greeks and Romans. Had our ancestors acted as the Committee of Public Instruction has hitherto acted; had they neglected the language of Ciero and Tacitus; had they confined their education to the old dialects of our own Island; had they printed nothing and taught nothing at Universities but the chronicles of Anglo-Saxons and romances in Norman-French, Would English have been what she is now? What Greek and Latin were to the contemporaries of More and Ascham our tongue is to the people of India."
2. "Within the last hundred and twenty years, a Nation which had previously been in a state as barbarous as that in which our ancestors were before crusades, has gradually emerged from the ignorance in which it was sunk and has taken its place among civilised communities. I speak of Russia. There is now in that country a large educated class, abounding with persons fit to serve the State in the highest functions and in no way inferior to the most accomplished men who adorn the best circles of Paris and London_ How was this change effected? Not by flattering national

> prejudices, not by filling the mind of the young Moscovite with old woman's stories which his rude fathers had believed—But teaching him those foreign languages in which the greatest mass of information had been laid up and then putting that information within his reach. The languages of Western Europe civilized Russia. I cannot doubt that they will do for the Hindoo what they have done for the Tartar."

The Government of India accepted the view of MACAULAY and on 7th March 1835 announced that "The Great object of British Government ought to be the promotion of European Literature and Science among the Natives of India. "Prsuant to this declaration three Universities were established in 1857 one at Bombay and others at Calcutta and Madras. Within a period of about 30 years the new system of education produced highly educated Indians and a desire for better existence generated in them. It was at that time that ALLAN OCTAVIAN HUME took initiative to establish an organisation came to be known as the Indian National Congress. Here again it was left to a European to take the lead. He wanted the most highly educated of the nation to meet each year and chalkout programme for the purpose of securing greater freedom, more impartial administration and a larger share in the management of the country. The first session of Congress was held in Bombay in the year 1885.

The Indian intellectuals started comparing the administration of India with that of England and started feeling dissatisfied with the shortcomings in Indian administration. They started demanding European Institutions culminating in a movement for independence and ultimately asked the British to QUIT INDIA. At last India became free. The proudest day of English history as Macaulay said in 1833 dawned on 18th July 1947 when the Indian Independence Act 1947 was passed by the British Parliament as follows:

- As from the fifteenth day of August, nineteen hundred and forty-seven, two independent Dominions shall be set up in India, to be known respectively as India and Pakistan,

- The said Dominions are hereafter in this Act referred as "the new Dominion", and the said fifteenth day of August is hereafter in this Act referred to be as "the appointed day".

The Indian National Congress had passed resolutions to reorganise the states on the basis of languages. But after independence the Government of free India run by the Indian National Congress did not evince much interest in the formation of linguistic states. Therefore, late P. Sriramulu started his fast unto death demanding formation of states on the basis of languages in accordance with the resolutions that had been adopted by the Indian Congress. He was not satisfied by the oral assurances given to him and he continued his fast and sacrificed his life.

Immediately after his death the Jawaharlal Nehru Government at the centre announced the constitution of a State Re-organisation Committee for the demarcation of the States based upon various languages spoken in different parts of the territory of India and as per its report the linguistic states were formed on 1st November 1956. The regional languages became the official languages of the respective states and it gave tremendous impetus and encouragement to the regional languages for it's all round developments long years have rolled by after the formation of linguistic states.

But the Indian languages are yet to attain the standards of European Languages in so far as science and technology are concerned. There is no progress except in collaborating with European countries. The question therefore is whether it is time to discontinue the education in European literature, science and technology, which brought about so much of revolutionary changes in all departments of Indian life. No doubt for administrative expediency the states have been reorganised and linguistic states has been formed. Does it mean that thereafter all educations must be only in regional languages? Will it elevate the knowledge of the people to the international standard or will it draw them back to pre-MACULAY period? The Bahujan samaj has a great stake in this matter. The European educated Upper Castes led the

Independence Movement and secured freedom from the yokes of the British.

It was the European education that helped them to achieve it. What about the Bahujan Samaj, which is still suffering under the iron yokes of the Upper Castes? They too will require European education to free themselves from the yokes and shackles of those who enjoy freedom today so that they may also live human beings with dignity and self-respect. Every year there should be a meeting of highly educated intellectuals belonging to the deprived and neglected parts of the people as what the Indian National Congress was doing before independence. These meetings should consider how to shape the destiny of their people, how to alleviate their sufferings and how to take them to a prosperous new life. There should be a Second Independence Movement for the purpose and it should be the responsibility of the highly educated intellectuals of these communities to lead such a movement.

SOCIAL STATUS QUO

In June this year, a Dalit panchayat chief, Adiamma was removed from her office in Karnataka. Her only crime was that she continued with her toilet cleaning job even after becoming president of the panchayat. A few years back a Dalit youth was forced to swallow human excreta in a Karnataka village. Similarly, in southern Tamil Nadu, a Dalit MLA was shoed away, abused and humiliated publicly, when he visited his constituency, simply because he was a Dalit and yet he had audacity to visit his constituency and hear people s grievances.

In most parts of rural Andhra Pradesh, Tamil Nadu, and Karnataka, hotel/tea shops maintain two-glass system one for Dalits and other for non-Dalits. In all the three States, practice of untouchability is rampant in its crudest form, uncomparable to rest of the India. The pattern of violence in this part of India contains medieval era characteristics, and is comparable only to the pattern of violence in western UP, Haryana and parts of Rajasthan bordering UP. A few years back, in district Mathura of UP, a Dalit youth and Jat girl were hanged from a banyan tree. This gory crime occurred in day time, witnessed by some 20,000 people. Their only crime was to enter in a wedlock, defying the caste norm. About an year back, Gujjars of district Dholpur, Rajasthan caught hold of a Dalit youth, punctured his nose, and put a thin rope, meant for stitching jute bags, through it.

The bleeding victim was paraded in the village streets. The victim, Rameshwar Jatav ran a small grocery shop, and had demanded ₹50 from Kamlesh Gujjar, who had bought items on credit. There is no dearth of such incidents to show the point. Every year, during the marriage season, we come across news items how a Dalit bridegroom was attacked for riding a mare. Also, the Dalit panchayat chief elected from reserved seats in this region, face similar social handicaps as witnessed in the southern States. What is common to both the regions? Climate, cropping pattern, language, dress and food-habits are all radically different.

It should have been only natural that the pattern of violence in both the regions was either radically different from each other, or similar to the pattern as witnessed at all-India level. Contrary to that, both the regions have a distinctly similar pattern of violence, distinctly dissimilar to the rest of India. Why? If there is any commonality in the two regions in question, distinct from the rest of India, it is the social composition of the ruling castes. In both the regions, Brahmins have a thin presence, and Kshatriyas are virtually non-existent. Traditionally, the upper Shudras have owned agrarian assets, but were subjected to politico-cultural dominance of Brahmins. In post-Independence period, slowly but steadily, they consolidated their political power as well, replacing Brahmins decisively.

Despite that, at cultural level, their dominance lacked socio-cultural legitimacy, neither Brahmins and nor Dalits, for their own different reasons, accepted them as the ruling castes. Traumatised by this unique varnal-caste logic of power and legitimacy, the upper Shudras tended to invoke fundamentals of the Chaturvarna value system, as it existed earlier. Since a social order of the medieval era cannot be enforced today, it only adds to frustration. In order to gain an upper varna-like dominance, violence is the most reliable and the final tool that the upper Shudras know. In both the regions in question, there exists a parallel system of governance, where regulatory authority of the modern State is subjected to the antiquated laws of Chaturvarna order.

If in a couple of decades, migration of upper Varna population from rural India to urban India is accomplished, and the upper Shudras take full control of rural India, the Italian fascists, in their graves may feel ashamed of being amateurs. The Dalits and the artisan OBCs, who together constitute about 57 per cent of India's total population, and who are the real proletariat, have a tough task at this juncture of history. While the struggle for a democratic social order has to fight the upper Shudras in rural India, it has to oppose the upper Varnas in urban India. As if that is not enough, its also has to fight the intellectual hegemony of both the ruling social blocks.

And the progressives expect the people to believe in the following:

- That it is not the social conflict or varna/caste dominance which is the fundamental crisis of Indian society, but the religious conflict;
- That the varnashram system is not a social order, but a religious system called Hinduism, and a party like the BJP, by invoking Hindus religious passion, is planning to install communal fascism, which we must prevent by bringing the Congress back to power;
- That an upper varna party like the BJP will use violence as the political weapon to suppress opposition, and the upper Shudras parties, will use democratic methods to deal with opponents and;
- That fascism as a political doctrine, as it evolved in Italy, can be more atrocious, more violent, more vicious than the ideology of the varnashram social order, and therefore we must all adopt a new phrase of fascism to define the anti-democracy doctrine. The intelligentsia of the country must understand that this is not the closing years of 18th century when a Shankaracharya would come and redefine charging

> elephant as mithya, and the people of India will lap it as reality. Much changes have occurred during past over one millennium. There is Amedkarism also for the Dalits to shape a vision. When Dr BR Ambedkar was raising the caste question, he was being told that Independence of the country was more important than the social question, and once freedom was accomplished, the caste question would be addressed. When Independence was achieved, Dr Ambedkar joined the Nehru Cabinet with the hope that the caste question will be addressed then. But he was told then that national reconstruction was more important, and once this was achieved, the resolution of caste question would be accompanied.

More than five decades have passed since then, but the varna/caste dominance remains. Once again, when the question of social transformation is being raised, people are being told that they must join secular brigade first to defeat communal fascism; probably they mean that the social questions can be tackled later. This is unacceptable. One cannot fight something which does not exist. The varnal-caste conflict is the fundamental question of India, and the agenda of communal fascism is only a mischievous construct, scripted only to retain the varnal-caste hegemony, and to ensure the social status quo.

SUB-CASTES AMONG DALITS

INHUMAN QUALITIES OF HINDUISM

Graded inequality, Ban on inter dining, forced endogamy, polluting touch, and restriction on occupation are enumerated as evils of Hindu caste system, and it is claimed that these are absent in castes of SCs, STs and BCs. Dr. Ambedkar's theory of "Genesis of Castes" is quoted to support this view. Bojja Tharakam has dealt with this at length. Let his 'tributes to DV' be construed as a courtesy and not as change of his views. In any case, I feel, to concentrate on genesis of caste, is to divert our attention to a wrong direction. The main question is whether the castes among avarnas and savarnas, today, belong to different categories.

KANSHIRAM'S WORK

The rosy picture painted by the editor about chamars of UP is, I am afraid, not all that true. Whatever is achieved politically is not because of strengthening of chamar jati, but due to cooperation of all the various small castes. You only have to see the caste structure of seats of MPs contested by Kanshiram during last Loksabha elections, or for that matter even in recent Vidhansabha elections. Kanshiram and Mayavati have not tried to strengthen only chamar caste, as is presumed by our editor.

They have asked to strengthen all bahujans to come together and work for common good of all bahujans including dalits. They never worked for "separate but equal" castes. They always worked to bring all together, demolishing walls among the castes, never ever, they advocated salvation of any individual caste or that of an individual person within a caste.

WHAT IS KANSHIRAM'S 'JATI TODO SAMAJ JODO'

Dr. Ambedkar confirmed in 'Annihilation of Castes', that the sanction behind the sastras must end. He had given special emphasis on the 'Manu' a smriti said to be written by a brahmin pundit Sumati Bhargava at the time of counter-revolution started by Pushyamitra Shunga about 185 BC. Dr. Ambedkar attacked. It must be understood that though it is said to be religious scripture, Dr. Ambedkar considered it to be a political book, rather a law book, or you may call it the Constitution of Ancient and Medieval slave India. Only in Ambedkar's India a new Constitution is provided to this country, and that too not entirely to the satisfaction of its maker. So the fundamental way is to make the bahujan samaj understand that they are not Hindus and hence they must stop considering themselves as Hindus. They shall not follow the tenets of Manu smriti. This is happening gradually, You find that the Adivasis, though they are being coerced by the manuvadis into believing that they must follow Hindu gods and Hindu religious worship etc., are talking freely of Ambedkarism and are turning gradually away from BSO. This process is the process of 'Samaj jodo'.

This can be attributed to the work of Kanshiram in post Ambedkar era. Again I have to make it clear that at this stage, without jeopardizing stand for religious and social unity, we can only strive for political unity; the religious and social unity will have to wait. I feel, our editor, also means to achieve only political unity at this time, when he says, "What we need is not the 'unity' that destroys any identity, but an understanding and harmony which would help maintain and foster such identities to fight the oppressor. "

DALIT UNITY IS NOT ENOUGH

Without in any way denigrating the efforts of those who are striving for Dalit Unity, I feel, even if all the Dalits of India, of all castes, shades and colours, unite, they cannot achieve any power without the help of other oppressed castes, as they are only about 16% or so. And if there is no power, caravan of Ambedkar will be on retrograde journey. Many non-dalit castes are realizing the mischief done by Caste system, they are having dialogue with Dalits and uniting with them, as is seen in North Indian states.

To think that those who talk of 'Unity' belong to a 'dominant caste' and so have an unfair vested interest in 'unity', will rather be an injustice to their efforts. The dominance they achieved is not the cause of their 'Unity talks', but it is the result of it. Before Phuley, Shahu and Ambedkar thought of Unity, the condition of all dalit castes was more or less same, none was dominant and all were subservient to BSO.

SHOULD WE NOT DESTROY OUR IDENTITY?

Are various leaders ready to give up their identity on argument that Dalit liberation must get priority over all other demands? One does not have tc give up ones identity, if we are talking at this stage of only political unity. But if we unite only politically at this stage, a time will come, when we have to unite religiously and socially also. At that time, I would like to ask these leaders, "Can they afford not to dissolve their identities?" If they did, their castes would be wiped out by the BSO.

One has only to see the way these sub-castes are fighting among themselves just for crumbs, they have forgotten that their real enemy, BSO, is safe and secure in its own citadel. Even at this stage, infighting among the sub-castes is counter productive and injurious to the interest of their own caste. It is the leaders of BSO, who make them fight by showing a carrot to the stooges. It is a post Poona pact situation of proliferating chamachas, big and small. The members of Ambedkarite public have by now acquired enough knowledge and experience to identify these stooges and keep away from them. If some one likes to remind the people of this situation, let him not be labeled as selfish and his warnings condemned as being of "educated- meaning brain washed", person of a 'dominant' caste.

9

Changes in Health and Medicine

UNDERSTANDING HEALTH, MEDICINE, AND SOCIETY

The extent of a person's physical, mental, and social well-being refers to the extent of a person's physical, mental, and social well-being. This definition, taken from the World Health Organization's treatment of health, emphasizes that health is a complex concept that involves not just the soundness of a person's body but also the state of a person's mind and the quality of the social environment in which she or he lives.

The quality of the social environment in turn can affect a person's physical and mental health, underscoring the importance of social factors for these twin aspects of our overall well-being. The social institution that seeks to prevent, diagnose, and treat illness and to promote health in its various dimensions is the social institution that seeks both to prevent, diagnose, and treat illness and to promote health as just defined. Dissatisfaction with the medical establishment has been growing.

Part of this dissatisfaction stems from soaring health-care costs and what many perceive as insensitive stinginess by the health insurance industry, as the 2009 battle over health-care reform showed.

Some of the dissatisfaction also reflects a growing view that the social and even spiritual realms of human existence play a key role in health and illness. This view has fueled renewed interest in alternative medicine. We return later to these many issues for the social institution of medicine.

THE SOCIOLOGICAL APPROACH TO HEALTH AND MEDICINE

We usually think of health, illness, and medicine in individual terms. When a person becomes ill, we view the illness as a medical problem with biological causes, and a physician treats the individual accordingly. A sociological approach takes a different view. Unlike physicians, sociologists and other public health scholars do not try to understand why any one person becomes ill. Instead, they typically examine rates of illness to explain why people from certain social backgrounds are more likely than those from others to become sick.

Here, our social location in society—our social class, race and ethnicity, and gender—makes a critical difference. The fact that our social backgrounds affect our health may be difficult for many of us to accept. We all know someone, and often someone we love, who has died from a serious illness or currently suffers from one. There is always a "medical" cause of this person's illness, and physicians do their best to try to cure it and prevent it from recurring. Sometimes they succeed; sometimes they fail. Whether someone suffers a serious illness is often simply a matter of bad luck or bad genes: we can do everything right and still become ill. In saying that our social backgrounds affect our health, sociologists do not deny any of these possibilities.

They simply remind us that our social backgrounds also play an important role. A sociological approach also emphasizes that a society's culture shapes its understanding of health and illness and practice of medicine. In particular, culture shapes a society's perceptions of what it means to be healthy or ill, the reasons to which it attributes illness, and the ways in which it tries to keep its members healthy and to cure those who are sick. Knowing about a society's culture, then, helps us to understand how it perceives health and healing. By the same token, knowing about a society's health and medicine helps us to understand important aspects of its culture. An interesting example of culture in this regard is seen in Japan's aversion to organ transplants, which are much less common in that nation than in other wealthy nations. Japanese families dislike disfiguring the bodies of the dead, even for autopsies, which are also much less common in Japan than other nations.

This cultural view often prompts them to refuse permission for organ transplants when a family member dies, and it leads many Japanese to refuse to designate themselves as potential organ donors. As culture changes over time, it is also true that perceptions of health and medicine may also change. Sociology and the Sociological Perspective that physicians in top medical schools a century ago advised women not to go to college because the stress of higher education would disrupt their menstrual cycles.

This nonsensical advice reflected the sexism of the times, and we no longer accept it now, but it also shows that what it means to be healthy or ill can change as a society's culture changes. A society's culture matters in these various ways, but so does its social structure, in particular its level of economic development and extent of government involvement in health-care delivery.

Poor societies have much worse health than richer societies. At the same time, richer societies have certain health risks and health problems, such as pollution and liver disease, that poor societies avoid. The degree of government involvement in health-care delivery also matters: the United States lags behind many Western European nations in several health indicators, in part because the latter nations provide much more national health care than does the United States. Although illness is often a matter of bad luck or bad genes, then, the society we live in can nonetheless affect our chances of becoming and staying ill.

SOCIOLOGICAL PERSPECTIVES ON HEALTH AND MEDICINE

The major sociological perspectives on health and medicine all recognize these points but offer different ways of understanding health and medicine that fall into the functional, conflict, and symbolic interactionist approaches. Together they provide us with a more comprehensive understanding of health, medicine, and society than any one approach can do by itself. Table, "Theory Snapshot" summarizes what they say.

Table. Theory Snapshot

Theoretical perspective	Major assumptions
Functionalism	Good health and effective medical care are essential for the smooth functioning of society. Patients must perform the "sick role" in order to be perceived as legitimately ill and to be exempt from their normal obligations. The physician-patient relationship is hierarchical: the physician provides instructions, and the patient needs to follow them.
Conflict theory	Social inequality characterizes the quality of health and the quality of health care. People from disadvantaged social backgrounds are more likely to become ill and to receive inadequate health care. Partly to increase their incomes, physicians have tried to control the practice of medicine and to define social problems as medical problems.
Symbolic interactionism	Health and illness are *social constructions:* Physical and mental conditions have little or no objective reality but instead are considered healthy or ill conditions only if they are defined as such by a society. Physicians "manage the situation" to display their authority and medical knowledge.

The Functionalist Approach

As conceived by Talcott Parsons, the functionalist perspective on health and medicine emphasizes that good health and effective medical care are essential for a society's ability to function. Ill health obviously impairs our ability to perform our roles in society, and if too many people are unhealthy, society's functioning and stability suffer. This was especially true for premature death, said Parsons, because it prevents individuals from fully carrying out all their social roles and thus represents a "poor return" to society for the various costs of pregnancy, birth, child care, and socialization of the individual who ends up dying early. Poor medical care is likewise dysfunctional for society, as people who are ill face greater difficulty in becoming healthy and people who are healthy are more likely to become ill.

For a person to be considered *legitimately* sick, said Parsons, several expectations must be met. He referred to these expectations as the sick rolesick role expectations of how people are supposed to think and act when they are ill.. First, sick people should not be perceived as having caused their own health problem. If we eat high-fat food, become obese, and have a heart attack, we evoke less sympathy than if we had practiced good nutrition and maintained a proper weight. If someone is driving drunk and smashes into a tree, there is much less sympathy than if the driver had been sobre and skidded off the road in icy weather. Second, sick people must want to get well.

If they do not want to get well or, worse yet, are perceived as faking their illness or malingering after becoming healthier, they are no longer considered legitimately ill by the people who know them or, more generally, by society itself. Third, sick people are expected to have their illness confirmed by a physician or other health-care professional and to follow the professional's advice and instructions in order to become well. If a sick person fails to do so, she or he again loses the right to perform the sick role.

If all of these expectations are met, said Parsons, sick people are treated as sick by their family, their friends, and other people they know, and they become exempt from their normal obligations to all of these people. Sometimes they are even told to stay in bed when they want to remain active. Physicians also have a role to perform, said Parsons. First and foremost, they have to diagnose the person's illness, decide how to treat it, and help the person become well. To do so, they need the cooperation of the patient, who must answer the physician's questions accurately and follow the physician's instructions. Parsons thus viewed the physician-patient relationship as hierarchical: the physician gives the orders and the patient follows them. Parsons was certainly right in emphasizing the importance of individuals' good health for society's health, but his perspective has been criticized for several reasons.

- First, his idea of the sick role applies more to acute illness than to chronic illness. Although much of his discussion implies a person temporarily enters a sick role and leaves it soon after following adequate medical care, people with chronic illnesses can be locked into a sick role for a very long time or even permanently.
- Second, Parsons's discussion ignores the fact that our social location in society in the form of social class, race and ethnicity, and gender affects both the likelihood of becoming ill and the quality of medical care we receive.
- Third, Parsons wrote approvingly of the hierarchy implicit in the physician-patient relationship.

Many experts say today that patients need to reduce this hierarchy by asking more questions of their physicians and by taking a more active role in maintaining their health. To the extent that physicians do not always provide the best medical care, the hierarchy that Parsons favoured is at least partly to blame.

The Conflict Approach

The conflict approach emphasizes inequality in the quality of health and of health-care delivery. As noted earlier, the quality of health and health care differ greatly around the world and within the United States.

Society's inequities along social class, race and ethnicity, and gender lines are reproduced in our health and health care. People from disadvantaged social backgrounds are more likely to become ill, and once they do become ill, inadequate health care makes it more difficult for them to become well. The evidence of inequities in health and health care is vast and dramatic. The conflict approach also critiques the degree to which physicians over the decades have tried to control the practice of medicine and to define various social problems as medical ones.

Their motivation for doing so has been both good and bad. On the good side, they have believed that they are the most qualified professionals to diagnose problems and treat people who have these problems. On the negative side, they have also recognized that their financial status will improve if they succeed in characterizing social problems as medical problems and in monopolizing the treatment of these problems. Once these problems become "medicalized," their possible social roots and thus potential solutions are neglected. Several examples show conflict theory's criticism. Alternative medicine is becoming increasingly popular but so has criticism of it by the medical establishment.

Physicians may honestly feel that medical alternatives are inadequate, ineffective, or even dangerous, but they also recognize that the use of these alternatives is financially harmful to their own practices. Eating disorders also show conflict theory's criticism. Many of the women and girls who have eating disorders receive help from a physician, a psychiatrist, a psychologist, or another health-care professional. Although this care is often very helpful, the definition of eating disorders as a medical problem nonetheless provides a good source of income for the professionals who treat it and obscures its cultural roots in society's standard of beauty for women.

Obstetrical care provides another example. In most of human history, midwives or their equivalent were the people who helped pregnant women deliver their babies. In the 19th century, physicians claimed they were better trained than midwives and won legislation giving them authority to deliver babies. They may have honestly felt that midwives were inadequately trained, but they also fully recognized that obstetrical care would be quite lucrative. In a final example, many hyperactive children are now diagnosed with ADHD, or attention-deficit/hyperactivity disorder. A generation or more ago, they would have been considered merely as overly active. After Ritalin, a drug that reduces hyperactivity, was developed, their behaviour came to be considered a medical problem and the ADHD diagnosis was increasingly applied, and tens of thousands of children went to physicians' offices and were given Ritalin or similar drugs.

The definition of their behaviour as a medical problem was very lucrative for physicians and for the company that developed Ritalin, and it also obscured the possible roots of their behaviour in inadequate parenting, stultifying schools, or even gender socialization, as most hyperactive kids are boys. Critics of the conflict approach say that its assessment of health and medicine is overly harsh and its criticism of physicians' motivation far too cynical. Scientific medicine has greatly improved the health of people in the industrial world; even in the poorer nations, moreover, health has improved from a century ago, however inadequate it remains today.

Although physicians are certainly motivated, as many people are, by economic considerations, their efforts to extend their scope into previously nonmedical areas also stem from honest beliefs that people's health and lives will improve if these efforts succeed. Certainly there is some truth in this criticism of the conflict approach, but the evidence of inequality in health and medicine and of the negative aspects of the medical establishment's motivation for extending its reach remains compelling.

The Interactionist Approach

The interactionist approach emphasizes that health and illness are *social constructions*. This means that various physical and mental conditions have little or no objective reality but instead are considered healthy or ill conditions only if they are defined as such by a society and its members. The ADHD example just discussed also shows interactionist theory's concerns, as a behaviour that was not previously considered an illness came to be defined as one after the development of Ritalin. In another example, in the late 1800s opium use was quite common in the United States, as opium derivatives were included in all sorts of over-the-counter products. Opium use was considered neither a major health nor legal problem. That changed by the end of the century, as prejudice against Chinese Americans led to the banning of the opium dens they frequented, and calls for the banning of opium led to federal legislation early in the 20th century that banned most opium products except by prescription. In a more current example, an attempt to redefine obesity is now under way in the United States.

Obesity is a known health risk, but a "fat pride" movement composed mainly of heavy individuals is arguing that obesity's health risks are exaggerated and calling attention to society's discrimination against overweight people. Although such discrimination is certainly unfortunate, critics say the movement is going too far in trying to minimize obesity's risks. The symbolic interactionist approach has also provided important studies of the interaction between patients and health-care professionals. Consciously or not, physicians "manage the situation" to display their authority and medical knowledge. Patients usually have to wait a long time for the physician to show up, and the physician is often in a white lab coat; the physician is also often addressed as "Doctor," while patients are often called by their first name.

Physicians typically use complex medical terms to describe a patient's illness instead of the more simple terms used by laypeople and the patients themselves. Management of the situation is perhaps especially important during a gynecological exam. When the physician is a man, this situation is fraught with potential embarrassment and uneasiness because a man is examining and touching a woman's genital area.

Under these circumstances, the physician must act in a purely professional manner. He must indicate no personal interest in the woman's body and must instead treat the exam no differently from any other type of exam. To further "desex" the situation and reduce any potential uneasiness, a female nurse is often present during the exam. Critics fault the symbolic interactionist approach for implying that no illnesses have objective reality. Many serious health conditions do exist and put people at risk for their health regardless of what they or their society thinks. Critics also say the approach neglects the effects of social inequality for health and illness. Despite these possible faults, the symbolic interactionist approach reminds us that health and illness do have a subjective as well as an objective reality.

HEALTH AND MEDICINE IN INTERNATIONAL PERSPECTIVE

As with many topics in sociology, understanding what happens in other societies and cultures helps us to understand what happens in our own society. This part's discussion of health and health care across the globe, then, helps shed some light on what is good and bad about U. S. health and medicine.

INTERNATIONAL DISPARITIES IN HEALTH AND ILLNESS

The nations of the world differ dramatically in the quality of their health and health care. The poorest nations suffer terribly. Their people suffer from poor nutrition, unsafe water, inadequate sanitation, a plethora of diseases, and inadequate health care. One disease they suffer from is AIDS. Some 33 million people worldwide have HIV/AIDS, and two-thirds of these live in sub-Saharan Africa. Two million people, most of them from this region, died in 2008 from HIV/AIDS. All of these problems produce high rates of infant mortality and maternal mortality and high death rates. For all of these reasons, people in the poorest nations have shorter life spans than those in the richest nations.

A few health indicators should indicate the depth of the problem. An important indicator, infant mortality for nations grouped into four income categories. The striking contrast between the two groups provides dramatic evidence of the health problems poor nations face.80 children in the poorest nations die before their first birthday for every 1,000 live births, the poor nations have serious problems indeed. The world differs in access to adequate sanitation facilities. Whereas this percentage is at least 98% in the wealthy nations of North America, Western Europe, and Australia and New Zealand, it is less than 33% in many poor nations in Africa and Asia.

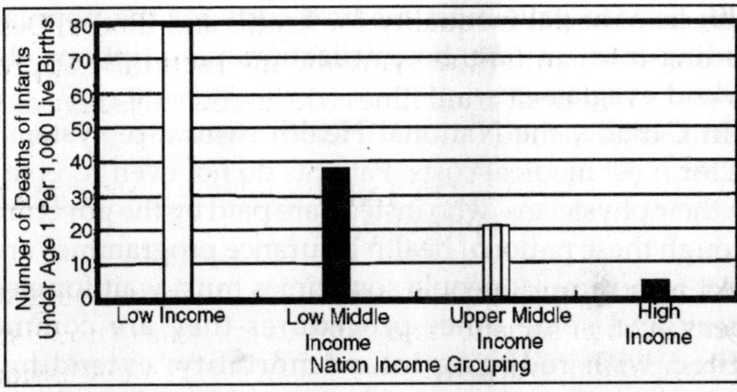

Fig. Infant Mortality for Low Income, Lower Middle Income, Higher Middle Income, and High Income Nations, 2008

Aging and the Elderly presented an international map on life expectancy. That map was certainly relevant for understanding aging around the globe but is also relevant for understanding worldwide disparities in health and health care. We reproduce this map here. Not surprisingly, the global differences in this map are similar to those for adequate sanitation, "Percentage of Population With Access to Adequate Sanitation Facilities, 2008". North America, Western Europe, and Australia and New Zealand have much longer life expectancies than Africa and Asia, where some nations have expectancies below 50 years. The society we live in can affect our life span by more than a quarter of a century.

HEALTH CARE IN INDUSTRIAL NATIONS

Industrial nations throughout the world, with the notable exception of the United States, provide their citizens with some form of national health care and national health insurance. Although their health-care systems differ in several respects, their governments pay all or most of the costs for health care, drugs, and other health needs. In Denmark, for example, the government provides free medical care and hospitalization for the entire population and pays for some medications and some dental care. In France, the government pays for some of the medical, hospitalization, and medication costs for most people and all of these expenses for the poor, unemployed, and children under the age of 10. In Great Britain, the National

Health Service pays most medical costs for the population, including medical care, hospitalization, prescriptions, dental care, and eyeglasses.

In Canada, the National Health Insurance system also pays for most medical costs. Patients do not even receive bills from their physicians, who instead are paid by the government. Although these national health insurance programmes are not perfect-for example, people sometimes must wait for elective surgery and some other procedures-they are commonly credited with reducing infant mortality, extending life expectancy, and more generally for enabling their citizenries to have relatively good health. In all of these respects, these systems offer several advantages over the health-care model found in the United States.

THEORIES OF HEALTH AND ILLNESS IN INDIA

Theories about health and illness deal with the ideas people use to explain how to maintain a healthy state and why they become ill. Ideas about illness causation may include such ideas as breach of taboo, soul loss, germs, upset in the hot-cold balance of the body, or a weakening of the body's immune system.

Theories of illness causation derive from the underlying cognitive orientation of a cultural group, and therapeutic practice usually follows the same cultural logic. Anthropologists often divide theories of illness into two broad categories: personalistic and naturalistic.

In a personalistic system, illness is believed to be caused by the intervention of a sensate agent who may be a supernatural being or a human being with special powers. The sick person's illness is considered to be a direct result of the malign influence of these agents. In naturalistic causation, illness is explained in impersonal terms. When the body is in balance with the natural environment, a state of health prevails. However, when that balance is disturbed, illness results. Often, people invoke both types of causation in explaining an episode of illness, and treatment may entail two corresponding types of therapy. The personalistic theories of illness, illness may be linked to transgressions of a moral and spiritual nature. If someone has violated a social norm or breached a religious taboo, he or she may invoke the wrath of a deity, and sickness-as a form of divine punishment-may result. Possession by evil spirits is also thought to be a cause of illness in many cultures. This may be due to inappropriate behaviour on the part of the patient-failure to carry out the proper rituals of respect for a dead ancestor, for example-or it may be simply due to bad luck.

Sometimes, one person's envy of another's good fortune is believed to exert a malign influence through the "evil eye," which can result in illness or other calamities. Witches and sorcerers are malevolent human beings who manipulate secret rituals and charms to bring calamity upon their enemies. Recovery from an illness arising from personalistic causes usually involves the use of ritual and symbolism, most often by practitioners who are specially trained in these arts. Naturalistic theories of disease causation tend to view health as a state of harmony between a human being and his or her environment; when this balance is upset, illness will result.

The humoural system is a naturalistic approach to illness whose roots are over two thousand years old. Humoural concepts of health and illness are widely found in India, southeast Asia, China, and, in a somewhat different form, in Latin and South America. Maintaining humoural balance involves attention to appropriate diet and activity, including regulating one's diet just as to the seasons. Illnesses may be categorized into those due to excess heat and those due to excess cold. Treatment of an illness of overheat would involve measures such as giving cooling foods and application of cool compresses.

In India, the ancient system of Ayurveda is based on naturalistic ideas of illness causation. Therapy in Ayurveda includes a vast pharmacopeia of preparations made from herbs and minerals, and dietary advice also forms part of every prescription. Ayurveda is actively practised in India today and has shaped the way Indians think about their bodies in health and in illness. An important set of theories about health and illness, often called "vitalist" theories, is widespread in China, South Asia, and Southeast Asia. When vital forces within the body flow in a harmonious pattern, a positive state of health is maintained. Illness results when this smooth flow of energy is disrupted, and therapeutic measures are aimed at restoring a normal flow of energy in the body. In China this vital force is known as "chi"; in India it is called "prana. " In China the ancient art of acupuncture is based on this understanding of the body.

Acupuncture needles are inserted at various points along the "meridians," or energy orientations, of the body. The stimulation of the needles helps to restore a proper flow of energy within the body. In India, yoga is used therapeutically to restore a balanced energy flow through body and mind. Biomedicine is founded on a naturalistic set of theories about the body, and these theories are continually evolving. One of the core theories of contemporary biomedicine, the germ theory of disease, is of relatively recent origin. The miasma theory of disease, poisonous emanations from rotting vegetation or carcasses were believed to cause disease. By the mid-1800s, controversy still raged as to whether miasma or a waterborne pathogen was the cause for cholera.

The "body-as-machine" metaphor has been a powerful way of conceptualizing the body within biomedicine, and a core assumption of the value system of biomedicine is that diagnosis and treatment should be based on scientific data. However, treatment approaches are often not rigorously analysed scientifically before being employed therapeutically. For example, angina pectoris has been treated in a variety of ways, including with the use of xanthines, khellin, vitamin E ligation of the internal mammary artery, and implantation of this artery. These treatments were used for many years before controlled trials finally showed that the efficacy of these treatments were no better than placebo alone.

Ritual and symbolism play important roles in the healing process in biomedicine, as they do in other healing systems. Taking a prescribed medication, for example, has a symbolic as well as a pharmacological effect. Symbolically, taking the medication may indicate to others that the person is unwell and is deserving of concern and sympathy. Surgical treatments such as coronary bypass surgery employ complex equipment and are performed in specialized settings. These settings and equipment all have powerful symbolic associations as well as technical functions. Rituals are patterned forms of behaviour that have symbolic significance, that often help to provide a context of meaning in a strange or frightening situation. Both patients who undergo the surgery and surgeons who perform the surgery are involved in rituals that serve to order a life-changing event.

The processes of obtaining informed consent, getting a patient prepped for surgery, and complex stages of post-operative care all have ritual as well as technical functions. Alternative therapies have been rapidly gaining in popularity worldwide. These therapies are diverse, ranging from traditional treatments adapted from their lands of origin, such as acupuncture and shiatsu, to newly developed forms of therapy such as therapeutic touch. Many alternative therapies have underlying theories of illness causation that are quite different from that of biomedicine. In therapies such as acupuncture, reiki, and shiatsu the concept of vital energy, or chi, is the basis for the practice.

Successful therapy is that which regulates and harmonizes energy flows. In iridology, particular areas on the iris of the eye are thought to correspond to specific body organs, and a diagnosis of malfunction of the organs can be made by an examination of the iris. Conceptually, this theory of illness links to an ancient philosophical system of "homologies" that makes connections between the cosmic and the terrestrial; between the outer environment and the inner; and between the external body and the internal body. All theories of health and illness serve to create a context of meaning within which the patient can make sense of his or her bodily experience. A meaningful context for illness usually reflects core cultural values, and allows the patient to bring order to the chaotic world of serious illness and to regain some sense of control in a frightening situation.

MEDICINE AND HEALTH CARE IN INDIA

Healthcare in India features a universal health care system run by the constituent states and territories of India. The Constitution charges every state with "raising of the level of nutrition and the standard of living of its people and the improvement of public health as among its primary duties". The National Health Policy was endorsed by the Parliament of India in 1983 and updated in 2002. However, the government sector is understaffed and under financed; poor services at state-run hospitals force many people to visit private medical practitioners.

Government hospitals, some of which are among the best hospitals in India, provide treatment at taxpayer expense. Most essential drugs are offered free of charge in these hospitals. Government hospitals provide treatment either free or at minimal charges. For example, an outpatient card at AIIMS costs a one time fee of rupees 10 and thereafter outpatient medical advice is free. In-hospital treatment costs depend on financial condition of the patient and facilities utilized by him but are usually much less than the private sector.

For instance, a patient is waived treatment costs if he is below poverty line. Another patient may seek for an air-conditioned room if he is willing to pay extra for it. The charges for basic in-hospital treatment and investigations are much less compared to the private sector. The cost for these subsidies comes from annual allocations from the central and state governments. Primary health care is provided by city and district hospitals and rural primary health centres. These hospitals provide treatment free of cost. Primary care is focused on immunization, prevention of malnutrition, pregnancy, child birth, postnatal care, and treatment of common illnesses. Patients who receive specialized care or have complicated illnesses are referred to secondary and tertiary care hospitals. In recent times, India has eradicated mass famines, however the country still suffers from high levels of malnutrition and disease especially in rural areas. Water supply and sanitation in India is also a major issue in the country and many Indians in rural areas lack access to proper sanitation facilities and safe drinking water. However, at the same time, India's health care system also includes entities that meet or exceed international quality standards. The medical tourism business in India has been growing in recent years and as such India is a popular destination for medical tourists who receive effective medical treatment at lower costs than in developed countries.

HEALTHCARE INFRASTRUCTURE

The Indian healthcare industry is seen to be growing at a rapid pace and is expected to become a ₹280 billion industry by 2020. The Indian healthcare market was estimated at ₹35 billion in 2007 and is expected to reach over ₹70 billion by 2012 and ₹145 billion by 2017. The Investment Commission of India the healthcare sector has experienced phenomenal growth of 12 per cent per annum in the last 4 years. Rising income levels and a growing elderly population are all factors that are driving this growth. In addition, changing demographics, disease profiles and the shift from chronic to lifestyle diseases in the country has led to increased spending on healthcare delivery.

Even so, the vast majority of the country suffers from a poor standard of healthcare infrastructure which has not kept up with the growing economy. Despite having centres of excellence in healthcare delivery, these facilities are limited and are inadequate in meeting the current healthcare demands. Nearly one million Indians die every year due to inadequate healthcare facilities and 700 million people have no access to specialist care and 80% of specialists live in urban areas. In order to meet manpower shortages and reach world standards India would require investments of up to ₹20 billion over the next 5 years. Forty per cent of the primary health centres in India are understaffed.

WHO statistics there are over 250 medical colleges in the modern system of medicine and over 400 in the Indian system of medicine and homeopathy. India produces over 250,000 doctors annually in the modern system of medicine and a similar number of ISM&H practitioners, nurses and para professionals. Better policy regulations and the establishment of public private partnerships are possible solutions to the problem of manpower shortage. India faces a huge need gap in terms of availability of number of hospital beds per 1000 population. With a world average of 3.96 hospital beds per 1000 population India stands just a little over 0.7 hospital beds per 1000 population.. Moreover, India faces a shortage of doctors, nurses and paramedics that are needed to propel the growing healthcare industry.

India is now looking at establishing academic medical centres for the delivery of higher quality care with leading examples of The Manipal Group and All India Institute of Medical Sciences already in place. As incomes rise and the number of available financing options in terms of health insurance policies increase, consumers become more and more engaged in making informed decisions about their health and are well aware of the costs associated with those decisions. In order to remain competitive, healthcare providers are now not only looking at improving operational efficiency but are also looking at ways of enhancing patient experience overall. India has approximately 600,000 allopathic doctors registered to practice medicine. This number however, is higher than the actual number practicing because it includes doctors who have emigrated to other countries as well as doctors who have died. India licenses 18,000 new doctors a year..

CENTRAL GOVERNMENT'S ROLE

Critics say that the national policy lacks specific measures to achieve broad stated goals. Particular problems include the failure to integrate health services with wider economic and social development, the lack of nutritional support and sanitation, and the poor participatory involvement at the local level. Central government efforts at influencing public health have focused on the five-year plans, on coordinated planning with the states, and on sponsoring major health programmes. Government expenditures are jointly shared by the central and state governments. Goals and strategies are set through central-state government consultations of the Central Council of

Health and Family Welfare. Central government efforts are administered by the Ministry of Health and Family Welfare, which provides both administrative and technical services and manages medical education. States provide public services and health education. The 1983 National Health Policy is committed to providing health services to all by 2000. In 1983 health care expenditures varied greatly among the states and union territories, from ₹13 per capita in Bihar to ₹60 per capita in Himachal Pradesh, and Indian per capita expenditure was low when compared with other Asian countries outside of South Asia.

Although government health care spending progressively grew throughout the 1980s, such spending as a percentage of the gross national product remained fairly constant. In the meantime, health care spending as a share of total government spending decreased. During the same period, private-sector spending on health care was about 1.5 times as much as government spending.

EXPENDITURE

In the mid-1990s, health spending amounted to 6% of GDP, one of the highest levels among developing nations. The established per capita spending is around ₹320 per year with the major input from private households. State governments contribute 15.2%, the central government 5.2%, third-party insurance and employers 3.3%, and municipal government and foreign donors about 1.3, just as to a 1995 World Bank study. Of these proportions, 58.7% goes towards primary health care and 38.8% is spent on secondary and tertiary inpatient care.

The rest goes for nonservice costs. The fifth and sixth five-year plans included programmes to assist delivery of preventive medicine and improve the health status of the rural population. Supplemental nutrition programmes and increasing the supply of safe drinking water were high priorities. The sixth plan aimed at training more community health workers and increasing efforts to control communicable diseases. There were also efforts to improve regional imbalances in the distribution of health care resources. The Seventh Five-Year Plan budgeted ₹33.9 billion for health, an amount roughly double the outlay of the sixth plan. Health spending as a portion of total plan outlays, however, had declined over the years since the first plan in 1951, from a high of 3.3% of the total plan spending in FY 1951-55 to 1.9% of the total for the seventh plan. Mid-way through the Eighth Five-Year Plan, however, health and family welfare was budgeted at ₹20 billion, or 4.3% of the total plan spending for FY 1994, with an additional ₹3.6 billion in the nonplan budget.

PRIMARY SERVICES

Health care facilities and personnel increased substantially between the early 1950s and early 1980s, but because of fast population growth, the number of licensed medical practitioners per 10,000 individuals had fallen by the late 1980s to three per 10,000 from the 1981 level of four per 10,000. In 1991 there were approximately ten hospital beds per 10,000 individuals. For comparison, in China there are 1.4 doctors per 1000 people.

Primary health centres are the cornerstone of the rural health care system. By 1991, India had about 22,400 primary health centres, 11,200 hospitals, and 27,400 clinics. These facilities are part of a tiered health care system that funnels more difficult cases into urban hospitals while attempting to provide routine medical care to the vast majority in the countryside. Primary health centres and subcentres rely on trained paramedics to meet most of their needs. The main problems affecting the success of primary health centres are the predominance of clinical and curative concerns over the intended emphasis on preventive work and the reluctance of staff to work in rural areas.

In addition, the integration of health services with family planning programmes often causes the local population to perceive the primary health centres as hostile to their traditional preference for large families. Therefore, primary health centres often play an adversarial role in local efforts to implement national health policies. In 1989 by the Ministry of

Health and Family Welfare, the total number of civilian hospitals for all states and union territories combined was 10,157. In 1991 there was a total of 811,000 hospital and health care facilities beds. The geographical distribution of hospitals varied just as to local socio-economic conditions. In India's most populous state, Uttar Pradesh, with a 1991 population of more than 139 million, there were 735 hospitals as of 1990. In Kerala, with a 1991 population of 29 million occupying an area only one-seventh the size of Uttar Pradesh, there were 2,053 hospitals.

Although central government has set a goal of health care for all by 2000, hospitals are distributed unevenly. Private studies of India's total number of hospitals in the early 1990s were more conservative than official Indian data, estimating that in 1992 there were 7,300 hospitals. Of this total, nearly 4,000 were owned and managed by central, state, or local governments. Another 2,000, owned and managed by charitable trusts, received partial support from the government, and the remaining 1,300 hospitals, many of which were relatively small facilities, were owned and managed by the private sector. The use of state-of-the-art medical equipment was primarily limited to urban centres in the early 1990s. A network of regional cancer diagnostic and treatment facilities was being established in the early 1990s in major hospitals that were part of government medical colleges.

By 1992 twenty-two such centres were in operation. Most of the 1,300 private hospitals lacked sophisticated medical facilities, although in 1992 approximately 12% possessed state-of-the-art equipment for diagnosis and treatment of all major diseases, including cancer. The fast pace of development of the private medical sector and the burgeoning middle class in the 1990s have led to the emergence of the new concept in India of establishing hospitals and health care facilities on a for-profit basis.

By the late 1980s, there were approximately 128 medical colleges-roughly three times more than in 1950. These medical colleges in 1987 accepted a combined annual class of 14,166 students. Data for 1987 show that there were 320,000 registered medical practitioners and 219,300 registered nurses. Various studies have shown that in both urban and rural areas people preferred to pay and seek the more sophisticated services provided by private physicians rather than use free treatment at public health centres.

TRADITIONAL PRACTICES

Indigenous or traditional medical practitioners continue to practice throughout the country. The two main forms of traditional medicine practised are the ayurvedic system, which deals with mental and spiritual as well as physical well-being, and the unani herbal medical practice. A vaidya is a practitioner of the ayurvedic tradition, and a hakim is a practitioner of the unani or Greek tradition. These professions are frequently hereditary.

A variety of institutions offer training in indigenous medical practice. Only in the late 1970s did official health policy refer to any form of integration between European-trained medical personnel and indigenous medical practitioners. In the early 1990s, there were ninety-eight ayurvedic colleges and seventeen unani colleges operating in both the governmental and non-governmental sectors.

HEALTH INSURANCE

The majority of the Indian population is unable to access high quality healthcare provided by private players as a result of high costs. Many are now looking towards insurance companies for providing alternative financing options so that they too may seek better quality healthcare. The opportunity remains huge for insurance providers entering into the Indian healthcare market since 75% of expenditure on healthcare in India is still being met by 'out-of-pocket' consumers.

Even though only 10% of the Indian population today has health insurance coverage, this industry is expected to face tremendous growth over the next few years as a result of several private players that have entered into the market. Health insurance coverage among urban, middle- and upper-class Indians, however, is significantly higher and stands at approximately 50%. The Insurance Regulatory and Development Authority is the governing body responsible for promoting insurance business and introducing insurance regulations in India. The share of public sector companies in health insurance premiums was 76% and that of private sector companies was 24% for the period 2005-06. Health insurance premiums collected over 2005-06 registered a growth of 35% over the previous year.

In 2001 the IRDA introduced provisions for Third Party Administrators to support the administration and management of health insurance products offered by insurance companies. TPAs are facilitators in the coordination process between the health insurance provider and the hospital. Currently there are 27 TPAs registered under the IRDA. Health insurance has a way of increasing accessibility to quality healthcare delivery especially for private healthcare providers for whom high cost remains a barrier. In order to encourage foreign health insurers to enter the Indian market the government has recently proposed to raise the foreign direct investment limit in insurance from 26% to 49%. Increasing health insurance penetration and ensuring affordable premium rates are necessary to drive the health insurance market in India.

ISSUES

Disease

India suffers from high levels of disease including Malaria, and Tuberculosis where one third of the world's tuberculosis cases are in India. In addition, India along with Nigeria, Pakistan and Afghanistan is one of the four countries worldwide where polio has not as yet been eradicated. Ongoing government of India education about HIV has led to decreases in the spread of HIV in recent years. The number of people living with AIDS in India is estimated to be between 2 and 3 million. However in terms of the total population this is a small number. The country has had a sharp decrease in the estimated number of HIV infections; 2005 reports had claimed that there were 5.2 million to 5.7 million people afflicted with the virus.

Pollution

The World Health Organization 900,000 Indians die each year from drinking contaminated water and breathing in polluted air. As India grapples with these basic issues, new challenges are emerging for example there is a rise in chronic adult diseases such as cardiovascular illnesses and diabetes as a consequence of changing lifestyles.

Malnutrition

Half of children in India are underweight, one of the highest rates in the world and nearly same as Sub-Saharan Africa. India contributes to about 5.6 million child deaths every year, more than half the world's total.

Water and Sanitation

Water supply and sanitation in India is a matter of concern. As of 2003, it was estimated that only 30% of India's wastewater was being treated, with the remainder flowing into rivers or groundwater. The lack of toilet facilities in many areas also presents a major health risk; open defecation is widespread even in urban areas of India, and it was estimated in 2002 by the World Health Organisation that around 700,000 Indians die each year from diarrhoea. No city in India has full-day water supply. Most cities supply water only a few hours a day. In towns and rural areas the situation is even worse.

MEDICAL TOURISM

India is quickly becoming a hub for medical tourists seeking quality healthcare at an affordable cost. Nearly 450,000 foreigners sought medical treatment in India last year with Singapore not too far behind and Thailand in the lead with over a million medical tourists. As the Indian healthcare delivery system strives to match international standards the Indian healthcare industry will be able to tap into a substantial portion of the medical tourism market. Already 13 Indian hospitals have been accredited by the Joint Commission International. Accreditation and compliance with quality expectations are important since they provide tourists with confidence that the services are meeting international standards. Reduced costs, access to the latest medical technology, growing compliance to international quality standards and ease of communication all work towards India's advantage. It is not uncommon to see citizens of other nations seek high quality medical care in the US over the past several decades; however in recent times the pattern seems to be reversing.

As healthcare costs in the US are rising, price sensitivity is soaring and people are looking at medical value travel as a viable alternative option. In the past the growth potential of the medical travel industry in India has been hindered by capacity and infrastructure constraints but that situation is now changing with strong economic progress in India as well as in other developing nations. With more and more hospitals receiving JCI accreditations outside the US, concerns on safety and quality of care are becoming less of an issue for those choosing to travel for medical treatment at an affordable cost.

The combined cost of travel and treatment in India is still a fraction of the amount spent on just medical treatment alone in western countries. In order to attract foreign patients many Indian hospitals are promoting their international quality of healthcare delivery by turning to international accreditation agencies to standardize their protocols and obtain the required approvals on safety and quality of care.

IMPORTANT POINTS

- A sociological approach emphasizes the relationship between health, medicine, and society. Our social backgrounds influence our health and access to health care, while the culture and social structure of a society influences its perceptions of health and illness and ways of healing.
- Sociological perspectives on health and illness fall into the functional, conflict, and interactionist approaches encountered. The functional view emphasizes the importance of health for a society's stability and the roles that people play when they

are sick. The conflict view stresses inequality in the quality of health and health-care delivery and efforts by physicians to monopolize the practice of medicine to increase their profits. Health and illness are social constructions subject to people's and society's interpretations. The interactionist view also studies how medical professionals and patients interact and the way professionals manage understandings of such interaction.

- Health and the quality of health care differ widely around the world and reflect global stratification. The earth's poorest nations have extremely high rates of infant mortality and life-threatening diseases such as AIDS and very low life expectancy. Despite efforts of organizations like the World Health Organization, the poor health of the poor nations' residents remains a serious problem.
- The United States ranks ahead of most of the world's nations in most health indicators, and health in the United States has greatly improved in the last century. At the same time, the United States lags behind most other industrial nations in important health indicators such as infant mortality and life expectancy. Moreover, serious disparities exist within the United States in the social distribution of health, as evidenced by the study of social epidemiology.
- Social class, race and ethnicity, and gender all affect the quality of health. Poor people lack health insurance and access to health, face high amounts of stress, live in unhealthy social and physical environments, and are more apt to engage in unhealthy lifestyles. For all of these reasons, their health is worse than that of the nonpoor. African Americans, Hispanics, and Native Americans all fare worse than whites on many health indicators, in large part because of their poverty and history of discrimination. Women fare worse than men on several heath indicators, but men have lower life

expectancies because of their higher rates of certain life-threatening illnesses. These rates are thought to be due to men's biology, unhealthy lifestyles brought on by their masculine socialization, and unwillingness to seek medical treatment.

- Social factors also help explain different rates of mental illness. The poor have higher rates of mental disorders than the nonpoor because of the stress of poverty and other negative life conditions. Women are more likely than men to be depressed and to suffer from some other disorders, but men are more likely to have antisocial personality disorders with symptoms that make them a threat to others. Clear racial and ethnic differences in mental disorders have not been found, perhaps because the strong family bonds and religious faith of many minorities help protect them from disorders that would otherwise be expected from their poverty and discrimination. In looking at Mexican-Americans, there's some evidence that living in American society raises the risks of mental disorders.
- The history of medicine reflects a move from religious and spiritual approaches to healing to scientific approaches. In prehistoric societies priests tried to appease the angry gods or chase away the evil spirits who were thought to cause physical and mental illness. Ancient civilizations made great advances in our understanding of health and illness, and the rise of scientific medicine beginning in the 1600s helped pave the path for today's scientific approach.
- Despite these medical advances, health care in the United States today faces several problems. The United States is alone in not offering universal national health insurance; its absence is thought to help account for the country's low ranking in the industrial world on major health indicators, as significant numbers of our poor and minorities lack health insurance. Managed care has also come under

criticism for restricting coverage of important medical procedures and prescription medicines. Racial and gender bias in health care is another problem that has adverse effects on the nation's health. Other quality-of-care problems include tired physicians, a lack of emergency-room physicians, and numerous mistakes made in hospitals. Disagreement over alternative medicine reflects the historic battle between the medical establishment and other healers, while self-referral and other issues raise important questions for medical ethics. Meanwhile, health-care fraud costs the nation some ₹100 billion annually and remains an important problem for the nation to address.

10

Social Movements

AN INTRODUCTION

Social movements in the United States and other nations have been great forces for social change. At the same time, governments and other opponents have often tried to thwart the movements' efforts. To understand how and why social change happens, we have to understand why movements begin, how they succeed and fail, and what impact they may have.

UNDERSTANDING SOCIAL MOVEMENTS

To begin this understanding, we first need to understand what social movements are. A social movement, an organized effort by a large number of people to bring about or impede social change may be defined as an organized effort by a large number of people to bring about or impede social change. Defined in this way, social movements might sound similar to special-interest groups, and they do have some things in common. But a major difference between social movements and special-interest groups lies in the nature of their actions.

Special-interest groups normally work *within the system* via conventional political activities such as lobbying and election campaigning. In contrast, social movements often work *outside the system* by engaging in various kinds of protest, including demonstrations, picket lines, sit-ins, and sometimes outright violence. Conceived in this way, the efforts of social movements amount to "politics by other means," with these "other means" made necessary because movements lack the resources and access to the political system that interest groups typically enjoy.

TYPES OF SOCIAL MOVEMENTS

Sociologists identify several types of social movements just as to the nature and extent of the change they seek. This typology helps us understand the differences among the many kinds of social movements that existed in the past and continue to exist today. One of the most common and important types of social movements is the *reform* movement, which seeks limited, though still significant, changes in some aspect of a nation's political, economic, or social systems.

It does not try to overthrow the existing government but rather works to improve conditions within the existing regime. Some of the most important social movements in U. S. history have been reform movements. These include the abolitionist movement preceding the Civil War, the woman suffrage movement that followed the Civil War, the labour movement, the Southern civil rights movement, the Vietnam antiwar movement, the contemporary women's movement, the gay rights movement, and the environmental movement. A *revolutionary* movement goes one large step further than a reform movement in seeking to overthrow the existing government and to bring about a new one and even a new way of life.

Revolutionary movements were common in the past and were responsible for the world's great revolutions in Russia, China, and several other nations. Reform and revolutionary movements are often referred to as *political* movements because the changes they seek are political in nature. Another type of political movement is the *reactionary* movement, so named because it tries to block social change or to reverse social changes that have already been achieved. The antiabortion movement is a contemporary example of a reactionary movement, as it arose after the U. S. Supreme Court legalized most abortions in *Roe v. Wade* and seeks to limit or eliminate the legality of abortion. Two other types of movements are *self-help* movements and *religious* movements. As their name implies, self-help movements involve people trying to improve aspects of their personal lives; examples of self-help groups include Alcoholics Anonymous and Weight Watchers. Religious movements aim to reinforce religious beliefs among their members and to convert other people to these beliefs.

THE ORIGINS OF SOCIAL MOVEMENTS

To understand how and why social movements begin, we need answers to two related questions. First, what are the social, economic, and political conditions that give rise to social movements? They do not arise in a vacuum, and certain macro problems in society must exist for movements to begin. Second, once social movements do begin, why are some individuals more likely than others to take part in them? Answers to this question usually focus on personality and other micro factors. As suggested, start with these micro factors and then turn to the macro conditions that make movements possible in the first place.

Micro Factors: Emphasis on the Individual

Over the years social scientists have tried to explain why some individuals are more likely than others to join social movements. Their explanations centre on several factors.

The Question of Irrationality

One issue is whether social movement involvement is *rational* or *irrational*. Early thinkers such as Gustavo LeBon, a French intellectual, thought that social movement involvement and, more generally, crowd behaviour were the product of *irrational impulses*. Writing in the wake of the French Revolution of 1789, these thinkers worried that social order was breaking down.

LeBon in particular blamed crowds for turning normally rational individuals into irrational and emotional actors who are virtually hypnotized by the crowd's mind-set. American sociologists early in the 20th century adopted LeBon's view. In so doing, they viewed social movement participation as more *expressive*, or emotional, than *instrumental*, or directed at achieving specific goals. Just after the mid-20th century, Ralph H. Turner and Lewis M. Killian presented their *emergent norm* view of collective behaviour, which downplayed the irrationality emphasized in earlier formulations.

Turner and Killian, when people start interacting in collective behaviour, they are not sure initially how they are supposed to behave. As they discuss their potential behaviour and other related matters, norms governing their behaviour emerge, and social order and rationality then guide behaviour. Adopting this view, most sociologists today feel that people taking part in social movements are indeed acting rationally and instrumentally, not just expressively. Although they have emotions, that does not mean their behaviour is any less rational or political.

Relative Deprivation

Another important line of thought has centred on relative deprivationrelative deprivation. The feeling by individuals that they are deprived relative to some other group or to some ideal state they have not reached., or the feeling by individuals that they are deprived relative to some other group or to some ideal state they have not reached. This view was popularized by James C. Davies and Ted Robert Gurr, both of whom built upon the earlier work of social psychologists who had studied frustration and aggression. When a deprived group perceives that social conditions are improving, wrote Davies, they become hopeful that their lives are getting better.

But if these conditions stop improving, they become frustrated and more apt to turn to protest, collective violence, and other social movement activity. Both Davies and Gurr emphasized that people's *feelings* of being relatively deprived were more important for the involvement in collective behaviour than their level of actual deprivation. Relative deprivation theory was initially very popular, but scholars later pointed out that frustration often does not lead to protest, as people can instead blame themselves for the deprivation they feel and thus not protest. Scholars who favour the theory point out that people will ordinarily not take part in social movements unless they feel deprived, even if many who do feel deprived do not take part.

Social Isolation Versus Social Attachments

A final micro issue has been whether the individuals participating in social movements are isolated from society or very much a part of it. Are they loners, or are they involved in social networks of friends, coworkers, and others? *The Politics of Mass Society,* William Kornhauser wrote that because modern societies are impersonal with weak social ties, individuals who are loners become involved in social movements to provide them the friendships and social bonding they otherwise lack.

Kornhauser's mass society theory mass society theory William Kornhauser's view that social isolation prompts involvement in collective behaviour and social movements was popular for a time, but much research finds that the people who join social movements are in fact very much a part of society instead of loners. They have many friends and belong to several organizations, and these friendship and organizational ties help "pull" them into social movements.

Macro Factors: Emphasis on Social Structure

Structural explanations of social movements try to understand why social movements are more likely to arise in some historical periods and locations than in others. In effect, they try to show how certain social, economic, and political conditions give rise to social movements. We discuss some of these explanations here.

Smelser's Structural-Strain Theory

One of the most popular and influential structural explanations is Neil Smelser's structural-strain theory structural-strain theory Neil Smelser's view that social movements and other collective behaviour occur and persist when six conditions are present: structural conduciveness, structural strain, generalized beliefs, precipitating factors, mobilization for action, and weak social control.. Smelser wrote that social movements and other collective behaviour occur when several conditions are present. One of these conditions is *structural strain,* which refers to problems in society that cause people to be angry and frustrated. Without such structural strain, people would not have any reason to protest, and social movements do not arise.

Another condition is *generalized beliefs,* which are people's reasons for why conditions are so bad and their solutions to improve them. If people decide that the conditions they dislike are their own fault, they will decide not to protest. Similarly, if they decide that protest will not improve these conditions, they again will not protest. A third condition is the existence of *precipitating factors,* or sudden events that ignite collective behaviour. In the 1960s, for example, several urban riots started when police were rumored to have unjustly arrested or beaten someone.

Although conditions in inner cities were widely perceived as unfair and even oppressive, it took this type of police behaviour to ignite people to riot. Smelser's theory became very popular because it pointed to several factors that must hold true before social movements and other forms of collective behaviour occur. At the same time, collective behaviour does not always occur when his factors do hold true. The theory has also been criticized for being a bit vague; for example, it does not say how much strain a society must have for collective behaviour to take place.

Resource Mobilization Theory

Resource mobilization theory resource mobilization theory. The view that social movements are a rational response to perceived grievances and that they arise from efforts by social movement leaders to mobilize the resources, especially the time, money, and energy, of aggrieved peoples and to direct them into effective political action is a general name given to several related views of social movements that arose in the 1970s. This theory assumes that social movement activity is a rational response to unsatisfactory conditions in society. Because these conditions always exist, so does discontent with them. Despite such constant discontent, people protest only rarely. If this is so, these conditions and associated discontent cannot easily explain why people turn to social movements. What is crucial instead are efforts by social movement leaders to mobilize the resources—most notably, time, money, and energy—of the population and to direct them into effective political action.

Also important are *political opportunities* for action that arise when, say, a government weakens because of an economic or foreign crisis. Resource mobilization theory has been very influential since its inception in the 1970s. However, critics say it underestimates the importance of harsh social conditions and discontent for the rise of social movement activity. Conditions can and do worsen, and when they do so, they prompt people to engage in collective behaviour.

As just one example, cuts in higher education spending and steep increases in tuition prompted students to protest on campuses in California and several other states in late 2009 and early 2010. Critics also say that resource mobilization theory neglects the importance of emotions in social movement activity by depicting social movement actors as cold, calculated, and unemotional. This picture is simply not true, critics say, and they further argue that social movement actors can be both emotional and rational at the same time, just as people are in many other kinds of pursuits.

THE LIFE CYCLE OF SOCIAL MOVEMENTS

Although the many past and present social movements around the world differ from each other in many ways, they all generally go through a life cycle marked by several stages that have long been recognized.

Stage 1 is *emergence*: This stage is obviously when social movements begin for one or more of the reasons. Stage 2 is *coalescence*. At this stage a movement and its leaders must decide how they will recruit new members and they must determine the strategies they will use to achieve their goals. They also may use the news media to win favourable publicity and to convince the public of the justness of their cause. Stage

3 is *institutionalization* or *bureaucratization*. As a movement grows, it often tends to become bureaucratized, as paid leaders and a paid staff replace the volunteers that began the movement. It also means that clear lines of authority develop, as they do in any bureaucracy. More attention is also devoted to fund-raising.

As movement organizations bureaucratize, they may well reduce their effectiveness by turning from the disruptive activities that succeeded in the movement's earlier stages to more conventional activity by working within the system instead of outside it.

At the same time, if movements do not bureaucratize to at least some degree, they may lose their focus and not have enough money to keep on going. Stage 4 is the *decline* of a social movement.

Social movements eventually decline for one or more of many reasons. Sometimes they achieve their goals and naturally cease because there is no more reason to continue. More often, however, they decline because they fail.

Both the lack of money and loss of enthusiasm among a movement's members may lead to a movement's decline, and so might *factionalism*, or strong divisions of opinion within a movement. The government may also "co-opt" a movement by granting it small, mostly symbolic concessions that reduce people's discontent but leave the conditions that originally motivated their activism largely intact. As noted earlier, movements also may decline because of government repression.

HOW SOCIAL MOVEMENTS MAKE A DIFFERENCE

By definition, social movements often operate outside of the political system by engaging in protest. Their rallies, demonstrations, sit-ins, and silent vigils are often difficult to ignore. With the aid of news media coverage, these events often throw much attention on the problem or grievance at the centre of the protest and bring pressure to bear on the government agencies, corporations, or other targets of the protest. As noted earlier, there are many examples of profound changes brought about by social movements throughout U. S. history. The abolitionist movement called attention to the evils of slavery and increased public abhorrence for that "peculiar institution." The woman suffrage movement after the Civil War eventually won women the right to vote with the ratification of the 19th Amendment in 1920.

The labour movement of the late 19th and early 20th centuries established the minimum wage, the 40-hour workweek, and the right to strike. The civil rights movement of the 1950s and 1960s ended legal segregation in the South, while the Vietnam antiwar movement of the 1960s and 1970s helped increase public opposition to that war and bring it to a close. The contemporary women's movement has won many rights in social institutions throughout American society, while the gay rights movement has done the same for gays and lesbians. Another contemporary movement is the environmental movement, which has helped win legislation and other policies that have reduced air, water, and ground pollution.

Although it seems obvious that social movements have made a considerable difference, social movement scholars until recently have paid much more attention to the origins of social movements than to their consequences. Recent work has begun to fill in this gap and has focused on the consequences of social movements for the political system, for various aspects of the society's culture, and for the lives of the people who take part in movements. Regarding political consequences, scholars have considered such matters as whether movements are more successful when they use more protest or less protest, and when they focus on a single issue versus multiple issues.

The use of a greater amount of protest seems to be more effective in this regard, as does a focus on a single issue. Research has also found that movements are more likely to succeed when the government against which they protest is weakened by economic or other problems. In another line of inquiry, movement scholars disagree over whether movements are more successful if their organizations are bureaucratic and centralized or if they remain decentralized and thus more likely to engage in protest. Regarding cultural consequences, movements often influence certain aspects of a society's culture whether or not they intend to do so and, as one scholar has said, "it is perhaps precisely in being able to alter their broader cultural environment that movements can have their deepest and lasting impact".

Social movements can affect values and beliefs, and they can affect cultural practices such as music, literature, and even fashion. Movements may also have biographical consequences. Several studies find that people who take part in social movements during their formative years are often transformed by their participation. Their political views change or are at least reinforced, and they are more likely to continue to be involved in political activity and to enter social change occupations. In this manner, writes one scholar, "people who have been involved in social movement activities, even at a lower level of commitment, carry the consequences of that involvement throughout their life".

IMPORTANT POINTS

- Social change involves the transformation of cultural norms and values, behaviour, social institutions, and social structure. As societies become more modern, they become larger, more heterogeneous, and more impersonal, and their sense of community declines. Traditions decline as well, while individual freedom of thought and behaviour increases. Some sociologists view modernization positively, while others view it negatively. Tönnies in particular lamented the shift from the Gemeinschaft of premodern societies to the Gesellschaft of modern societies. Durkheim also recognized the negative aspects of modernization but at the same time valued the freedom of modern societies and thought they retain a good amount of social solidarity from their division of labour.
- A functionalist understanding of social change emphasizes that it's both natural and inevitable. Talcott Parsons's equilibrium model recognized that

gradual change is desirable and ordinarily stems from such things as population growth and technological advances, but that any sudden social change disrupts society's equilibrium. Taking a very different view, conflict theory stresses that sudden social change is often both necessary and desirable to reduce inequality and to address other problems in society. Such social change often stems from intentional efforts by social movements to correct perceived deficiencies in the social, economic, and political systems.

- Several sources of social change exist. These include population growth and changes in population composition, changes in culture and technology, changes in the natural environment, and social and ethnic conflict.
- Demography is the study of population. It encompasses three central concepts: fertility, morality, and migration, which together determine population growth. Fertility and mortality vary by race and ethnicity, and they also vary around the world, with low-income nations having both higher fertility and higher mortality than high-income nations.
- The world's population is growing by about 80 million people annually. Population growth is greatest in the low-income nations of Africa and other regions, while in several industrial nations it's actually on the decline because birth rates have become so low. The world's population reached 6.8 billion by the beginning of the 21st century and is projected to grow to more than 9 billion by 2050, with most of this occurring in low-income nations. The annual rate of population growth will decline in the years ahead.
- Thomas Malthus predicted that the earth's population would greatly exceed the world's food supply. Although his prediction did not come true,

hunger remains a serious problem around the world. Although food supply is generally ample thanks to improved technology, the distribution of food is inadequate in low-income nations. Fresh water in these regions is also lacking. Demographic transition theory helps explain why population growth did not continue to rise as much as Malthus predicted. As societies become more technologically advanced, first death rates and then birth rates decline, leading eventually to little population growth.

- Urbanization is a consequence of population growth. Cities first developed in ancient times after the rise of horticultural and pastoral societies and "took off" during the Industrial Revolution as people moved to be near factories. Urbanization led to many social changes then and continues today to affect society.
- Sociologists have long been interested in the city and have both positive and negative views of urbanization and city life. Contemporary research supports Wirth's hypothesis that tolerance for nontraditional beliefs and behaviours will be higher in urban areas than in rural areas.
- Social movements have been important agents for social change. Common types of social movements include reform movements, revolutionary movements, reactionary movements, and self-help and religious movements.
- Explanations of social movements address both micro and macro factors. Important issues at the micro level include the question of irrationality, the importance of relative deprivation, and the impact of social isolation. Macro theories address the social, economic, and political conditions underlying collective behaviour. Two of the most important such theories are Smelser's structural-strain theory and resource mobilization theory.
- Most social movements go through a life cycle of four stages: emergence, coalescence, bureaucratization,

and decline. Decline stems from several reasons, including internal divisions and repressive efforts by the state.

- Social movements have political, cultural, and biographical consequences. Research finds that movements are more successful in the political arena when they use more rather than less protest and when they focus on a single issue rather than multiple issues.

11

Culture and Society

CULTURE AND THE SOCIOLOGICAL PERSPECTIVE

As this evidence on kissing suggests, what seems to us a very natural, even instinctual act turns out not to be so natural and biological after all. Instead, kissing seems best understood as something we learn to enjoy from our culture.

The artifacts and ways of thinking, feeling, and acting that are part of any society., or the symbols, language, beliefs, values, and artifacts that are part of a society. Because Society, Sociology and the Sociological Perspective, refers to a group of people who live in a defined territory and who share a culture, it is obvious that culture is a critical component of any society.

If the culture we learn influences our beliefs and behaviours, then culture is a key concept to the sociological perspective. Someone who grows up in the United States differs in many ways, some of them obvious and some of them not so obvious, from someone growing up in China, Sweden, South Korea, Peru, or Nigeria. Culture influences not only language but the gestures we use when we interact, how far apart we stand from each other when we talk, and the values we consider most important for our children to learn, to name just a few. Without culture, we could not have a society.

The profound impact of culture becomes most evident when we examine behaviours or conditions that, like kissing, are normally considered biological in nature. Consider morning sickness and labour pains, both very familiar to pregnant women before and during childbirth, respectively.

These two types of discomfort have known biological causes, and we are not surprised that so many pregnant women experience them. But we *would* be surprised if the husbands of pregnant women woke up sick in the morning during their wives' pregnancies or experienced severe abdominal pains while their wives gave birth.

These men are neither carrying nor delivering a baby, and there is no logical—that is, biological—reason for them to suffer either type of discomfort. And yet anthropologists have discovered several societies in which men about to become fathers experience precisely these symptoms. They are nauseous during their wives' pregnancies, and they experience labour pains while their wives give birth. The term *couvade* refers to these symptoms, which do not have any known biological origin. Yet the men feel them nonetheless, because they have learned from their culture that they *should* feel these types of discomfort. And because they should feel these symptoms, they actually do so.

Perhaps their minds are playing tricks on them, but that is often the point of culture. As sociologists William I. and Dorothy Swaine Thomas once pointed out, if things are perceived as real, then they are real in their consequences. These men learn how they should feel as budding fathers, and thus they feel this way. Unfortunately for them, the perceptions they learn from their culture are real in their consequences. The example of drunkenness further shows how cultural expectations influence a behaviour that is commonly thought to have biological causes. In the United States, when people drink too much alcohol, they become intoxicated and their behaviour changes.

Most typically, their inhibitions lower and they become loud, boisterous, and even rowdy. We attribute these changes to alcohol's biological effect as a drug on our central nervous system, and scientists have documented how alcohol breaks down in our body to achieve this effect. This explanation of alcohol's effect is OK as far as it goes, but it turns out that *how* alcohol affects our behaviour depends on our culture. In some societies anthropologists have studied, people drink alcohol until they pass out, but they never get loud or boisterous; they might not even appear to be enjoying themselves. In other societies, they drink lots of alcohol and get loud but not rowdy. In some societies, including our own, people lose sexual inhibitions as they drink, but in other societies they do not become more aroused. The anthropological evidence is very clear: alcohol as a drug does affect human behaviour, but culture influences the types of effects that occur. We learn from our culture how to behave when drunk just as we learn how to behave when sobre.

CULTURE VERSUS BIOLOGY

These examples suggest that human behaviour is more the result of culture than it is of biology. This is not to say that biology is entirely unimportant. As just one example, humans have a biological need to eat, and so they do. But humans are much less under the control of biology than any other animal species, including other primates such as monkeys and chimpanzees. These and other animals are governed largely by biological instincts that control them totally. A dog chases any squirrel it sees because of instinct, and a cat chases a mouse for the same reason. Different breeds of dogs do have different personalities, but even these stem from the biological differences among breeds passed down from one generation to another. Instinct prompts many dogs to turn around before they lie down, and it prompts most dogs to defend their territory. When the doorbell rings and a dog begins barking, it is responding to ancient biological instinct. Because humans have such a large, complex central nervous system, we are less controlled by biology.

The critical question then becomes, how much does biology influence our behaviour? Predictably, scholars in different disciplines answer this question in different ways. Most sociologists and anthropologists would probably say that culture affects behaviour much more than biology does. In contrast, many biologists and psychologists would give much more weight to biology. Advocating a view called socio-biology. The view that genes and other aspects of human biology influence human behaviour and values., some scholars say that several important human behaviours and emotions, such as competition, aggression, and altruism, stem from our biological makeup. Sociobiology has been roundly criticized and just as staunchly defended, and respected scholars continue to debate its premises.

Why do sociologists generally favour culture over biology? Two reasons stand out. First, and as kissing and the other examples show, many behaviours differ dramatically among societies in ways that show the strong impact of culture. Second, biology cannot easily account for why groups and locations differ in their rates of committing certain behaviours. For example, what biological reason could explain why suicide rates west of the Mississippi River are higher than those east of it or why the U. S. homicide rate is so much higher than Canada's? Various aspects of culture and social structure seem much better able than biology to explain these differences. Many sociologists also warn of certain implications of biological explanations.

First, they say, these explanations implicitly support the status quo. Because it is difficult to change biology, any problem with biological causes cannot be easily fixed. Consider evidence that women do worse than men on the math SAT exam and are less likely to be mathematically gifted. Some researchers attribute this difference to women's lower testosterone levels or to their brain structures. Suppose either explanation is true. What, then, can we do to improve women's math SAT scores? Operate on their brains? Give them more testosterone?

Obviously either option is morally unethical and practically impossible. If these are the only options, then there is little hope for improving women's math ability, and gender inequality in math will continue. Suppose instead, as many educators think, that the gender math difference stems from social and cultural factors, including the way girls and boys are brought up, the amount of attention teachers pay to them, and gender stereotyping in children's books. None of these factors will be easy to change, but at least it is more possible to change them than to change biological conditions. Sociology's perspective on gender and math performance thus promises at least some hope in reducing gender inequality in math performance. A second possible implication of biological explanations that concerns some sociologists harkens back to an earlier time.

This was a time when perceived biological differences among races and religions were used to justify forced sterilization and mass violence, including genocide, against certain groups. As just one example, in the early 1900s, some 70,000 people, most of them poor and many of them immigrants or African Americans, were involuntarily sterilized in the United States as part of the eugenics.

The view, popular in the early 20th century, that certain categories of people were biologically inferior and hence should be sterilized movement, which said that certain kinds of people were biologically inferior and must not be allowed to reproduce.

The Nazi Holocaust a few decades later used a similar eugenics argument to justify its genocide against Jews, Catholics, gypsies, and gays. With this history in mind, some scholars fear that biological explanations of human behaviour might still be used to support views of biological inferiority.

THE ELEMENTS OF CULTURE

Culture was defined earlier as the symbols, language, beliefs, values, and artifacts that are part of any society. As this definition suggests, there are two basic components of culture: ideas and symbols on the one hand and artifacts on the other. The first type, called non-material culture. The symbols, language, norms, and values that constitute a major part of a society's culture., includes the values, beliefs, symbols, and language that define a society.

The second type, called material. An element of culture consisting of society's material objects, or artifacts., includes all the society's physical objects, such as its tools and technology, clothing, eating utensils, and means of transportation. These elements of culture are discussed next.

SYMBOLS

Every culture is filled with symbols. Things that stand for something else and that often evoke various reactions and emotions., or things that stand for something else and that often evoke various reactions and emotions. Some symbols are actually types of nonverbal communication, while other symbols are in fact material objects. Sociology and the Sociological Perspective emphasizes, shared symbols make social interaction possible. Let's look at nonverbal symbols first. A common one is shaking hands, which is done in some societies but not in others.

It commonly conveys friendship and is used as a sign of both greeting and departure. Probably all societies have nonverbal symbols we call gesturesge. Movements of the hand, arm, head, and other parts of the body that are meant to convey ideas or emotions non-verbally., movements of the hand, arm, or other parts of the body that are meant to convey certain ideas or emotions. However, the same gesture can mean one thing in one society and something quite different in another society. In the United States, for example, if we nod our head up and down, we mean yes, and if we shake it back and forth, we mean no. In Bulgaria, however, nodding means no, while shaking our head back and forth means yes! In the United States, if we make an "O" by putting our thumb and forefinger together, we mean "OK," but the same gesture in certain parts of Europe signifies an obscenity.

"Thumbs up" in the United States means "great" or "wonderful," but in Australia it means the same thing as extending the middle finger in the United States. Certain parts of the Middle East and Asia would be offended if they saw you using your left hand to eat, because they use their left hand for bathroom hygiene. Some of our most important symbols are objects. Here the U. S. flag is a prime example. For most Americans, the flag is not just a piece of cloth with red and white stripes and white stars against a field of blue. Instead, it is a symbol of freedom, democracy, and other American values and inspires pride and patriotism. During the Vietnam War, however, the flag became to many Americans a symbol of war and imperialism. Some burned the flag in protest, prompting angry attacks by bystanders and negative coverage by the news media. Other objects have symbolic value for religious reasons. Three of the most familiar religious symbols in many nations are the cross, the Star of David, and the crescent moon, which stand for Christianity, Judaism, and Islam, respectively. Whereas many cultures attach no religious significance to these shapes, for many people across the world they evoke very strong feelings of religious faith. Recognizing this, hate groups have often desecrated these symbols. As these examples indicate, shared symbols, both nonverbal communication and tangible objects, are an important part of any culture but also can lead to misunderstandings and even hostility. These problems underscore the significance of symbols for social interaction and meaning.

LANGUAGE

Perhaps our most important set of symbols is language. In English, the word *chair* means something we sit on. In French, the word *chaise* means the same thing. As long as we agree how to interpret these words, a shared language and thus society are possible. By the same token, differences in languages can make it quite difficult to communicate. For example, imagine you are in a foreign country where you do not know their language and they do not know yours. Worse yet, you forgot to bring your dictionary that translates their language into yours, and vice versa, and your iPhone battery has died. You become lost.

How will you get help? What will you do? Is there any way to communicate your plight? As this scenario suggests, language is crucial to communication and thus to any society's culture. Children learn language from their culture just as they learn about shaking hands, about gestures, and about the significance of the flag and other symbols. Humans have a capacity for language that no other animal species possesses. Our capacity for language in turn helps make our complex culture possible. In the United States, some people consider a common language so important that they advocate making

English the official language of certain cities or states or even the whole country and banning bilingual education in the public schools. Critics acknowledge the importance of English but allege that this movement smacks of anti-immigrant prejudice and would help destroy ethnic subcultures.

In 2009, voters in Nashville, Tennessee, rejected a proposal that would have made English the city's official language and required all city workers to speak in English rather than their native language. Language, of course, can be spoken or written. One of the most important developments in the evolution of society was the creation of written language. Some of the preindustrial societies that anthropologists have studied have written language, while others do not, and in the remaining societies the "written" language consists mainly of pictures, not words.

This variation with data from 186 preindustrial societies called the Standard Cross-Cultural Sample, a famous data set compiled several decades ago by anthropologist George Murdock and colleagues from information that had been gathered on hundreds of preindustrial societies around the world. In Figure, "The Presence of Written Language", we see that only about one-fourth of the SCCS societies have a written language, while about equal proportions have no language at all or only pictures.

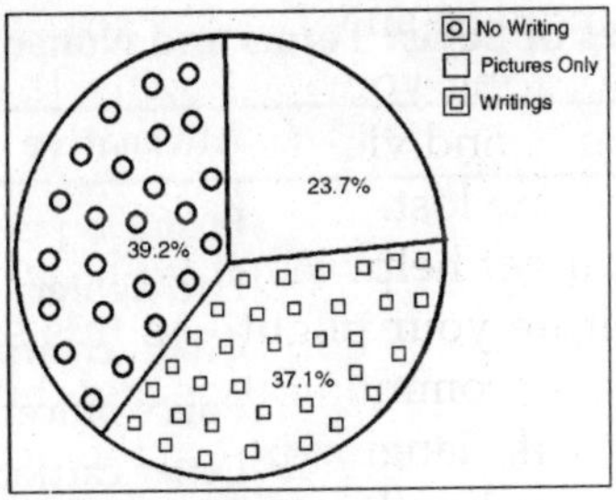

Fig. The Presence of Written Language (Percentage of Societies)

To what extent does language influence how we think and how we perceive the social and physical worlds? The famous but controversial Sapir-Whorf hypothesis Sapir-Whorf hypothesis. The view that language influences the thoughts and perceptions of people in a society., named after two linguistic anthropologists, Edward Sapir and Benjamin Lee Whorf, argues that people cannot easily understand concepts and objects unless their language contains words for these items. Language thus influences how we understand the world around us. For example, people in a country such as the United States that has many terms for different types of kisses are better able to appreciate these different types than people in a country such as Japan, which, as we saw earlier, only fairly recently developed the word kissu for kiss.

Another illustration of the Sapir-Whorf hypothesis is seen in sexist language, in which the use of male nouns and pronouns shapes how we think about the world. In older children's books, words like fireman and mailman are common, along with pictures of men in these jobs, and critics say they send a message to children that these are male jobs, not female jobs. If a teacher tells a second-grade class, "Every student should put his books under his desk," the teacher obviously means students of both sexes but may be sending a subtle message that boys matter more than girls. For these reasons, several guidebooks promote the use of nonsexist language. Table, "Examples of Sexist Terms and Nonsexist Alternatives" provides examples of sexist language and nonsexist alternatives.

Table. Examples of Sexist Terms and Nonsexist Alternatives

Term	Alternative
Businessman	Business person, executive
Fireman	Fire fighter
Chairman	Chair, chairperson
Policeman	Police officer
Mailman	Letter carrier, postal worker
Mankind	Humankind, people
Man-made	Artificial, synthetic
Waitress	Server
He (as generic pronoun)	He or she; he/she; s/he
"A professor should be devoted to his students"	"Professors should be devoted to their students"

The use of racist language also shows the Sapir-Whorf hypothesis. An old saying goes, "Sticks and stones may break my bones, but names will never hurt me." That may be true in theory but not in reality. Names can hurt, especially names that are racial slurs, which African Americans growing up before the era of the civil rights movement routinely heard. The Sapir-Whorf hypothesis, the use of these words would have affected how whites perceived African Americans. More generally, the use of racist terms may reinforce racial prejudice and racial stereotypes.

NORMS

Cultures differ widely in their norms. Socially acceptable ways of behaving., or standards and expectations for behaving. We already saw that how people behave when drunk stems from society's expectations of how they should behave when drunk. Norms of drunken behaviour influence how we behave when we drink too much. Norms are often divided into two types, formal norms. Norms that are very important and usually written down; also called laws and mores and informal. Relatively unimportant norms, often unwritten, that still affect people's behaviour.. Formal norms, also called *mores* and *laws*, refer to the standards of behaviour considered the most important in any society.

Examples in the United States include traffic laws, criminal codes, and, in a college context, student behaviour codes addressing such things as cheating and hate speech. Informal norms, also called *folkways* and *customs*, refer to standards of behaviour that are considered less important but still influence how we behave. Table manners are a common example of informal norms, as are such everyday behaviours as how we interact with a cashier and how we ride in an elevator. Many norms differ dramatically from one culture to the next. Some of the best evidence for cultural variation in norms comes from the study of sexual behaviour.

Among the Pokot of East Africa, for example, women are expected to enjoy sex, while among the Gusii a few hundred miles away, women who enjoy sex are considered deviant. In is Beag, a small island off the coast of Ireland, sex is considered embarrassing and even disgusting; men feel that intercourse drains their strength, while women consider it a burden. Even nudity is considered terrible, and people on Beag keep their clothes on while they bathe. The situation is quite different in Mangaia, a small island in the South Pacific. Here sex is considered very enjoyable, and it is the major subject of songs and stories. While many societies frown on homosexuality, others accept it.

Among the Azande of East Africa, for example, young warriors live with each other and are not allowed to marry. During this time, they often have sex with younger boys, and this homosexuality is approved by their culture. Among the Sambia of New Guinea, young males live separately from females and engage in homosexual behaviour for at least a decade.

It is felt that the boys would be less masculine if they continued to live with their mothers and that the semen of older males helps young boys become strong and fierce. Other evidence for cultural variation in norms comes from the study of how men and women are expected to behave in various societies.

For example, many preindustrial societies are simple hunting and gathering societies. In most of these, men tend to hunt and women tend to gather. Many observers attribute this gender difference to at least two biological differences between the sexes. First, men tend to be bigger and stronger than women and are thus better suited for hunting. Second, women become pregnant and bear children and are less able to hunt. Yet a different pattern emerges in some hunting and gathering societies. Among a group of Australian aborigines called the Tiwi and a tribal society in the Philippines called the Agta, both sexes hunt.

After becoming pregnant, Agta women continue to hunt for most of their pregnancy and resume hunting after their child is born. Some of the most interesting norms that differ by culture govern how people stand apart when they talk with each other. In the United States, people who are not intimates usually stand about three to four feet apart when they talk. If someone stands more closely to us, especially if we are of northern European heritage, we feel uncomfortable. Yet people in other countries—especially Italy, France, Spain, and many of the nations of Latin America and the Middle East—would feel uncomfortable if they were standing three to four feet apart. To them, this distance is too great and indicates that the people talking dislike each other. If a U. S. native of British or Scandinavian heritage were talking with a member of one of these societies, they might well have trouble interacting, because at least one of them will be uncomfortable with the physical distance separating them.

Rituals

Different cultures also have different ritualsrituals Established procedures and ceremonies that often mark transitions in the life course., or established procedures and ceremonies that often mark transitions in the life course. As such, rituals both reflect and transmit a culture's norms and other elements from one generation to the next. Initiation and commencement ceremonies in colleges and universities are familiar examples of time-honoured rituals. In many societies, rituals help signify one's gender identity.

For example, girls around the world undergo various types of initiation ceremonies to mark their transition to adulthood. Among the Bemba of Zambia, girls undergo a month-long initiation ceremony called the *chisungu,* in which girls learn songs, dances, and secret terms that only women know. In some cultures, special ceremonies also mark a girl's first menstrual period. Such ceremonies are largely absent in the United States, where a girl's first period is a private matter. But in other cultures the first period is a cause for celebration involving gifts, music, and food.

Boys have their own initiation ceremonies, some of them involving circumcision. That said, the ways in which circumcisions are done and the ceremonies accompanying them differ widely. In the United States, boys who are circumcised usually undergo a quick procedure in the hospital.

If their parents are observant Jews, circumcision will be part of a religious ceremony, and a religious figure called a *moyel* will perform the circumcision. In contrast, circumcision among the Maasai of East Africa is used as a test of manhood. If a boy being circumcised shows signs of fear, he might well be ridiculed. Are rituals more common in preindustrial societies than in modern ones such as the United States? Consider the Nacirema, studied by anthropologist Horace Miner more than 50 years ago.

In this society, many rituals have been developed to deal with the culture's fundamental belief that the human body is ugly and in danger of suffering many diseases. Reflecting this belief, every household has at least one shrine in which various rituals are performed to cleanse the body. Often these shrines contain magic potions acquired from medicine men. The Nacirema are especially concerned about diseases of the mouth. Miner writes, "Were it not for the rituals of the mouth, they believe that their teeth would fall out, their gums bleed, their jaws shrink, their friends desert them, and their lovers reject them".

Many Nacirema engage in "mouth-rites" and see a "holy-mouth-man" once or twice yearly. Spell Nacirema backward and you will see that Miner was describing American culture. As his satire suggests, rituals are not limited to preindustrial societies. Instead, they function in many kinds of societies to mark transitions in the life course and to transmit the norms of the culture from one generation to the next.

Changing Norms and Beliefs

Our examples show that different cultures have different norms, even if they share other types of practices and beliefs. It is also true that norms change over time within a given culture. Two obvious examples here are hairstyles and clothing styles. When the Beatles first became popular in the early 1960s, their hair barely covered their ears, but parents of teenagers back then were aghast at how they looked. If anything, clothing styles change even more often than hairstyles.

Hemlines go up, hemlines go down. Lapels become wider, lapels become narrower. This colour is in, that colour is out. Hold on to your out-of-style clothes long enough, and eventually they may well end up back in style. A more important topic on which norms have changed is abortion and birth control. Despite the controversy surrounding abortion today, it was very common in the ancient world. Much later, medieval theologians generally felt that abortion was not murder if it occurred within the first several weeks after conception.

This distinction was eliminated in 1869, when Pope Pius IX declared abortion at any time to be murder. In the United States, abortion was not illegal until 1828, when New York state banned it to protect women from unskilled abortionists, and most other states followed suit by the end of the century. However, the sheer number of unsafe, illegal abortions over the next several decades helped fuel a demand for repeal of abortion laws that in turn helped lead to the *Roe v. Wade* Supreme Court decision in 1973 that generally legalized abortion during the first two trimesters.

Contraception was also practiced in ancient times, only to be opposed by early Christianity. Over the centuries, scientific discoveries of the nature of the reproductive process led to more effective means of contraception and to greater calls for its use, despite legal bans on the distribution of information about contraception. In the early 1900s, Margaret Sanger, an American nurse, spearheaded the growing birth-control movement and helped open a birth-control clinic in Brooklyn in 1916. She and two other women were arrested within 10 days, and Sanger and one other defendant were sentenced to 30 days in jail.

Efforts by Sanger and other activists helped to change views on contraception over time, and finally, in 1965, the U. S. Supreme Court ruled in *Griswold v. Connecticut* that contraception information could not be banned. As this brief summary shows, norms about contraception changed dramatically during the last century. Other types of cultural beliefs also change over time. Since the 1960s, the U. S. public has changed its views about some important racial and gender issues. The percentage of Americans who would vote for a qualified black person as president rose almost 20 points from the early 1970s to the middle of 1996, when the GSS stopped asking the question. If beliefs about voting for an African American had not changed, Barack Obama would almost certainly not have been elected in 2008. Several years of the GSS, shows that the percentage saying that women should take care of running their homes and leave running the country to men declined from almost 36% in the early 1970s to only about 15% in 1998, again, when the GSS stopped asking the question.

Values of what is desirable or undesirable and right or wrong are another important element of culture and involve judgments of what is good or bad and desirable or undesirable. A culture's values shape its norms. In Japan, for example, a central value is group harmony. The Japanese place great emphasis on harmonious social relationships and dislike interpersonal conflict. Individuals are fairly unassertive by American standards, lest they be perceived as trying to force their will upon others.

When interpersonal disputes do arise, Japanese do their best to minimize conflict by trying to resolve the disputes amicably. Lawsuits are thus uncommon; in one case involving disease and death from a mercury-polluted river, some Japanese who dared to sue the company responsible for the mercury poisoning were considered bad citizens.

Individualism in the United States

In the United States, of course, the situation is quite different. The American culture extols the rights of the individual and promotes competition in the business and sports worlds and in other areas of life. Lawsuits over the most frivolous of issues are quite common and even expected. Phrases like "Look out for number one!" abound. If the Japanese value harmony and group feeling, Americans value competition and individualism. Because the Japanese value harmony, their norms frown on self-assertion in interpersonal relationships and on lawsuits to correct perceived wrongs.

Because Americans value and even thrive on competition, our norms promote assertion in relationships and certainly promote the use of the law to address all kinds of problems. This difference between the two nations' cultures with data from the 2002 World Values Survey which was administered to random samples of the adult populations of more than 80 nations around the world. One question asked in these nations was, "On a scale of one to ten, please indicate your views on competition." The percentages of Americans and Japanese who responded with a "one" or "two" to this question, indicating they think competition is very beneficial. Americans are about three times as likely as Japanese to favour competition.

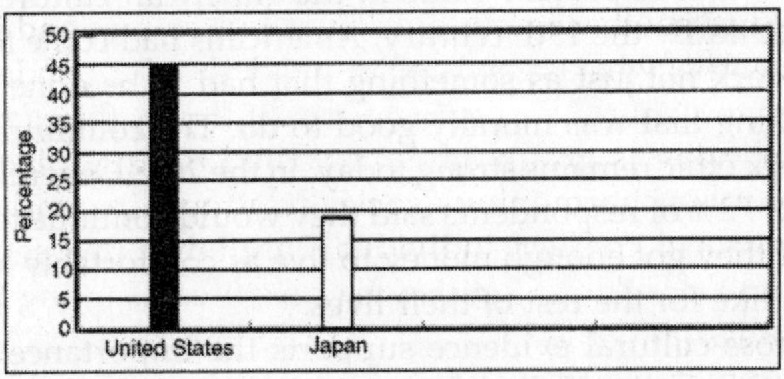

Fig. Percentage That Thinks Competition is Very Beneficial

The Japanese value system is a bit of an anomaly, because Japan is a modern nation with very traditional influences. Its emphasis on group harmony and community is more usually thought of as a value found in preindustrial societies, while the U. S. emphasis on individuality is more usually thought of as a value found in modern cultures. Anthropologist David Maybury-Lewis describes this difference as follows: "The heart of the difference between the modern world and the traditional one is that in traditional societies people are a valuable resource and the interrelations between them are carefully tended; in modern society things are the valuables and people are all too often treated as disposable."

In modern societies, continues Maybury-Lewis, individualism and the rights of the individual are celebrated and any one person's obligations to the larger community are weakened. Individual achievement becomes more important than values such as kindness, compassion, and generosity. Other scholars take a less bleak view of modern society, where they say the spirit of community still lives even as individualism is extolled. In American society, these two simultaneous values sometimes create tension. In Appalachia, for example, people view themselves as rugged individuals who want to control their own fate. At the same time, they have strong ties to families, relatives, and their neighbours. Thus their sense of independence conflicts with their need for dependence on others.

The Work Ethic

Another important value in the American culture is the work ethic. By the 19th century, Americans had come to view hard work not just as something that had to be done but as something that was morally good to do. The commitment to the work ethic remains strong today: in the 2008 General Social Survey, 72% of respondents said they would continue to work even if they got enough money to live as comfortably as they would like for the rest of their lives.

Cross-cultural evidence supports the importance of the work ethic in the United States. Using earlier World Values Survey data, The percentage of people in United States and three other nations from different parts of the world—Mexico, Poland, and Japan—who take "a great deal of pride" in their work. More than 85% of Americans feel this way, compared to much lower proportions of people in the other three nations.

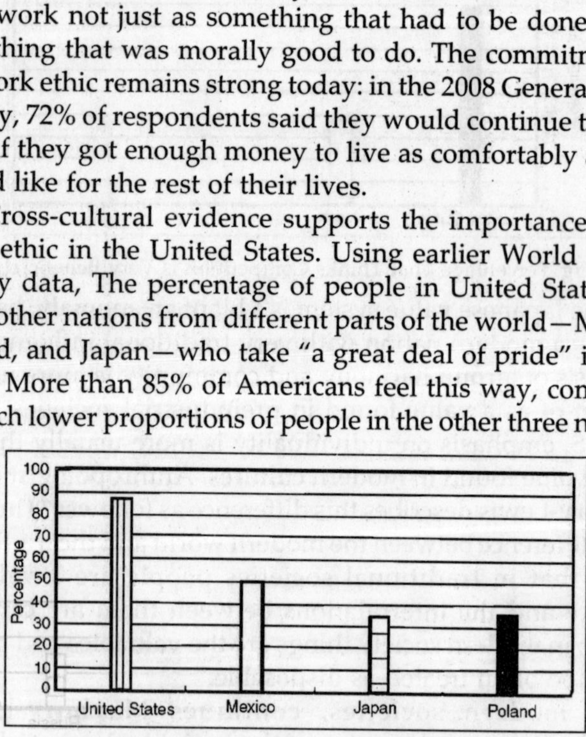

Fig. Percentage of People Who Take a Great Deal of Pride in Their Work

Closely related to the work ethic is the belief that if people work hard enough, they will be successful. Here again the American culture is especially thought to promote the idea that people can pull themselves up by their "bootstraps" if they work hard enough. The WVS asked whether success results from hard work or from luck and connections. The proportions of people in the four nations just examined who most strongly thought that hard work brings success. Once again we see evidence of an important aspect of the American culture, as U. S. residents were especially likely to think that hard work brings success.

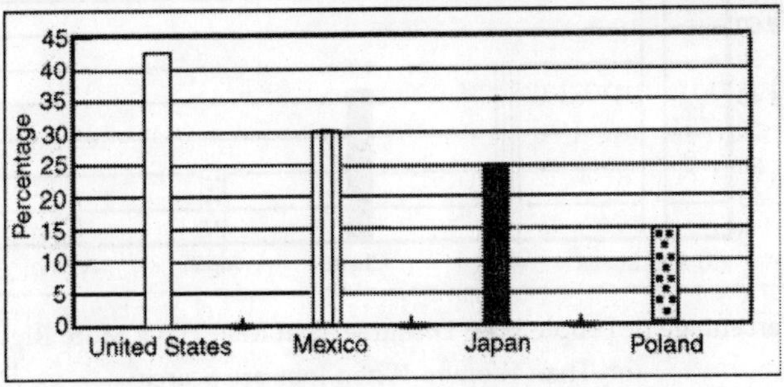

Fig. Percentage of People Who Think Hard Work Brings Success

If Americans value the work ethic and also believe hard work brings success, then they should be more likely than people in most other nations to believe that poverty stems from not working hard enough. As expected, Americans are much more likely to attribute poverty to not working hard enough.

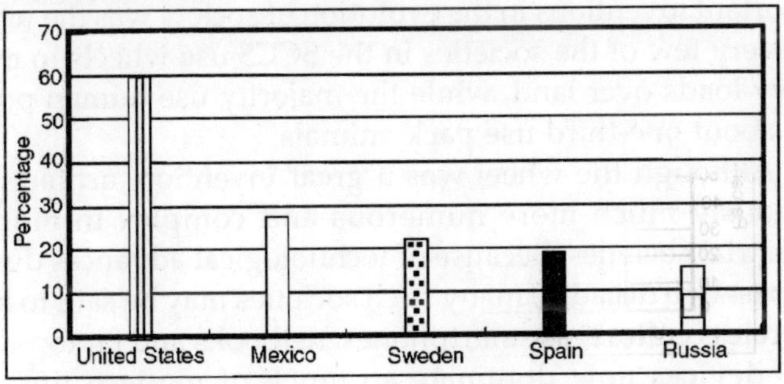

Fig. Percentage of People Who Attribute Poverty to Laziness and Lack of Willpower

We could discuss many other values, but an important one concerns how much a society values employment of women outside the home. The WVS asked respondents whether they agree or disagree that "when jobs are scarce men should have more right to a job than women." U. S. residents are more likely than those in nations with more traditional views of women to disagree with this statement.

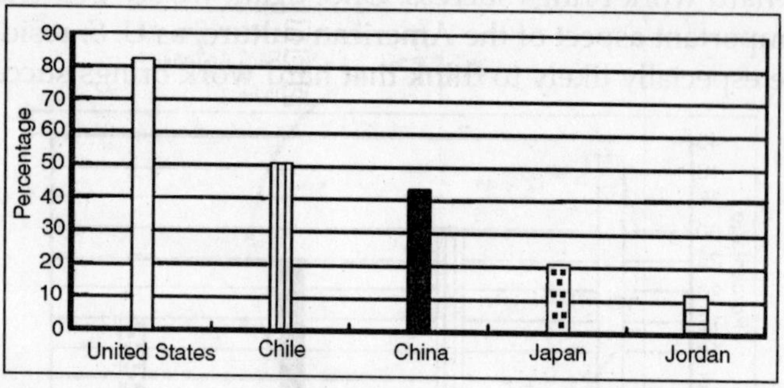

Fig. Percentage of People Who Disagree That Men Have More Right to a Job Than Women When Jobs are Scarce

ARTIFACTS

The last element of culture is the artifacts. The material objects that constitute a society's material culture., or material objects, that constitute a society's material culture. In the most simple societies, artifacts are largely limited to a few tools, the huts people live in, and the clothing they wear. One of the most important inventions in the evolution of society was the wheel. The very few of the societies in the SCCS use wheels to move heavy loads over land, while the majority use human power and about one-third use pack animals.

Although the wheel was a great invention, artifacts are obviously much more numerous and complex in modern industrial societies. Because of technological advances during the past two decades, many such societies may be said to have a wireless culture, as smartphones, netbooks and laptops, and GPS devices now dominate so much of modern life. The artifacts associated with this culture were unknown a generation ago. Technological development created these artifacts and also new language to describe them and the functions they perform. Today's wireless artifacts in turn help reinforce our own commitment to wireless technology as a way of life, if only because children are now growing up with them, often even before they can read and write. Sometimes people in one society may find it difficult to understand the artifacts that are an important part of another society's culture.

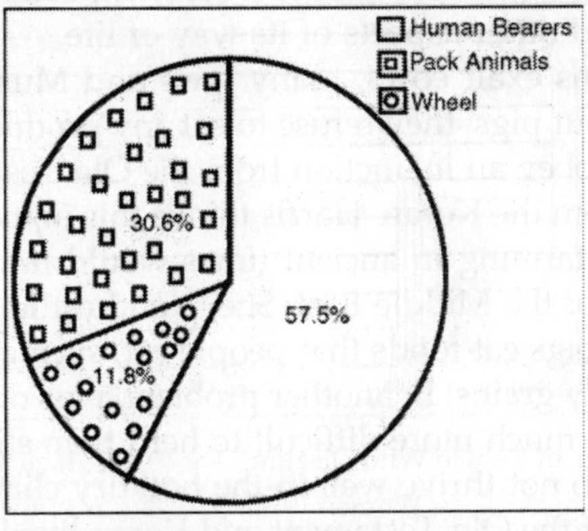

Fig. Primary Means of Moving Heavy Loads

If a member of a tribal society who had never seen a cell phone, or who had never even used batteries or electricity, were somehow to visit the United States, she or he would obviously have no idea of what a cell phone was or of its importance in almost everything we do these days. Conversely, if we were to visit that person's society, we might not appreciate the importance of some of its artifacts. In this regard, consider once again India's cows. People from India consider cows holy, and they let cows roam the streets of many cities.

In a nation where hunger is so rampant, such cow worship is difficult to understand, at least to Americans, because a ready source of meat is being ignored. Anthropologist Marvin Harris advanced a practical explanation for India's cow worship. Millions of Indians are peasants who rely on their farms for their food and thus their existence. Oxen and water buffalo, not tractors, are the way they plow their fields. If their ox falls sick or dies, farmers may lose their farms. Because, as Harris observes, oxen are made by cows, it thus becomes essential to preserve cows at all costs. In India, cows also act as an essential source of fertilizer, to the tune of 700 million tons of manure annually, about half of which is used for fertilizer and the other half of which is used as fuel for cooking. Cow manure is also mixed with water and used as flooring material over dirt floors in Indian households. For all of these reasons, cow worship is not so puzzling after all, because it helps preserve animals that are very important for India's economy and other aspects of its way of life.

If Indians exalt cows, many Jews and Muslims feel the opposite about pigs: they refuse to eat any product made from pigs and so obey an injunction from the Old Testament of the Bible and from the Koran. Harris thinks this injunction existed because pig farming in ancient times would have threatened the ecology of the Middle East. Sheep and cattle eat primarily grass while pigs eat foods that people eat, such as nuts, fruits, and especially grains. In another problem, pigs do not provide milk and are much more difficult to herd than sheep or cattle. Next, pigs do not thrive well in the hot, dry climate in which the people of the Old Testament and Koran lived.

Finally, sheep and cattle were a source of food back then because beyond their own meat they provided milk, cheese, and manure, and cattle were also used for plowing. In contrast, pigs would have provided only their own meat. Because sheep and cattle were more "versatile" in all of these ways, and because of the other problems pigs would have posed, it made sense for the eating of pork to be prohibited. In contrast to Jews and Muslims, at least one society, the Maring of the mountains of New Guinea, is characterized by "pig love." Here pigs are held in the highest regard.

Bibliography

Bayly, C.A.: *Rulers, Townsmen, and Bazaars: North Indian Society in the Age of British Expansion,* Cambridge: Cambridge University Press, 2000.

Bhambhri, C.P.: *Constitutional, Educational, and Inherited Social Imbalances,* New Delhi: National Institute of Educational Planning and Administration, 2004.

Bhaskar, D.: *Organization for Change: A Systems Analysis of Family Planning in Rural India,* New Delhi: Family Planning Association, 2005.

Bhikhu, P.: *Crisis and Change in Contemporary India,* New Delhi: Sage, in association with The Book Review Literary Trust, 1998.

Carrithers, M.: *The Assembly of Listeners: Jains in Society,* Cambridge: Cambridge University Press, 2005.

Downs, F.: *Christianity in North East India,* Delhi: Indian Society for Promoting Christian Knowledge, 2004.

Embree, T.: *Utopias in Conflict: Religion and Nationalism in Modern India,* Berkeley: University of California Press, 2005.

Eugene, F.: *Politics and Social Conflict in South India: The Non-Brahman Movement and Tamil Separatism,* Berkeley: University of California Press, 1997.

Hasnain, N.: *Shias and Shia Islam in India: A Study in Society and Culture,* New Delhi: Harnam, 1999.

Heinsath, C.: *Indian Nationalism and Hindu Social Reform,* Princeton: Princeton University Press, 1996.

Jeffrey, R.: *People, Princes, and Paramount Power: Society and Politics in Indian Princely States,* New Delhi: Oxford University Press, 1998.

John, V.: *Church and Political Upheaval in Mizoram: A Study of the Impact of Christianity on the Political Development in Mizoram*, Aisawl: Mizo History Association, 1995.

Karashima, N.: *Towards a New Formation: South Indian Society under Vijayanagar Rule*, New Delhi: Oxford University Press, 1996.

Kumar, R.: *The Social History of Modern India*, New Delhi: Oxford University Press, 2001.

Mahalingam, T.V.: *Administration and Social Life under Vijayanagar*, Madras: University of Madras, 2004.

Minakshi, C.: *Administration and Social Life under the Pallavas*, Madras: University of Madras, 1997.

Mishra, J.: *Social and Economic Conditions under the Imperial Rashtrakutas*, New Delhi: Commonwealth, 1997.

Mohammed, S.: *Islamic Fundamentalism in India*, Chandigarh: Twenty-First Century India Society, 1996.

Muthiah, S.: *A Social and Economic Atlas of India*, New Delhi: Oxford, University Press, 1999.

Raye, R.: India: *A Compendium*, New York: American Geographical Society, 2002.

Richard M.: *Social Roles of Sufis in Medieval India*, Princeton: Princeton University Press, 1998.

Sharma, R.: *Light on Early Indian Society and Economy*, Bombay: Manaktalas, 1999.

Singhvi, A.K.: *Thar Desert in Rajasthan: Land, Man, and Environment*, Bangalore: Geological Society of India, 1996.

Stein, B.: *Peasant, State, and Society in Medieval South India*, New Delhi: Oxford University Press, 2000.

Thapar, R.: *From Lineage to State: Social Formations in the Mid-First Millennium B.C. in the Ganga Valley*, New Delhi: Oxford University Press, 1994.

Index